Angeleno Days

❖   ❖   ❖

Angeleno Days

An Arab American Writer on Family,

Place, and Politics

Gregory Orfalea

The University of Arizona Press
Tucson

The University of Arizona Press
© 2009 Gregory Orfalea
All rights reserved

www.uapress.arizona.edu

Library of Congress Cataloging-in-Publication Data
Orfalea, Gregory, 1949–
Angeleno days : an Arab American writer on family,
place, and politics / Gregory Orfalea.
p. cm.
Essays originally published in the Los Angeles times
magazine from 1999–2003.
ISBN 978-0-8165-2773-1 (pbk. : alk. paper)
1. Orfalea, Gregory, 1949–   — Family. 2. Orfalea,
Gregory, 1949–   — Homes and haunts — California — Los
Angeles. 3. American literature — Arab American
authors — Biography. I. Title.
PS3565.R427Z46 2009
814'.54 — dc22   2008036915

Publication of this book is made possible in part by
the proceeds of a permanent endowment created with
the assistance of a Challenge Grant from the National
Endowment for the Humanities, a federal agency.

14 13 12 11 10 09   6 5 4 3 2 1

for Gar
the Ah to this Oh

❧

:·. :·. :·.

Contents

Angeleno Days

Introduction

Toward the end of the 1990s, mired in a civil service job in Washington, D.C., I began to experience a yearning for Southern California, the place of my birth and youth, that was so powerful it pretty much took over my life. It is natural that falling into the trench of middle age, people begin to look back to their youth with a terrible fondness and not a little anxiety. Youth is, of course, gone. One's own children, if not a cold look in the mirror, are replacing it day by day. In my case, something more insistent and deeper than nostalgia was taking place. I began for the first time in my life to define what it was that made me, after spending half my life in the East, irreducibly a Westerner. I began to plumb the meaning of home. Finally, I came to understand the vast changes in the City of the Angels that had birthed me, and how that brutal, beautiful city along the Pacific sea had inexorably shaped me and those I loved, not only in Los Angeles but those whom my wife and I had brought to life three thousand miles away. Raised "East," two of our three boys are now working in California post-college. The third may not be far behind.

I don't mean my motives for writing this book to sound too calculated. In fact, the pull of the Far West was as strong and mysterious as any that drew the Forty-Niners to the gold fields a century and a half ago—probably stronger. There was just this burning need, aided and abetted by my sense that Washington was a city that had lost its soul.

When the chance to return to teaching and the Southland came in 2004, I jumped at it. My alienation from the sterility and venality of the Capital and the sense that I was lost down a bureaucratic rabbit hole was nearly complete. My Washingtonian wife balked, however. Though we had taken our boys for many delightful summer and Christmas trips to California, she dreaded change as much, it seemed, as I longed for it. Security was very important to her. I understood over time this to be a classic East Coast–West Coast temperamental divide. Though opposite souls, we were not, mercifully, opposing, and the love managed to continue. Though 2004 was a watershed year in my life, I had already begun to reflect back on Los Angeles from my perch in Washington as to what it had given and taken in a series of memoirs that were published by the *Los Angeles Times Magazine* and its extraordinary editor, Alice Short. Begun with a haunted walk through my father's now abandoned garment factory in what had once been a teeming, vibrant L.A. garment district downtown ("Kingdom of Rags"), Alice slowly coaxed memoirs out of me that were progressively more serious and painful. They evolved from discussions by mail and phone and in person when I returned to Los Angeles for various family crises, celebrations, or government duties. After touring the burned-out buildings of the 1992 Rodney King riots in South Central L.A. for my federal housing agency, Alice asked me over lunch, "Were you ever there before?" Yes, I told her; I had taught children once in South Central. "Did you write about that for your government paper?" No, I said; you don't write about personal things for the government. "Well, write them for me," she said. That launched the difficult journey that became "The Teacher's Prayer." Inside my memoir-pusher was a hard-nosed journalist — Alice insisted I camp out at the Hall of Records in Norwalk, and it was there I found out that several of my former students had been killed young.

The series ended with the toughest assignment: to come to grips, as much as such a thing is possible, with the San Fernando Valley murder-suicide of my sister and father. I am convinced that no one but Alice Short, who had taken the exact opposite journey of mine from East to West for college, could have pulled that piece out of me: "An Act of Forgiveness." I confess to running away from the subject for nearly twenty years.

I have lost two childhood paradises in my life — my own in California, when I came of age and left — and the childhood of our boys in the warm Washington neighborhood around Chevy Chase Circle, a paradise that was over when two of them went off to college and I fell back on my hollow day job with this inchoate yearning to return to the West. After a time, life is pain; I've not doubted that bleak assessment. Yet at the same time, paradoxically, the carapace of suffering that is life is cracked here and there, and we call those cracks joy. I think now something rather contrary — that the joy is truly the core of life, a core we have a hard time breaking into, a core that cracks sometimes of its own accord upward to break our pain. How strange it is that we convince ourselves life is pain period, when in fact it is joy at the core, insufferable joy that mocks our surface suffering by its very existence and the sad, nagging way we deny it. Coming home, I was following those fault lines, lonely and joyful in the same moment.

For all its extraordinary vitality and diversity on the east edge of the Asian rim, Los Angeles is not much celebrated by writers, at least not by writers of literary works, certainly not the way Bellow celebrated Chicago or I.B. Singer, Bernard Malamud, and Louis Auchincloss celebrated New York City. Of course, L.A. flickers in the background, if not the foreground, of more movies than anyone can count, and perhaps that is one reason serious authors have either left it or been vacuumed into the Hollywood mill. The few writers birthed in and around the City of Angels not swallowed by celluloid seem to escape to New York — Joan Didion and Lawrence Weschler come to mind. The author of the greatest novel ever written on Los Angeles — *Ask the Dust* — wrote the book in the Depression when he was hungry, starving even, living on Bunker Hill downtown, just before he gave his soul to the camera and screenwriting. He was the Italian American, John Fante. When I took a class of mine to Union Station by train, hiking up Bunker Hill to try and find Fante's rooming house where he wrote *Ask the Dust*, we found nothing but the Santa Monica Freeway.

A surprising number of eminent writers, from F. Scott Fitzgerald to Aldous Huxley to Ray Bradbury, have commented on L.A. as a social phenomenon in occasional pieces, and these can be seen in the fascinating collection *Writing Los Angeles*, edited by David Ulin. Kevin Starr's multivolume history of California has much that is informative and important about Los Angeles. But few native Angelenos have paid the city steady literary attention; D.J. Waldie's pithy yet sympathetic rendering of his hometown, the ultra-suburb of Lakewood, in the book *Holy Land* is a recent exception, and of course no one has quite scored the shadows extending far and deep from an otherwise sunny city as has that Sacramento girl Joan Didion. When you read Didion's L.A., like it or not, you are reading the nation. Mike Davis has given the city a lot of well-deserved hell. In my own case, I've felt a personal calling to pay Los Angeles some respect, cold, hot, or grudging; one wages this little war daily in the East, where it seems L.A. is constantly pancaked to the make-believe world of just one of its industries, as if Washington wasn't without façade or New York without Mammon. One gets tired of this rote and intellectually lazy pummeling of Los Angeles ("La la land," "Oh, you must have been West, you've gotten a tan!"), especially when one has dipped one's toes in enough shallowness in the East to line an empty pool. Hang around any Senate cloakroom or corridor of the Stock Exchange. People trump place, as my friend the Cuban American writer Pablo Medina has said. As I am someone for whom family is life itself — and a thing growing beyond blood — the reader will find several portraits of remarkable people in the first section of this book. Show me whom you love and I will show you who you are, said Mussorgsky. In my case, there's a Lebanese peddler grandmother who lived in the Wilshire District (appearing in "Nazera"), my barber of 40 years ("The Barber of Tarzana"), my father ("Contact"), and our special-gifts son, Luke ("Straight Shooters"). There is also Daniel Pearl, an alter ego of sorts, killed barbarically in Pakistan ("Valley Boys").

And yet a place does have a soul, blackened or not, and for all its complexities, Los Angeles (and surrounding California) is the place that shaped my soul and that perennially speaks to me — the place where, as Joan Didion said, "the mind is troubled by some buried but ineradicable suspicion that things had better work out, because here, beneath that immense bleached sky, is where we run out of continent."

When the University of Arizona Press asked me to put together a selection of nonfiction to date, it was quite a challenge. For one thing, the work here spans a quarter-century. Some of the early pieces were written before the advent of the personal computer on a manual typewriter. Our oldest son, Matthew, boosted the project immeasurably by hunting down pieces I had forgotten I had written; after his patient gathering, we began the winnowing process. What remains here is roughly one-third of my published essays and memoirs, including a few pieces in print for the first time.

The work fell into two categories — memoirs about Los Angeles and my extended family and friends there, and essays on Arab Americans, their political concerns, and their literature. As L.A. has probably overtaken Detroit as the U.S. city with the largest Arab American population (400,000), these subjects wade into each other. It is not completely haphazard that the San Gabriel Mountains bow like a Muslim at the end of Part One and swallow my family at the beginning of Part Two.

A word on memoir: as the dominant mode in the first section and perhaps of the book as a whole, memoir runs the risk of conveying self-absorption. But I have always felt that memoir has the potential if done right to do just the opposite, to be what I would call "expansive memoir," the permeable story of an individual life in intimate dialogue with others and indeed the social and political life of the times. Described in this way, the action of a self is never in isolation; or rather, in faithfully recording the truth about oneself, one has a better chance at leaching the truth of our condition. You preserve a jacket by folding it inside out; so too, a life. I also believe—and this may have something to do with the Arab American family I grew up in—that you discover self *through* others. This is a direct challenge to the Emersonian notion of selfhood.

One does not set out to be a *"vox populi,"* or even a *"vox civili."* One bares the soul not in a sensational way, but as one feels one's way in the dark, by finding handholds on the rock, by moving towards even the thinnest light. Maybe, just maybe, with courage and devotion, you have earned the right to slide the veil off the society's hidden face. Put another way, the writer of expansive or engaged memoir subjects his or her actions and inclinations to no less scrutiny than that of a society. As Robert Bly once intimated, the best political poem is a quarrel with oneself.

Which book of St. Augustine, after all, moves us more—his *De doctrina christiana* ("On Christian Doctrine") or his *Confessions*, the first self-story, or autobiography, in human history? Of course it's the latter, the original "soul on fire" of Western literature. What tells me more about the power of peer pressure and mob violence than Augustine's relentlessly honest fourth-century A.D. portrayal of his stripping a neighbor's pear tree with friends, "the Wreckers," or sitting by the obscene excitement of his best friend as they watch men being eaten alive in the Coliseum? Is there a more immediate study of seventeenth-century London than that eyewitness of the 1666 Great London Fire, Samuel Pepys? Or of Western literati who passed through France in the thirties than diarist Anaïs Nin?

Some stories, to be sure, are too compelling in themselves for fiction —and some very good fiction writers have outdone themselves with a "true" story saved for decades, sometimes till the end of a life. I'm thinking now of that searing study of a blow-up fire in Montana, which took the lives of several of the author's friends even as it barely spared his— Norman Maclean's masterpiece, *Young Men and Fire*, unfinished at his death, yet cut off with stunning finality at the foot of his wife. And for all Pat Conroy's florid jolts to the heart in fiction, his outstanding book, to my mind, is his painstaking—and painful—celebration of college basketball, *My Losing Season*, in which the shadow of a wildly abusive father stalks him till a barely peaceful end. On the joyous side, it's hard to imagine Lynne Cox besting her tale of stripping down to Spandex each dark morning for two decades to follow a wonderful, arduous deep-sea obsession in *Swimming to Antarctica*. If it were fiction, that story would be just plain far-fetched.

One writes what one must; all else is prefatory. One writes to breathe, to remove objects from the windpipe or fat from the heart. We all sustain traumas and, something new for this society, a natural death may be becoming increasingly rare. In societies wracked by war, such as Iraq or Afghanistan — wars at least in part of our making — swift death is a part of daily life. Our war is more internal, though we have for the first time in nearly two hundred years — since the earliest years of the Republic — taken a hard hit from an enemy abroad, one we hardly knew existed. But still the ongoing war is inner and for that we are called to have as much courage as a soldier. I have tried out of some merciless drive to understand and to keep balance while walking edges life thrust under my feet. I once thought my life too happy to call for much comment. But watch out! Life has a way of filling such vacuums.

Who thinks as a boy fielding ground balls that he will one day face the shooting deaths of his closest loved ones? Or schizophrenia, euthanasia, family drug addiction, the killing of his students? These shocks of fate are not things sought out, and in general writing about them is far from pure therapy — it brings its own agony, as well as anger and backlash from others caught in the tragedies, too. Occasionally, down the road, there may be a healing and quiet deliverance. Memoir can cauterize the wound. Still, my mother refused to read "An Act of Forgiveness," and I had to literally negotiate certain words through an intermediary — my brother — for her to even consent to it's being published. I confess to granting her wishes — though not to everything. As Tobias Wolff once hinted to me, if a writer pulled his punches for every loved one who might be hurt, he wouldn't write a thing of worth. But granting that, I am sure Wolff would himself agree that memoir needs long gestation and that it may be wise to allow a close relative a look at it, and then to weigh objections before making tough decisions on a final form. Those without strong family ties suffer less with such things; for those of us with them, these are extremely difficult decisions. This is the occupational hazard of a nonfiction memoir writer. If it is a matter of losing the love and devotion — not to mention jeopardizing the health — of someone close, no one is going to set that in motion for a paragraph or several paragraphs. That may be less the issue than we sometimes think. It is nigh impossible to predict the gamut of reaction to sensitive realities made public; it's impossible, even, to be completely thorough in inquiring into the possibilities. If one is lucky, one's family and friends give courage, rather than take it.

The denouement to this elliptical explanation of something that is finally inexplicable is that my mother did finally read the piece about the deaths of her only daughter and husband four years after it was published and gave a quiet nod. It hurt terribly, she said, but perhaps it might help someone. I couldn't ask for more.

Part Two of this book deals with my life as an American of Arab descent and with Middle East issues. It also explores some of the exciting new literature of such Arab Americans in this country. I tried to pick representative pieces, as well as those dealing with pressing, current problems such as Iraq, Lebanon's third destruction in twenty-five years, and Palestine (a problem that is never not pressing). I toyed with the idea of excerpting parts of my two books on Arab American history and culture, but rejected that in favor of offering work not available under cover elsewhere. I was the first Arab American to walk Capital Hill day to day on behalf of the community and have written about it extensively in *The Arab Americans: A History*. American literature has never been too kind to those who take strong political stands, with some exceptions (Twain, Arthur Miller). To take on what at the time was anathema in the American political system and still is, to some extent — that is, Palestinian rights and America's and Israel's role in suppressing them — probably wasn't the most practical decision I ever made, but I don't regret it. I try and address some of the pitfalls in "Facing the Wall: Arab Americans and Publishing," realizing that discourse on these matters for Arab Americans is finally opening up, should open up; I've heard enough horror stories of others to know my own are not unique and that in itself is troubling. The wall, though hardly collapsed, has begun to be breached since 9/11. If this book does one thing, blowing a good-sized hole in that wall would be a source of real satisfaction.

It will become obvious to the reader that I have had a personal obsession with Arab-Jewish interaction, both positive and negative. Los Angeles was a good place to grow up to come at this because, unlike in

New York City, the two communities lived together, intermingled in neighborhoods (mine were Anaheim and Tarzana), and worked together, especially in the garment, construction, and film industries. Though it is true that Syrian Jews and Arabs both toiled in the New York garment factories, the huge number and political influence of American Jews in New York marginalized the Arab American community there. This never happened in Los Angeles, where the two communities are closer in number and not as politically extreme (granting that the assassination of an Arab American leader by the JDL occurred in L.A.—Alex Odeh).

My takes on the Arab-Jewish conundrum are as various as a direct address to a Jewish actress ("To Hope"), an imaginative memoir of Daniel Pearl ("Valley Boys"), and a repudiation of Palestinian suicide bombing ("No. Not This.").

I confront the 9/11 catastrophe directly in "We Were the People" and "Snuffing the Fire of Radical Islam." The attacks, which forced me out of my Washington government office, filter through several essays. (Oddly enough, "Straight Shooters" appeared exactly on September 11, 2001, in the *Washington Post*, the one piece of good news my friend Tim Shriver said he found that day.) It seems to me, even eight years and two invasions later, that we have yet to deal with why al-Qaeda launched the attack: that sense of the invasiveness of American arms and culture dominating corrupt regimes and, of course, shunting the Palestine problem to the side. We continue to bat at the shadows of terror, to the great detriment of our soul and safety, not to mention the payment in treasure and blood of our youth. We need to focus on root inequities, see things as they are and not how we wish them to be.

I have long tried to help unearth the rich literature of Arab Americans, spark it in every way I could, and bring it to the larger literary community of the nation. For a long time, Arab American literary obscurity limned the community's political marginality, but that, too, is changing. I've extensively rewritten the essay that broke some ground on Arab stereotyping in the novel and brought it up to the promising trends of late. I had a great deal of fun sharing with the reader how and why a gripping real event can be twisted into fiction in "Shall We Gather in the Mountains?" Though I've written about and reviewed the work of writers as various as the Israeli Amos Kenan, the Russian poet Andrei Vosnesensky, and America's William Stafford, I chose to focus this offering on work dealing with Arab American writers, such as the wonderful Naomi Shihab Nye, as well as matters of my own aesthetics ("Why Write?").

Most of my early work had to be left out. For purely sentimental reasons, I would like to have included the piece that won me an award at Georgetown as an undergraduate, "Coming to Grips with a Greased Pole," which scours the coming-of-age of a political consciousness in the Vietnam War–era, as well as the normal hijinks of a college student of that era. One old piece I couldn't find at first to reject it: the strike proclamation read by the president of our student body just after the Kent State shootings in Ohio in the spring of 1970. A collection such as this is an assault, to some extent, on the lost, but this one in its red mimeograph ink should stay lost. Among the many editors and others who shepherded this work through the years, sometimes against the grain but with real commitment and hope, I'd like to thank Alice Short, former editor of the *Los Angeles Times Magazine*; Lawrence Goldstein of the *Michigan Quarterly Review*; Robert Fogarty of the *Antioch Review*; Bill Webb of the *Washington Post*; Michael Kinsley, former editor of the *Los Angeles Times*; Kathryn Haddad of *Mizna*; Holly Arida and Anan Ameri of the Arab American National Museum; Aziz Shihab of the *Arab Star*; Fuad Moughrabi of the *Journal of Palestine Studies*; Ben Bennani of *Paintbrush*; Eric Hooglund and the late Daniel Goodwin of the Smithsonian Institution Press; Anne Gordon of the *Cleveland Plain Dealer Sunday Magazine*; and Karen Braziller of Persea Books. My writer friends remain constant and their readings of this material, in whole or in part, helped shape the final ship: John Hildebrand, Pablo Medina, Rick Cannon, Tobias Wolff, Steven Salaita, Garrett Hongo, Naomi Shihab Nye, and Patricia Serrafian Ward. Gary Paul Nabhan was my noble lamplighter on the road to a publisher. The University of Arizona Press, in the persons of editorial director Christine Szuter and senior editor Patti Hartmann—along with Anna Mirocha, Nancy Arora, Keith LaBaw, Kathryn Conrad, and Holly Schaffer—with great devotion, sensitivity, and intelligence brought this book to birth. I should add patience for an unwieldy manuscript slowly swallowed, digested, and nourished into shape. Thanks to childhood comrades, especially my lawyer Ed Siegler, and Marco Pardo, John Millsfield, and Marty Martinez. Karen Pointer and Frank Ellsworth gave parts of the manuscript a careful look. A deep nod to Dr. Daniel Young, Dr. Frederick Brewster, and Susan Levin—healers in every sense of the word. My students Patrick Kelly of Pomona College and Lucy Thiboutot at Georgetown supplied useful material. Thanks to Stephanie Necca for her tireless work in typing the manuscript and to our neighbors Alan Moin, Sabrina Ousmaal, and their dear daughter, Mitra, for constant goodwill.

Special thanks to my brother, Mark, and uncle Gary Awad for careful and sensitive attention to the most emotionally charged pieces of this work; to my mother, Rose, for everything; to our son Matthew for his hard work tracking down and organizing his father's far-flung and often buried material; to sons Andy and Luke for encouragement throughout; and to my wife, Eileen, as always, for her love, forgiveness, and bravery.

I

Los Angeles Memoirs

Kingdom of Rags

Speak to me, Santee and Los Angeles streets! Of a world of color flying by on a metal rack. Skeletons of dress patterns shivering on a shoulder. I am listening. For the sound of buttons jumping in a box, men groaning under bolts of cloth. I was the man, or a boy, flying by with color, shaking the buttons like the dice of my future, groaning with the men under worsted. And now half my life is gone, and Santee Street is silent. I put my ear to the wind.

The wind-wing of his pale blue T-bird. In my young summers and on weekends I was drafted to ride with my father to the factory downtown. I don't think it was an order. We were a *schmate* family, a brood familiar with rags. A century ago, my father's Syrian father was the original linen merchant in Cleveland. My eye for beauty, both natural and false, must owe something to the display window, on Colorado Boulevard, of Awad of Pasadena, my maternal grandfather's Corday handbag place. It was as automatic for us children to work in a garment factory as it is today for kids to jigger the joystick of a computer game.

In 1955, my father, with "outside" man Earl Racine, began his first dress firm, LeGreg of California, a stylish conjoining of the names of his two children, Leslie and Greg. Dad's first "make" was an orange sleeveless dickey. And we weren't alone. There were dozens of women's garment factories in the lofts and warehouses fanning out from the epicenter of the Cooper Building at Ninth and Los Angeles streets. They were named as we were named, for wives and children: Jan Sue, Nancy B., Patty Woodard, Young Edwardian, Edith Flagg, Jody Tootique. And they all were selling the sun in a garment: *Forget vacation. Slip this on.*

LeGreg had some real hits: a striped tent dress that coyly hid baby-making of the '50s, sleeveless blouses and full bouffant skirts (six dollars retail for a set!), something a Texas chain called Margo's named, in ads, "a pleat treat." A Maine boutique enlisted *Women's Wear Daily* as an agent, asking the publisher to call LeGreg's to order the "hot item," a sailor-collared chemise.

But the rag trade was always precarious, and by 1963, the business had capsized. As my father once said, "I'm not in one business, I'm in five," meaning that for each of the four seasons, plus "holiday," a manufacturer had to restyle his dress line. In this garment pentathlon, if you slipped during one season—if, for example, one hot style was made poorly by the contractor, had a bad "fit," or was undersold—the garments all flooded back and your kingdom was in a heap. You and yours were unstitched.

But rag people came back. That was the meaning of rags; you were used to reuse.

Dad named his new company "Mr. Aref," as if afraid to entrust his luck to anyone but himself. He took no partners. It worked. The company was the first to style and make "the granny," soon de rigueur for every protesting coed. It landed him in *Time* magazine. His designer, George Wilner, revealed the genesis of that number: "A small retailer from Glendale brought me something in calico he said his daughter's friends had made, and that the kids liked it. We found some leftover calico print fabric, some ruffle, and in two hours I had it styled empire, with cuffs, like Empress Josephine, cut and stitched. Marty Bogash, our head of sales, took it on the Broadway, to Walt Dixon, the buyer, and we sold ten thousand dollars of the granny in one day. It took off like a rocket!"

By the end of the '60s, Mr. Aref was a $1-million operation with seventy employees. The company bought out another venerable firm, Ro-Nel, and started two other labels, By George! and Madison 7.

Ah, the first sacrament of the day: Howard's Coffee Stand, a little nook at the entrance to the Cooper Building.

"Cream uhn shoogaar, Aref?"

"Yes, Howard. As always."

"As always. Donut?"

"Donut, as always."

"As always, donut."

I liked the way Howard's baritone pronounced "shoogaar," as if he were giving the manufacturer his last sweetness of the day.

Then Dad and I strode down the gauntlet of showcases that lined the hallway entry to the Cooper Building. Dad would whistle at his own showcase and call the mannequin "Doll," and I would thrill at how prominent was our tent-dressed temptress.

Once the "goods" (anything made was good) were clipped of threads, I took them to shipping. I tried to first fill the orders of my Aunt Vinny (Circle Fashions on Pico Boulevard) and Aunt Jeannette (Jeanie's Casuals on Reseda Boulevard). The family was in rags from start to finish, father creating the styles, grandfather stitching the cloth, and my aunts vending it.

Bobby, the black shipper, gave me a pile of clipboards. Soon he and I were "picking," swiftly unhooking dresses by size and color for each of the stores' orders. Fred, the Chinese American head of shipping, riffled through the dresses on the silver rack one last time, looking for any error — a collar mis-ironed, a missing button, double-checking our work. Then Bobby and I set to it, boxing and bagging. Soon the smell of the gummed wet brushes of the old tape machine filled the air, and the sound of tissue, and the boxes stacking.

Before noon when I went out on the street, I took my orders from several workers: Jesse and Jose, the cutters, wanted their patterns; our French designer Maria, who had a hunchback, asked for buttons and silk thread; Eddie Gold, our old bookkeeper, reminded me, "Paper spools! Paper spools, dear boy!"

Time for lunch. *Speak to me, Sam's, of franks grilled, sliced, basted with mustard!* Sam's, on Ninth below Spring Street just around the corner from Manufacturer's Bank, was always crammed. There was something about my father in these few moments of wild ease, jawing with the waitress, the vein along his temple relaxing for the first (and last) time in the day, his fork cutting the franks without bun as cleanly as he would cut cloth, that made me know I would never know anyone like him. The sheer life of him! The irreplaceable style!

After lunch, I picked up a pattern from the pattern maker on Spring Street, inhaling the acrid ink and dyes. I wheezed a bit, sensing in the ink a writing life. One by one, I ducked into the specialty shops for the spools and the thread and the buttons. Everything on the streets was in motion: dresses, racks, bolts, models' posteriors, the thighs of shippers. More than once I picked up a skeletal original pattern thrown off the rack by a pothole in a crosswalk, a casualty of beauty.

After Bobby and I had finished bagging or boxing our shipments for the day, I'd peer in on my father. I might see Cy Harris, the piece goods salesman, running the latest swatches through Aref's fingers. My father had the hands of a pianist. He knew cloth. He lived by feel. Same here.

At Christmas parties, Dad liked to dance between the racks with Janine, head of his Cal Mart showroom, a stunning, tall brunette with blue eyes. He also liked to twirl the sample-makers' mannequin, riddled with pins. Or churn it with George Wilner himself!

"We enthused each other," Wilner, a former professional dancer, remembered. "A big order made an explosion of joy. And it spread through the whole factory."

If we ran out of A & B bags, or a certain box size, I was sent to the eleventh floor of the Cooper Building, where Charm of Hollywood, the well-established rag business of my uncles Albert and Victor Orfalea, had the whole floor. Al and Vic and Aref were good to each other, rose together and sank together. Uncle Al's son would go on to start, with his father's savings from the ailing rag trade, Kinko's Copies.

By 1977, Mr. Aref and associated labels had come undone. It was part of a cloth cataclysm that left few garment houses downtown intact. How did a world die in so short a time? There are so many reasons, it is like trying to finger one termite for a collapsed foundation. Most relevant perhaps: Few children, and almost none of the grandchildren, of the rag owners grasped the baton of the life of a sweatshop. My father was plain worn out, and let me know that I was meant for better.

Was I? Is it? This writer's life — is it better? And did I retreat to a large bureaucracy out of fear of the rollercoaster fate of rags?

None of us in the younger generation kept the cloth faith. My cousin did pretty well starting Kinko's. Huge profits and employment created, yes, but — something you can wear? Can feel? My uncle Gary, the youngest son of my contractor grandfather, went to work for Unocal. There's something made there, to be sure, but it's no more yours than it is the creation of hundreds of thousands of other stockholders. And how do you get your hands on a tank of gas?

And me? Could I hold this article over my head and call it a rain cap?

Yet, in the dark hours after making nothing but meetings all day, I stitch a book. It is made, it has weight. And it makes no money. Just like all the beauty my father fabricated, finally. Do I want the reader to pull a book on like a good sweater? Yes! I want it to wear well. To comfort. To awaken. Even, like a good burlap, to itch.

Loft by loft, floor by floor, I ascend the Cooper Building. Only one manufacturer is left in the cavernous place of jobbers and ghosts. When I tell Edith Flagg who I am, her breath goes out. She remembers immediately my father's violent death a few years after he closed Mr. Aref.

Back East, my wife won't take the brass-buttoned, turquoise denim pants suit the last manufacturer gave me. It has an elastic waist, she says; it's for seniors. I put it up for auction at our church's fundraiser in the spring. Nobody bids.

I seem to have lost that outfit, as I did my father, without saying how beautiful everything he made was. Maybe the errant pants suit is dancing in a closet with my father's granny dress. Maybe some widowed grandmother pulled it out of a pile, put it on, and is now prowling the corridors of Congress.

It was a kingdom, not Congress. A kingdom of color, of feel, of voice, of tags. It was a kingdom of rags.

Valley Boys

I am an American with Arab roots; Daniel Pearl was an American writer with Jewish roots. We both grew up in the San Fernando Valley of Los Angeles. Knowing that alone tells me something about him.

Dan Pearl lived in Encino and went to Birmingham High School at Victory and White Oak; I lived next door in Tarzana and went to Crespi Carmelite High School at Ventura and White Oak. I did not know him, but I know him.

I know because he grew up in Encino that he loved oak trees, not the pin oaks of the East that stand up straight and tall and have little, sharp leaves, but what we call — we, being Daniel and I — live oaks, trees with a gnarly, sprawling set of branches that smell of Italian pasta, many low to the ground that a boy can haul himself up into and perch in on a summer day, and eat a banana or drink an Orange Julius purchased on "the boulevard" (Ventura Boulevard, the street of our youth).

The reason Encino is Encino is because there are oaks; Encino means "oak" in Spanish, and oaks are symbols of things that do not die. I'm not sure of the exact location of Daniel Pearl's family home, but I'll bet that on many a day he would drive his bicycle past the huge live oak that no one — not even Californian suburbanites — would remove from the middle of the street on Balboa as it goes into the hills. And he would have touched it with his hand as he passed, maybe right where I touched it when I passed as a boy, happy to know it was there and thriving in spite of all the tawdriness around us. He would have continued to do this as a teenager with his first car, squeezing by the Old Oak of Balboa with a hand out the window to touch its flank, knowing how rarely people let things live that should live.

I know Daniel Pearl because I went to his school's famous dances. My school, being a Catholic boys' school, did not have famous dances. My school had only terrifying dances, ones where the mothers lined you up on either side of the library and demanded that you dance with the jacketed girl far across the room against the Geography section.

But Daniel's Birmingham High School had a reputation for getting the great bands of L.A. to perform live. Could this be where he got his love of music, his facility with several musical instruments? Birmingham drew such bands as the Seeds, the Doors in their infancy, the Nitty Gritty Dirt Band ("Buy for me the rain, my darlin,' buy for me the rain"). Birmingham also had something we never had: girls that looked like girls — in fact, that looked better than girls, looked like women. They wore spangled miniskirts and we Crespi boys would pay our lucre at the door and spend hours working up the nerve to ask one of these dark angels to do the Mashed Potato or Surfer Stomp.

I know, or surmise, that Daniel, like I, had his heart broken in the Valley as teenagers have their hearts broken in valleys everywhere, but never so much as this Valley with its long boulevards of endless shops that faced each other like a phalanx of longing in the sun. It was not a place for someone with a brain. Or a particularly deep heart.

But it had its secret orange grove — Bothwell's, below the hill on the Tarzana–Woodland Hills border — and Daniel and I whizzed it. Daniel and I stole oranges, because that was one of the secret pleasures of a place once as overrun with oranges as the Valley was, before it was overrun by roads and malls. Daniel put his hand over the barbed wire or took the low-hanging fruit that was trying itself to escape as he drove by on his bicycle.

I rode my bike to Encino every day to go to school. I know Daniel knew those commercial back alleys because driving down them helped us imagine a world where people didn't just sleep and go elsewhere to work. Smelling ginger, soy, and strong coffee, we dreamed of journeys to places like China or France. At the same time, we paid respect where respect was due, for example, to the pies at Dupar's or Dead End Beach. I am sure Daniel loved the shore, and getting there. There was nothing like getting there on a Saturday over Malibu Canyon, inhaling all the sage and rosemary, your hands out the window, your voice wailing about "Dirty Water" (Boston) or some guy named Louie, until you saw, in the dip of hills, that blue egg of the ocean.

It pulled you elsewhere, you who had a desire to know, to understand, and to love those unlike you, even those who did not like you. You knew you had a gift for language. You married late, if you were Daniel or Greg, because you had been in thrall to the language and others and knowing and finding others where they ticked. But you were so grateful you did finally arrive. And you were on your knees to the Almighty who for some reason made Jew and Arab, Encino and Tarzana, America and Pakistan, love and hate, emptiness and longing for that boy coming your way with your gift.

I did not know Daniel Pearl but I know him. And I know that the people who killed him did not know him. Those who did this horrible thing do not know oranges or oaks, Encino or Tarzana; they do not know what America is or can be. They identified a person with one word. Daniel never identified anyone with one word. And even that word they got wrong. Because Daniel was an Arab, a wandering Arab, and I am a skeptical Jew. I do not believe that God is the province of any one people, any one faith, and that any faith and people who kill in his name are allied with death and not life, not oaks, not oranges, not olives or land or Kashmir or anywhere but darkness.

I was raised where Daniel Pearl was raised. I am very proud of him. I only wish I had raised my voice sooner, gone over there, offered myself up as an American with an Arab skin and said, "Take me and examine me. Is my blood any different from Daniel Pearl's? If so, execute me. If not, look at this vast human being, and fall on your knees."

The Barber of Tarzana

Who is one of the longest-operating barbers in California? Who once cut Al Jolson's hair? Who had his barbershop rammed by an arsonist? Who has been trying to make me stylish for forty years without success? ("You're not getting any younger. It's time to comb it forward. The Nero look!")

His name is Luigi Venti, eighty-four, of Venti's Elite Barbers in Tarzana. Elite, because when you go under the Venti blade, you become part of a fraternity that stretches back to 1939, the year Luigi—also known as Louie—graduated from barber college, the youngest registered haircutter in Los Angeles. He was seventeen years old. The Elite fraternity ranges from actor Harrison Ford to Olympic champion diver Dr. Sammy Lee, who long ago cut out my tonsils. It includes anyone who needed to sharpen up, at risk of bloodletting, in the vicinity of the Los Angeles Convention Center (1939 to 1941), Wilshire and Robertson boulevards (1942 to 1945), Burton Way and Doheny Drive (1946 to 1962), and Ventura Boulevard and Corbin Avenue (1963 to the present).

And it includes my hero, Bud Abbott. One day, when I was a twelve-year-old riding a lime green Schwinn down a phalanx of palms on Oakdale Street in Tarzana, I caught sight of him watering his modest lawn at Redwing Street. Luigi had told me "the great Abbott" lived there, and I always slowed, hoping to see him. That time, I lucked out. Abbott was in a bathrobe, holding the nozzleless, drooping hose like a defanged snake. The "lecturer," Abbott's definition of the comic straight man, looked up. I waved. Bud waved. I pedaled furiously to the barbershop, where I announced my sighting. Naturally, Luigi was pleased. Had I seen the sign, "Hi Neighbor!" on his mailbox? (No, I hadn't.) Well, that was all right. Next time.

Early on, Luigi developed a unique way to cut hair, a process he called "the four-phase system." In Phase One, the customer would receive a basic trim, a cleanup of the neck. In Phase Two, Louie would begin to cut hair, exposing the ears somewhat, taking about an inch off the top. In Phase Three, he would take the straight razor around the ears, producing an arc of flesh. And then came Phase Four. Total butchery. It was in the height of his ecstasy at Phase Four that Louie was known to reveal scalp. A head under the Venti hand at Phase Four had to be ready for anything. It was his Ninth, his Pietà, his "Remembrance of Things Past." Luigi could make a head at Phase Four resemble Dresden after the firebombing. Not a hair on the head remained more than a millimeter long.

For years Louie tried to persuade me to beg off Phase Four. Wouldn't I prefer an Ivy League cut, or the fullness of the Madison Avenue blow-dry? I knew what he was trying to do — avoid the ultimate pain of creating one's best. It's possible, too, that he had had it with the wrath of my mother.

My mother spread bad word over Louie. She liked me with short hair, mind you, but Phase Four?

Even when I let my hair grow long for a time in college, I eventually sought out Louie for my traditional Phase Four, a rebellion against the rebellion. "Why are you still going to him?" my mother would croak.

"Why does the Earth orbit the Sun? Why do swallows come back to Capistrano? Louie learned the normal cut at barber college. He was done with that early." She would throw her hands up and say that I was crazy. (Now, flying in from the East for family and a cut, I no longer get her frowns when I mention Louie's name. Now my head *is* Phase Four.)

Luigi could cut me with hedging shears for all I cared. I wanted to hear him play the mandolin or accordion in his shop. I wanted an update on Bud Abbott. I wanted the Mafia jokes, the one-liners coming fast and furious with the whole barbershop his stage, customers part of the act. Let the scissors do their worst, as long as time was killed.

The shop hasn't changed much since the '60s. There's no chrome here or back lacquer basins; the place, once done up in a faint combat green, is now off-white. Photos of Cagney, Sinatra, Wayne, and Abbott adorn the top of the store-length mirror that reflects the customers sitting as if facing a firing squad. Bottles of every type of hair lotion populate the faux wood build-ins. Above the maestro hangs a faded framed print of a mandolin-banjo and a guitar. Next to it is an old oil of Louie in his blackgoggled eyeglass days (the '70s, no doubt). At one time, the gold-colored Naugahyde barber chairs showed their stuffing.

There used to be five chairs at Venti's Elite Barbers: Luigi's, separated from the plebeians of the world behind a screen of rippled plastic, toward the back of the store; three empty chairs (a memorial to former customers?); and Don Rio's chair near the window.

For years, Don Rio was "the other barber," the straight man to Louie's comic. He never seemed to be as busy as Louie and often sat in the swivel chair, curled into himself like a vulture, a sly smile resisting the pull of gravity. Don got all of the little kids; his cuts were reliable, no surprises. You can imagine my delight when, at sixteen, I was elevated to "first chair" behind the ripples.

The Godfather was another fixture in the shop around that time. He would remain nameless, never budging for a haircut, a watermelon-bulge over his belt, meaty hands clasped there, hair combed immaculately with water. He never read the movie magazines strewn on the end tables, never smoked, hardly blinked his eyes. I think Luigi would direct comments at him just to make sure he was alive. It was said that the Godfather had made some dough in the rag business stitching up jeans and swimsuits, and when he found out that my father was in the same business, I got the only nod the man gave in a year.

Years after the Godfather died, I quietly asked Louie why he'd left the rag business. Luigi said cryptically: "He threw someone down the steps."

Don Rio, too, is gone. His place today is taken by Paul Spira. One of the original five chairs has been given away. Two chairs near the window are empty. But Paul is now behind the screen in the once exalted position (doing the sensitive dye and hairpiece work), and Luigi is on the other side, closer to the window.

"I just got promoted," Louie says. "Right out the window."

John Wayne impersonator Ermall Williamson enters the shop.

"How long have you come to Luigi?" I ask.

"About twenty-five years."

"Why?"

"I'm waiting for him to get it right."

"One thing about Erm, he's got lots of hair," says Louie, pointing with a comb to a thick white mane. "I used to use a certain hair tonic on him. Now I clean up his neck, take the curls out—the John Wayne special."

"Wayne was bald," cracks Erm. "From 1949 on, he wore a hairpiece."

"Louie," I query, "did you ever do any real Western stars? No offense, Erm."

"I did Jay Silverheels."

"Who?"

"Tonto. I told him, 'Now I'm gonna scalp *you*.' "

Luigi Venti was born in 1922 above his father's barbershop across from the L.A. Convention Center "by midwife, for five dollars. My dad took one look at me and wanted his money back."

"My father was a producer," Louie hums along, stropping the razor. "He had fifteen kids with two wives. The first wife died, leaving him with four children. The second wife, my mother, had eleven kids. I have a half-brother and three half-sisters."

Erm: "I had a half-sister. The other half was my brother."

Now it's Erm's turn in the chair. His wife, Betty, watches the whole show for free.

"You don't even give me the mirror anymore."

"I'll give ya a mirror when I get done with ya. Say, are you picking me up this evening?"

"Why, are you going to fall down?"

This goes on until Louie slaps the lilac vegetal on Erm's neck, pointing him, sadly, in the direction of Time.

A few days later, signature beret doffed to expose his turtle-like baldness, Luigi takes me next door for a cup of coffee and a letting-down of what little hair remains to us both.

"My grandfather worked for peanuts, pennies, as a stonemason in a quarry," he says. "Barbering not only made my father more money, it was a way to keep your hands clean. Then he heard about 'beautiful America.' In 1913, he left Palermo on a boat to New York, which was too cold. Chicago was too windy. But California? 'Ah, that'sa nice. That'sa like Sicily.' "

Luigi worshiped his father, who taught him to play the mandolin, violin, and accordion. He learned how to strop and use the straight razor "the proper way," and how to singe hair with a candle to stop the breakage of ends.

Though Louie was restless as a boy — in love with music that came from his father's shop, happy to spend half of his school career not in class but in choir — he praises his father's hard-working example. "None of my brothers were ever drunks or touched narcotics. My father didn't care what we made or did. He wanted honesty."

In seventh grade, he met Barbara Armiles-Dominguez. He carried her books for her; he walked her back home on Sundays from St. Vincent's at Adams and Figueroa. "We did a lot of walking together," he says, and his eyes still shine after sixty years of marriage. Louie and Barbara danced on the brink of war to Duke Ellington, Benny Goodman, Henry Busse, and the Dorsey Brothers. He proposed to her while sitting in his father's 1933 black Buick.

After barber college, Luigi worked in his father's shop for a time and then joined Lloyd's barbershop at Wilshire and Robertson. Cuts were fifty cents apiece.

At Lloyd's, and later at Kenny Robert's shop, he cut them all, and cut up with them. There was André Previn ("young, good looking, very quiet, decent, particular in dress"); Herb Ellis (Merv Griffin's guitarist); Primo Carnera, the boxer ("very punchy in the chair"); Clete Roberts, the newscaster ("he took me flying, he saw holes in Stalin's stockings"); Sen. James Roosevelt; Donald O'Connor ("he used to like my daughter"); Louis B. Mayer("very businesslike, always had a lot of people around, his chauffeur was a bodyguard. I was told not to talk to Mr. Mayer about his films"); Al Jolson. In 1942, a skinny Frank Sinatra came in for a shine and a cut: "He was getting diction lessons across the street to get rid of his Hoboken accent — the same place Rita Hayworth went to get rid of her Spanish accent." Many stars brought their children. Louie gave Tony Thomas (Danny's son) his first butch haircut. He clipped Ed Begley Jr., Desi Arnaz Jr., Michael Reagan. He even counts a few true-blue Mafia men among those whose ears he has lowered — Mickey Cohen and Bugsy Siegel. "Whenever one of them got clipped and left, a detective would come in and ask me what the guy said."

Louie opened Venti's Elite Barbers in 1963 in Tarzana. He has survived recessions, long hair, the Vietnam War, even maniacal customers. In 1993, after giving refuge to barbers whose shops had been set afire by an irate teenager, his own store was damaged three nights in a row when a truck, driven by the same kid, rammed through the front glass. (The kid eventually did some time; the fire at one of the other shops spread through an entire shopping center and caused 3.5 million dollars in damage.)

"I've been more careful cutting since then," Louie smiles wanly.

He has a special affection for musicians and still cuts the hair of guitarist Roc Hillman, a member of Tommy Dorsey's original band. Though Louie finds in music "the international language," he dismisses today's offerings, particularly rap, as "a narcotic chant": "Rap disturbs the mind. They're all gonna be deaf."

Which leads him to his chief concern: violence. "Here you have to pass a test to get a driver's license," he says. "How about with a gun? I hate to say it—bring back the death penalty. Show executions on TV. The best sermon is example. You can talk all you want, but people will be too scared to hurt others if they see someone hung. Look what we have here. Charles Manson gets fed three times a day. He [orchestrated the killing of] the best hair stylist in the United States, Jay Sebring. He's not working. I am! Crime and no punishment.

"In the Army, you work in line. In church, you're in line. We're not in line. The mental attitude of our youth? God help us if there's a war. They'll be shooting each other. If they do it here, imagine what they'll do there!"

And what about the lessons of barbering?

"I learned everybody is the same. It's the avenues that come out of our lives that change people. I remember happy people as children. Then they come back . . ." His voice trails off, unwilling, perhaps, to acknowledge the dead ends of adulthood. "People are born equally. But when they grow up, some of them have too many humps in the road."

I have known for a long time that I come to Luigi Venti for more than what his scissors do. There is his unfailing humor, certainly, but also a certain sound-mindedness, and, for all the stars he serves, a rare equanimity and fellowship. Louie could be talking about a fellow Crespi High School graduate of mine, or Al Jolson, and it's all the same. Everyone has hair, everyone loses hair.

I give him what I find in him—respect for the backdrop that defines the lights, the night sky that Bud Abbott once was for Costello's star shower. The setup man. The barber of the neck the beautiful girl will surround with her creamed hand.

He knows it's time to go and, almost on cue, time to speak one last time of Bud Abbott.

"Once, when he was sick, my wife and I drove to his house to give him his cut," Louie recalls, looking out his window at encroaching buildings. "He asked my wife to come sit next to him while I trimmed away. He was watching something on TV. It was an Abbott and Costello movie, *Buck Privates*. And as we watched, he grew a little astonished as he watched himself driving a car. 'I never drove a car in my life,' Abbott said to me. 'I had epilepsy. But they made me drive the car down a hill. The cameraman ran like he was going to be killed!' "

"What did he tell you about Lou Costello?" I ask Luigi.

"Oh, no. [The man who] introduced me to Bud told me, 'Don't talk about Lou. Since Lou died, [Bud] ain't nobody. He laid an egg in every show he did. He was actually mad at Lou Costello for dying!'

"To be honest, Bud Abbott had [little] money when he died. I had to drive him to the bank once to pull out some of his residuals. He gambled, and the government took all his dough in taxes." Luigi pauses. "Look, if they ever looked at me, at any of us, for taxes the way they looked at him . . ." Here he lifts his wrists as if he could be led away.

I tip Luigi outrageously and he smiles, presenting me once more with his signature plastic flat brush that loops on the index finger. It works and, like Louie, it's found nowhere else. He loads me up with baseball cards "for the boys."

Thus we are joined, wordsmith and hairsmith. We're at war with time still, admirers of the Great Abbott in a world gone mad for power, money, and fame. In his store we have all been straight men to Luigi's sainted harlequin. But in the world at large, it is different. In a better world, perhaps, a world of propriety and properness, Louie and I would be the clowns. But in this one, where madness is the norm, we are the straight men, the "lecturers," Bud's cherished "Neighbor!" to all errant shooting stars.

The Teacher's Prayer

In 1992, my employer sent me home — to the streets of Los Angeles — to tour communities torn apart by the riots. I was living in Washington, D.C., working for a federal housing agency, and I flew West to inspect a burned-out strip mall and tend to emergency housing, but my thoughts kept straying to "my kids." I'd been a teacher fifteen years earlier at Miramonte Elementary at East Sixty-Eighth Street and Compton Avenue, at the time the second-largest primary school in the United States. It was there that I witnessed my students' struggle between faith and fate, between art and the rind of reality.

I drove from LAX to Miramonte on a search I had promised myself years ago. I had never stopped being haunted by memories of young Angelenos swimming up concrete to their hard playing fields. Who among my students had survived? My search was dogged, too, by a kind of teacher's prayer: Had I made a difference in their lives? Here's what I found.

Eric the Thumb Sucker

When I returned after fifteen years, one of the first things that greeted me was the cinder-block wall that girds the Miramonte playground. One orange tree still lolled over that wall, at the approximate spot where teachers lost a foul ball to an incensed Doberman pinscher on the last day of school in 1977. Now the bark was thicker, the oranges fatter, the Doberman gone. And Eric was gone. Eric Dennis, who smashed my car against the cinder-block wall.

When I entered one of forty rooms as Miramonte's writer-in-residence on a grant from the California Arts Council, Eric Dennis was lodged in the toughest Educationally Handicapped class. The classroom seemed like a variation on a maximum-security prison. Most of the kids wandered — or lunged — around freely, the teacher reduced to a cattle prod, at best. In six meetings over the first few weeks, I could barely get someone to sit at a desk, much less write a line of poetry or drama.

At the seventh meeting, the teacher was absent and the substitute was angry. Denise stuffed Cheetos into her mouth; Ernest flashed his large teeth, needling chubby, sensitive Kim. Five times I tried to read a poem; five times it was swallowed in the din. Then I went to the chalkboard and, half out of despair, drew an irregular, closed figure, a blob.

"What's that?" Ernest shouted.

"That's my soul," I replied. "Why don't you draw yours?"

Pandemonium. Everyone rushed to the board and drew lines, squiggles or perfect boxes, often drawing over each other's work. The sub slapped a ruler on her desk and accused the students of acting like fools. Then Gloria, a quiet, shy girl, came up to me and whispered, "I'd write a poem, Mr. Poetry Man, if there were less people at the board," and I sensed a breakthrough.

"Would you speak it to me, Gloria?"

Ready to take dictation, I grabbed an old typewriter and plopped it on a desk. "I Don't Like My Shape," she began. "If I had good parents, I would like my shape." That broke the dam. Soon everyone lined up to speak his or her own poem to me, including Eric Dennis.

Eric was eleven but still sucked his thumb so furiously that there was a red sore at its base. He had bottomless chocolate eyes and a taciturn expression that bordered on fear, but he blabbered his poem so casually, and with such personal satisfaction, that it belied its subject: suicide.

> . . . And if my soul won't stay with me
> Until I die,
> I'll kill myself,
> And then I'll cry.

Several days later in the lunchroom, Eric said he wanted to change the ending of this poem to "I'll cry, and then I'll kill myself." I said I liked it better the first way.

"But I can't cry after I kill myself."

"Who said?"

"Ernest."

"Ernest doesn't know what you are capable of."

"Can I still cry after I kill myself?"

"Sure."

"How?"

"Have you ever fallen asleep, had a bad dream, and woke up crying? Well, when you're dead, you're asleep, just longer. Maybe you'd cry because you didn't really want to kill yourself. Do you?"

"No."

"Well, then, you were right the first time."

Eric became one of my favorites—and a powerful writer in that short set of seasons we shared. Though he almost never let a smile last, he stopped sucking his thumb and wrote with exuberance. One day, I launched a love poem exercise in his class, figuring no one knows more about love than one who hasn't got it. Or who had it and saw it go. I added a twist to get the students moving: Imagine yourself a city boy writing to a country girl, or vice versa. Eric—who insisted that his be "City Boy to City Girl"—stunned the class into silence as he shouted in ecstasy at the end:

> I'm gonna marry everybody
> till they have babies
> everybody in California
> I love the whole wide world!
> And I love my wife
> but we can't have no more kids
> cause we don't have the money
> to buy clothes—matter of fact
> we don't have the money to feed
> you that well
> and we can't feed horses, cows, dogs,
> pigs, elephants—
> and I love the whole wide world!

Over the course of the school year, I'd occasionally give kids, Eric among them, a lift home. One afternoon, he spilled chocolate cake all over the back seat of my car. The next day, I asked him to clean it up. He took the keys and, before long, I heard a crash in the parking lot. Sure enough, Eric had given into the temptation to drive a blue Mercury. I flew into a rage—which I immediately regretted, looking into those bottomless, pained eyes. Eric started sucking his thumb again and never wrote another poem. He avoided me and didn't apologize, even though I repeatedly asked him to write that two-word poem you say when you've done something wrong. On the last day of school, he told me he had written it, that it was at his house. "Just say it!" I blurted.

"I'm sorry," Eric said, and hurried away.

Years later, calling up a half-century of the city's deceased on a computer at the Hall of Records in Norwalk, I discovered the death — by blunt force trauma — of a twelve-year-old boy in Los Angeles on Dec. 30, 1978. It was strangely labeled "accident — fall to curb." His name was Eric Dennis.

There was no mother's name on the certificate. The father's phone number was unlisted. Yet I was pretty sure this was my Eric Dennis.

"I'm sorry, Eric," I murmured, walking out.

Julius Caesar Is Lonely

He was a bunch-haired clown, strutting his strange, fulminating poems like a budding dictator. He wrote a one-act play about a man on his deathbed surrounded by greedy heirs, and he was the first child ever to read his poems at Beyond Baroque, a literary café in Venice.

Israel Andrade, nine, was the one student remembered by all five of the Miramonte teachers I managed to track down.

Joanie Pollock Klein, who logged ten years teaching kindergarten before retiring to raise her own children, remembered Izzy nearly eating the mike at Beyond Baroque. Steve Schiewe, who put in seven years before taking over the family life insurance business in Beverly Hills, recalled that he sipped espresso that night in Venice to the rhythm of Israel's paean to loneliness, "Julius Caesar, Romans!" which starts "Ta ta, da da, da da / A poet said no / music, no song, ta ta, my house is burned . . . Oh Julius Caesar, the fire is going up your wife."

Izzy's self-confidence astounded everyone, and he drew applause after each of this poems. "The Cussing Hour" described a traffic jam in which a mother gets a ticket: "Let me tell you cussing / is no place to be." "Mark Park" used word play to evoke fear: "Mark Park heard a bark in the park / Mark park, walk in the dark."

Overnight Izzy was transformed from butt of scorn to school hero, imitated by many on the playground who tried to read with his dramatic caesuras.

His biggest triumph came at the end of the school year, when he wrote and starred in "Come to Sun," one of eight original one-act plays performed before the entire school. Izzy played the father, a "grouchy old man" who, as the play opens, yells from his bed: "Where's my supper? Don't you know I'm gonna die?" An angel, invisible to all others, invites the father to "come on" with her. "Why don't you call me 'old grouchy man'?" the father asks. Her reply: "You're not an old grouchy man—*inside.*"

Israel had found a home in his writing.

As I combed the records at Norwalk and discovered three Israel Andrades who had died over the past half-century, I prayed none of them were Izzy. Mercifully, no one fit his chronology. I gave out a low shout, sensing he had not gone to the sun yet and that he had found a way to express that precious, unlikely interior of his, somewhere, somehow, in the world of grouchy adults.

The Rain, The Rain, The Rain

Avery Metzenheimer must have known something. He graduated from the sixth grade with that sense of the routine that lay ahead in adult life:

> You get tired
> More than a telephone pole
> Getting wired
> You'll get tired, tired, tired.

But he knew how to play, and his poems always had a lilt, a music and a wink.

It was one of the many drought years in California. Avery's best effort—one of the best poems of the whole year—spoke to that drought, using his fondness for repetition and humanity:

> The rain, the rain, the rain
> I get not one pain
> And the elderly man carrying
> His cane
> You can see the snow
> And it will glow
> The rain, the rain, the rain
> I like to play football in the
> Rain
> When I fall I have no pain
> Nobody gets hurt
> It's this one boy named dirt
> The rain, the rain, the rain

Again I checked the records in Norwalk and believed I had found my student. Avery Metzenheimer appears never to have married, logging some years as a customer service representative before dying at 33 of a sarcoma in the left thigh.

Avery Metzenheimer and Eric Dennis were the only students—out of eight hundred—who asked me on that last day of school if I'd be coming back.

The Great Man Speaks

We watched President Jimmy Carter's inaugural speech in Adelyn Stovall's fourth-grade classroom. There was no great joy or excitement, no feeling of being at an event any greater than recess. One boy was slouched, his cheek in hand, his black pick sticking from his hair, like the listing periscope of a submarine. A girl stared with her hazel eyes into a kind of blank present.

But the occasion sparked that day's poetry lesson, when I asked the children to write a dramatic monologue of a great man speaking to a bush, or a can, or something. Gilbert Aguilar wrote a beaut, titled "The Great Man Speaks to Anything":

> He tells the gun not to kill
> The great man tells the rat
> not to steal
> He tells the horses not to die
> A great dog tells the cats not
> to eat rats
> He told the elephant not
> to eat too many peanuts
> He tells the spider, throw
> your box of web away.

Swimming With Charles

Charles Alva, one of my sixth-graders, loved the water. His soul, he wrote, looked like a "duck's foot." He had a few things to say about swimming as well:

> I feel like a cup of water
> and sometimes I feel

like a beach and it feels funny
because people are
swimming in me.

At 1:55 a.m. on March 31, 1994, a Charles Alva was shot in the neck at a parking lot in Paramount. If this was *my* Charles Alva, as I fear from his vital statistics, then all those people swimming in him were shot, too. This Charles Alva had made it to his junior year of high school before he dropped out. He worked as a parking lot attendant. He left behind a wife and, I believe, a poem about his soul that outlives him, as it will me, and maybe this book. It will remind us that we are refreshing to others if we try. When I swim, I swim with Charles, and those who swam in him. When I take my ticket now at the parking booth, I look in the eyes of the attendant to see who is swimming there.

World War III

Imagine four historical figures looking out over a wasteland in the wake of a nuclear war: Abraham Lincoln, George Washington, Coretta Scott King, and Helen of Troy. Cloyd Milton's fifth-graders imagined it; a retired Milton told me it was the best class that he had had in thirty years of teaching. The sophistication of their one-act play, *World War III*, still stuns me. It opens with Coretta Scott King:

Coretta: Wars are usually silly things.
Abraham: I agree with you very deeply.
George: Wars hurt people who are not in the wars.
Helen: Who cares about it if people get hurt?
People get hurt. People have to die sometimes.

Helen of Troy is a real Machiavelli, a needler and deflator. She pooh-poohs the others' piety: "You three say it's bad to have wars. But why not let them hurt themselves at their own game?" When a Russian stumbles onto the scene, George, Abe, and Coretta shoot him, but Helen pouts: "All I want to do is let people fight over me. Not fight over them."

The play concluded with a haunting exchange on the morality of war between a soldier and Abraham Lincoln's son. A student backstage blew up a paper bag and crushed it for the sound of a gunshot: Lincoln's son had shot the soldier and then run offstage, scared, a virtual Cain. The bodies rose slowly as the audience heard "All You Need Is Love" by the Beatles.

There was perfect quiet when the music stopped, then thunderous applause. Loretta Jones, a wonderfully self-possessed and wise eleven-year-old, took a bow as the chief playwright along with her helpers, Wendy Wells and Wanda Woods. The *Los Angeles Herald Examiner*, which covered our extravaganza of one-acts, *Not For Children Only*, mentioned *World War III* honorifically.

Wanda Woods was a poet in her own right: Her best work was titled "Cook":

When I cook chicken
the grease burns me.
As I hop around the floor
it burns me more.
I went to the doctor.
It's no help he could do.
It was always inside me
the rest of my life.
The day I died, the day it
stopped.

Good Luck, Delbert

One dry day toward the end of the school year, I took to a basketball court after class, trying unsuccessfully to dunk on the eight-foot-high basket and attracting a crowd. Delbert Smith, who possessed one of the quickest minds in the school, walked up.

Earlier in the year, Delbert had barely escaped a house fire that killed his mother. From that time on, like Eric Dennis, he periodically sucked his thumb. But he wrote fine poems all year long: "What would we live in if we didn't have the world? / Who would we play with?"

Delbert took a ball twenty-five feet out, smiling a wide, crooked-tooth smile.

"I'll get you an ice cream if you hit that one, Delbert," I called out.

"Really, Mr. Awfulla?" His dark eyes gleamed.

Delbert, ten, took aim, bent down, shot the ball like children do, from the ankles, and banked it in.

Others wanted to get into the act, and sooner or later they sank theirs, too. I was drawn to try, but after several attempts I had no success.

"Maybe you should just try and bank it in, Mr. Awfulla," Delbert offered.

"No, Delbert. Everyone has to do it his own way." I bounced the ball methodically. "All you have to do is take your time, bend easy, let 'er go cleanly . . . and . . . she'll fall through . . . sweet!" The ball went through right on the "sweet!"

The kids yipped like puppies and danced around me. Delbert was ecstatic, hugging me, and I made good on my promise down at the corner market.

That late spring day, walking back in the sun, has stayed with me. Nor can I forget the next day, when Delbert rushed toward me and pulled a poem from his pocket:

The Good Luck Shot

Good luck does not work
all the time
The basket is high
the wind is low
the shot will miss
try once more
this can't miss
with a kiss it will
go through the hoop
it's going it's going
it's gone

I confess: After months of searching the streets of South Central L.A., the Internet, many schools, databases, places of business and worship, even appealing to radio listeners through public service announcements, I could not physically locate Delbert or any of my other students.*

You live ones I did not find — you dead ones I did. You are here in the unshackled work of your youth. You may find me here, as well, in a not completely tame tangle of words, more your student than your teacher now. I am older, but I remember.

---

*A letter to the editor of the *Los Angeles Times Magazine*, where this memoir first appeared, affirmed that though he had to endure the foster care system, Delbert, indeed, was alive, with "the most positive personality I've ever come across." He had starred in track and football in high school, and later took two degrees from Cal State University at Long Beach. A poet and recorder of rap poetry, Delbert was working as a teacher.

Straight Shooters

For those tired of watching silly end-zone dances by professional football players and wondering if there is any untattooed skin on the body of an NBA basketball player, for those who have nodded off after the fourth dunk of the professional slam-dunk competition and have lost track of which team the latest hundred-million-dollar player is on, or going to, or sulking about, I've got the perfect antidote.

You'll find it in a church-run gym in Gaithersburg, Maryland, every winter. Each Saturday morning starting in January at St. Raphael's, the human spirit is on display with no smoking pinwheels, no call girls dressed as cheerleaders, no jet fighters streaking or dope fiends singing, no mikes stuck in mouths for comment.

It costs nothing but a Saturday morning. It demands nothing but the willing suspension of disbelief. It guarantees nothing but delight. It hurts, it high-fives the heart.

I'm talking about a little grace called Special Olympics basketball. It's not exactly a pickup game, one of the last vestiges of true sport left in the world, but it will pick you up. All that's needed is a hankie, or three. My twelve-year-old boy was out there.

His name is Luke. He has neurofibromatosis—a word I can barely pronounce—which was signaled by lots of café au lait spots on his body when he was born. In rare cases life-threatening, NF is a condition hard to describe. But I'll try. Say you had an electrical wire swathed by insulation that was a little frayed. Say you'd lose a little charge in your current through the fray. That's what NF kids have. Their brains are fine. Their tongues are fine. It's the connection between the two that isn't.

Because of this, half of NF kids can't talk well (Luke didn't speak till he was four) or read well, or add or subtract without very hard work. Many also can't catch a fastball or even a normal ball because NF kids have low muscle tone and poor hand-eye coordination. Throw an object to them and they often flinch. They need special schools with special teachers to show them how to hold out their hands to protect themselves. So we call them "special needs," though they are indeed kids with special gifts. And these kids take those needs and gifts to the Special Olympics.

At St. Raphael's, these disability "all-stars" are on display — the NF kids, those with Down syndrome, autism, cerebral palsy and other conditions, from Ivymount and Katherine Thomas (private schools in Rockville, Maryland) and Somerset Elementary (a public school in Bethesda). Watching them, your heart might ache because of the ice surrounding it hitting heat, but soon it loosens up, as do these kids, and you may be amazed at the things you won't find.

You will not find the Killer Instinct, so lauded in the pros, fostered in college and high school, among all "normal" children. There are a few swipes here and there, and even a push. But no KI.

Let me give you an example. There's little Mark, hyperactive, big teeth, alert eyes — a fine shooter and defender. He dribbles quickly down the shortened court to the six-feet-high basket, shoots and misses, then chases the rebounder down and fouls him. He cries out to the referee, "You have to call it! I fouled him! That's not good!"

Can you imagine Shaquille O'Neal fouling anyone and begging the ref to call it? And I don't mean in the last three seconds of the game, I mean when the game has just started!

Mark aside, you will not find a lot of defense in these games. In fact, for most of the kids, it's an accomplishment to dribble the ball to the right goal. Many just pick it up and fly, filled with the excitement of being able to do, for a few seconds, what their older brothers, sisters, cousins, or TV heroes do often and naturally.

It's generally a slow game, with occasional bursts of action, and everyone gets to approach the low basket at his or her own pace. Parents are ordered by Montgomery County Special Olympics coordinator Pam Yerg to sit on the stage of the church gym and cheer till their heads fall off. That we do. We do it for little Jessie, who hardly speaks but has this grand smile, who works hard to walk with or without a ball but pushes the basketball up to the rim to kiss it, barely. That is worth a cheer. No dunk deserves it better.

Then there's Adam, who is more taken with a parent's video-shooting than with the game on the court. When another player, like his friend Luke, makes a basket, Adam has an impresario's way of thrusting his arms out in a V and announcing, gently, floating in front of the makeshift stands, "Ladies and gentlemen, an outstanding effort!" When Adam himself makes a shot, he does the same thing, slowly walking, smiling, raising the Vs behind the swarm of children sweeping the other way.

I don't mean to be saccharine. These kids have things to learn, too. Like many "normal" children, they don't take to passing. They want to do it all themselves. We are Kobe Bryants at heart, eh? But as the games progress, the notion of passing off suddenly strikes them (as it did Kobe), and one by one they look for help, especially when one of the Big Boys hangs over them like a giant.

The Big Boys are brought in, one to each team of three disabled kids, to keep things moving. They are not supposed to shoot, but every now and then one of them does — a great big dunk usually — and that oohs and ahs everyone. It's good to have them. They learn courage, too. The children are put through the paces of drills. It's not chaos. They have to hit paper plates pasted up on the wall at various heights to learn to pass. They dribble around cones, do free throws, shuffle laterally. But the big excitement is the game.

And the thing that most amazes us is how quickly we adults, so utterly given to competition, see the competitiveness in ourselves melt away, or rather transform into something else — the drive to overcome not others but oneself, even if for only a few seconds.

Earlier in his life, I gave up on Luke playing ball sports. Too many times he was hit in the face before he saw the ball coming. Too many times he would flinch before you even threw it. I steered him to swimming, bicycling, even running, all of which he enjoys and does well. But Special Olympics showed me that patience and determination can win out and that disabled kids, too, can experience the simple pleasures of a round ball going through a netted hoop.

Luke dribbled as the lefty he is. He picked up the ball and ran with it and we all laughed. Then he banked one in, Adam saluted, Mark clapped (though he was on the other team), Jessie smiled, Pam Yerg shouted. And my wife and I gave thanks for days when slow kids give quick jabs of love and show us all that in back of the greenbacks and sour egos is the desire of a child to overcome gravity. With a ball. With a bat. With himself.

We Were the People

We were the people who lived on an island called North America. We lived, we loved, we built homes once made of stone and brick, but then we changed to stucco and drywall and a lower grade of wood. We were a people of porches, but over time we became a people of backyards.

We were a people who loved to travel and though we didn't invent the car, we mass-produced it and made it the replacement of the horse and buggy all over the world (except mountainous places like Afghanistan). We built great roads that crisscrossed our land. Some of these roads cut huge swaths through cities and towns and uprooted poor people or farmers. But everyone used these roads, even the poor people and the farmers (who learned other trades and adjusted). We taught the world the thrill of open windows and wind rushing through them that did not destroy but gave us a feeling of freedom, open spaces, limitlessness.

We were a people who loved the sea. We congregated in cities along seacoasts. We didn't start this way. Most of our people at the beginning ran off to land like a fish to water. We were drunk on land, the chance to raise our own food in the light of God and to know that we owned that land, that no one could take it from us. But eventually we grew so well — maybe it was the quality of the food and the abundance of it — that we invented things that seemed more exciting and less taxing than slopping hogs or repairing a fence. And pretty soon in our life as a nation we found ourselves more pulled to the sea than the land, more to the cities by the sea than those sunk in the center of the continent.

We loved speed. Increasingly. The more speed we discovered, the more speed we sought. Our cars, our boats, our planes, even songs. Amusements. We seemed to like to defy death in our games. Perhaps we felt we had so mastered the mechanics of such things that we could make razor-edge accommodations with death, just for the thrill. So we built amusement "parks" that were less green than traditional parks and more multicolored and speed driven. We built roller coasters that dipped steeper, whirlabouts that tilted weirder, even what appeared to be free-fall rides that landed, of course, in water. Occasionally, someone died on one of these rides, but rarely. We were all assured that that was a gross, once-in-a-lifetime malfunction of the system.

It hardly need be said that we were a people of freedom. We were born in a revolution against the ruling monarchy of the time, Great Britain, and we zealously guarded the newfound freedom we achieved — and, in fact, sparked a love of freedom throughout Europe, starting first in France. It was a bloody path to this freedom, to be sure, but once achieved, no one let it slip, because Americans were onto something. The human spirit liked to stretch its wings, and people felt happier determining their future themselves as much as was possible.

Thus, we became a people of self — self-definition, self-fulfillment, self-esteem. At the same time that we honed ourselves busily in pursuit of happiness, we realized there were others out there. Some were bronze-faced and some were dark umber-faced. It was hard enough to deal with others, but *these* others were trouble, indeed. The bronze-faced ones were done away with for the most part, and the umber-faced ones made subservient. This didn't sit right with many of our people because we were founded on the principle of "liberty and justice for all." So we had a terrible civil war. It took another century to begin to integrate the dark umber-faced people into the society at large, but as we did, we became a better, more just land and people felt better about themselves. It could be said that the dark umber-faced people liked the sea, and freedom, and speed, and travel, and backyards just as much as everyone else did.

We hated war and loved sport. Our sports accelerated when we didn't have much of a war to fight. We hit little round balls of leather and cork and larger balls of leather and air and egg-shaped things called pigskins and little white pock-marked goodies that really sailed down the green beyond the sand into the hole. We liked holes in our sports. Some zone of emptiness to fill. Rims, pockets, uprights, "down the pike," "the lip of the cup." We taught our children lots of sports when we weren't at war because we were an energetic, spirited people who liked to test each other, usually with good intentions, and we were in love with a well-toned body. And motion. And sport was the chief way we overcame our self-obsession, and it was there we learned teamwork and the beauty of people working in concert.

We hated war, but we were good at it. We were, in fact, fierce warriors once our dander was got up. Being on an island, we didn't much want to mess in others' pots. But sometimes it was unavoidable and when we gathered all our selves together as one, we were a fearsome sight. We jumped from planes with our faces smeared in grease and tried to look like the bronze faces we wiped out. We rescued the whole continent of Europe from many tyrants, and Japan, too. We did it in concert with some pretty ruthless regimes, to be sure, like the Soviet Union, but a greater good was there to be had, and we made the alliances we had to to get the job done. We were not afraid to lose lives for this cause, because for all our self-culture, at heart, and despite all our failings, we believed in the sanctity of the individual and the right of a person to breathe freely and determine his or her own destiny. We were the Individual People. We worshipped at the altar of freedom and said God was there, too.

We became a rich people beyond anything the world had seen. Some people had cars half the size of a city block. We built towers far above our cities and rockets that leapt off the Earth. Mansions, once rare, became tract homes. We located little ponds in our backyards, ponds of water we cleansed with chemicals. We extended our life spans with our inventions, found ways to have sex without having children, built explosives that could do in the Earth, partly out of a sense of protection. *See that, world? So don't tread on me.* Too bad others found a way to blow up everything, too, but the world was getting complicated. We spent billions of dollars to gather up rocks on the Moon, more or less just to say we'd done it. It seemed at times as if we were trying to scale God's own fortress and say to him: *See here. You created some magnificent upstart in the people from Maine to California!*

And we went on smoking in our backyards, steaming in our stock markets, flying in our cars (though with more and more of them we got slower). We gave a lot to the world, to be sure. We picked up Europe from the ashes with our dollars and our ingenuity. We helped people get electricity with dams, drained swamps here and there, sent out something called the Peace Corps. But for the most part, we stuck to our island. We tried to live and let live. We couldn't police the world, anyway. We built the United Nations, but steered clear of it as much as possible. We liked the idea of unity more than the reality of it. For the reality was disunity. And there was only so much we could do. Our chief emissary was something called rock music. We sent that all over the place. And food that could be cooked in a wink. Fast music and food and chips to eat or to power electrical brains. But otherwise, we stuck to our backyards.

For after Europe, we were not good at wars. Something was missing.

We were too far off the island in a hostile terrain with few people on our side. We would shout, "Why do you hate us? We believe in live and let live." But they replied, "If you did, why are you doing this here and that there?" They pointed out that oil was important to us and that we hooked up with unsavory people to keep it flowing. They showed us loving tungsten for our light bulbs and propping up this dictator or that to get it. They said we didn't understand that people were suffering under the thumb of dictatorships or repressions in places like Guatemala, China, and the West Bank and that for some crazy reason we were tied up with those people. We put up our hands and said, "No, you don't understand. There are good reasons we do what we do." But they just pointed to those who were suffering.

Someone was connecting the dots. One day, for the first time in our history since 1812, foreigners attacked our East Coast. They destroyed two of our largest buildings by crashing our own jets into them. We thought these people deranged, for they killed themselves in the process. Maybe they were and maybe they weren't. They also hurt our main concrete fort. About three thousand people were killed. We were no longer an island. We were bleeding from hatreds that came from afar but struck from within. We walked around, shaken. We all felt like the rubble from those buildings was on our chests. We wanted to be known for our benevolence toward the world — from afar, mind you — but the world said, "We want you up close. We want you to see us. You don't see us." And so they took us through their hell.

Cracked open, we poured ourselves out. Many of our firemen and policemen and rescue workers lost their lives trying to reach those in the burning buildings. It was amazing to watch how they gave themselves up without a moment's hesitation. It had been a long time since we'd seen something like it and it seemed for a time that the Individual People were fully out of their skins and given towards others.

What was wanted of us from here?

We were a very special people living on borrowed time, as all people are all over the world, except we never felt time pass. Now we feel time and reason flee. We were the people apart. But we aren't now. At a great cost we are the people we weren't. And who those people are remains to be seen. Whether we pick out of who we were the best or the worst, remains to be seen. All that is certain is that the river of suffering of the world has flowed into our harbors and at a very great cost, we are not who we were. We know we are no longer apart from it all; we are a part of it all. Our backyards are facing front.

Nazera

Father's mother was called "the Rock," as in the Rock of Gibraltar. When I was a kid and visited her Wilshire district home with the gabled roof on Mansfield—a street lined with tall palms and scarred-for-life sycamores—I figured Gibraltar was somewhere hidden in her garden, or the shed. I once asked her directly about the so-called rock she was supposed to be like. She shooed me off and crowed, "If I was a rock you wouldn't be here." Then she asked if I would like some coffee with milk in it. The parents scowled and she cackled like the Wicked Witch of the West. For all I know, she might have been a witch. She had a tattoo of a small blue cross about the size of a dime on the underside of her left wrist. It straddled two tendons there; near the cross were two blue dots. "That's because I went to a doctor who cut a boil off me," she said. She was proud of that marked wrist, and would hold it up to the light, like someone who had survived a suicide attempt.

"Nazera! Nazera!" she would sing and dance around and around, crying out her name before the gathered family as if she were a last dinosaur from an extinct world, and all better take note and savor the steps of her feet, for worse times were ahead. We would clap for her. Her gray hair, still long at her age of eighty-eight, swayed behind her. And the daughter who took care of her and suffered the brunt of her lifelong campaign against the meek, would shriek. Aunt Vernice did not talk, speak, answer, retort, utter, remark, or partake of any other commonplace verb. She shrieked and sang over the telephone, "Noooo, Roooose! Mom is at it again. Reeeeally!" Her mother took down her gray crowning glory and as the hair sashayed, a frazzled storm cloud, Aunt Vernice squealed like a filly. Nazera never danced like this in front of strangers. With them, she was demure.

But with the family, after a meal of grape leaves, *kibbi*, and vats of sour *leban*, she would wrap herself in a shawl she had crocheted in all colors of the rainbow and go happily into her own world. She used to give me a little claw-like iron bell that resembled the gold bell at Communion and ask that I ring it. I did. "Oh, that's nice!" she smiled. "I got that bell from a beggar in Cleveland for two vials of holy water."

And how did she get the holy water? "I blessed it myself."

Grandma Nazera was, in her time, a grape picker, moppet, huckster, notions peddler, and self-styled prophetess. She never claimed she was a saint. I make that claim, humbly, now that her motley of colors has drained off onto the dusty streets of the world and they have sold her home to a young couple who want to "restore" it. More than any home that my own family had, Nazera's represents childhood to me, and no tinkering with awnings, mending of moldings, or unstripping of the original wood can restore that quality.

Actually, no house could hold her, though the Mansfield one came close to doing so. No church could, either—she was raised a Melkite, married an Orthodox, and brought up her children as Roman Catholics because, in her words, "Sonny boy, that was the closest steeple in Cleveland." If it had been the Elks Club, we might all have been raised Elks.

By American standards, she was not a beauty, though at times her knowing eyes and smile bloomed, if not a rose on her cheeks, certainly a hibiscus. A photo of her sticks out in my mind. It was one of many brown photos hidden in an ebony end table that was never the end of anything, but always, so it seemed, in the center of her living room. In that special browned picture stands Grandfather, a tall, charming chap if there ever was one, with a noble, high forehead and gold fob chain hanging down from his vest. The young and short Nazera looks like she had just swallowed an olive pit. Black hair is tight on her head; her jowls are caved and her black eyes point the finger. The photographer must have taken a few belts after snapping that one. A more unlikely duo could not have touched this earth. They lived together for fifty-five years, enduring world wars, cancers, strokes, colostomies, Parkinson's disease, and other accoutrements of age. They were unsuited; they had six children, the last being my father.

But I am getting ahead of my story. I should say something about where she was born, though it wasn't long before she wrote that place off. It is a land that has not seen peace for five thousand years: Lebanon. She cracked into the world in a mountain village along the eastern Mediterranean, a village with an air so pure that asthmatics pilgrimage to it from around the globe, between various civil wars, bloodlettings,

confrontations between giants and giants, giants and pigmies, and pigmies and pigmies. The village is a stronghold of Melkite and Orthodox
Christians, many of a hermetic bent, and it is called Zahleh.

A jumpy, cold stream—the Bardowni River—rushes down the cen-
ter of the village. Fifty years after Nazera had last seen it, she could still
remember its sound: "It goes *chlchgllchgl*." When I visited Lebanon for
the first time, she gave me specific instructions as to how to get to her
house, what window to look out, and what tree I would find along the
Bardowni River just outside the window. When our group found the
house, now inhabited by a Muslim couple, we were allowed upstairs,
where one naked light bulb hung from a bilious green ceiling. I looked
out the designated window to find, sure enough, the ripe poplar and the
rushing stream she had mentioned. Legions of poplars hobnobbed it
down the river. She once said, "A broad leaf catches more rain."

Nazera spent her earliest years helping her father in his vineyard on
the outskirts of Zahleh and visiting her own grandmother on donkey-
back. She never tired of telling the story about how her grandmother
would know when she was coming by the donkey ears bobbing above
the stone wall. "*Mittle hamar*," Nazera would call, and wiggle her own
ears "like a jackass" on into her ninth decade.

The vineyard cost her a toe. One day, hopping on top of the lime-
stone wall that bounded the vines while her father and the workers
picked the fruit, she slipped. Falling to the ground, she smashed her toe
on a rock. A deformed, blackened, ingrown nail on the wrecked toe
announced her scrappiness to the world through open-toe slippers many
years later. To Grandmother, walls clearly were not meant for contemplation. And toes? They were made to dance with and to break!

She escaped death before she was seven, the year she and her father
left for America. Three Druze people approached her father at the vineyard one day as he was piling clusters of grapes in a basket, wiping his
forehead from sweat. They wanted to buy some grapes, they said. But
they gave her father, Barakat Jabaly, too large a coin. With a knowing
look, he called to little Nazera, "Go to get change!" She sought out the
cave where they slept during harvest and kept their wherewithal, but she
couldn't find the secret cache of gold. On her return, Barakat tried to
cover her mouth before she blurted it, but it was too late. The words
"gold" and "cave" were out.

That night, they awoke in the cave to sounds of rustling. "Don't make any noise," Barakat whispered. "Get on my back." Quickly, with stealth, he crawled with his daughter out of the cave right under the thieves' noses. "We left them dinner," Nazera smiled.

"The Druze," Grandma told me, "were thieves from day one." According to her, if you left so much as a wine jug in your vineyard, they'd sweep it up. Followers of a loner offshoot of Islam in the Chouf Mountains, the Druze managed to elicit her strongest venom. But to be fair, Grandma had plenty saved up for the Jews, the Arabs, the bankers, presidents Nixon and McKinley, the door-to-door Fuller Brush salesmen, and Lucille next door with the white hair who was cold and had bars on her windows.

Grandmother's assignation of guilt over the cave incident may have been induced by stories of the Druze massacres of 1860, twenty-six years before her birth. The period of the 1880s was one of relative calm in Zahleh, and robbery and arson could just as easily have been carried out by Bedouins or by vagrants of any religious stripe. As I grew, of course, Druze metamorphosed in my mind from fuse to human being when, as a teenager, I snapped my fingers to the rock and roll tunes of L.A.'s top disc jockey, a Druze named Casey Kasem.

Grandma's sister, Rose, had been a kind of Lebanese mail-order bride for one Boutros Hamrah in the United States. In 1893, when Nazera was seven years old, she and her father and her two brothers sailed from Beirut to New York to link up with Rose. Now émigrés, the children were also motherless.

When Nazera was an infant, Zahra Sahadi Jabaly had deserted her children and husband and fled to South America. It was said that Barakat was hot-tempered and liberal with the hand—in a word, a wifebeater. In her twenties as a governess for other children, Zahra died in Brazil of yellow fever. Though Zahra had run from abuse, the uncharacteristic abandonment of her children by an Arab mother at a harrowing time must have thrown Nazera's life permanently off kilter. But the fractured family had no time to think about that on the cold Atlantic; like everyone else in steerage, they were sick to their stomachs.

Fresh off the boat, or "F.O.B.," Nazera was prodded by immigration officials on Ellis Island: "Where are you from?" "Syria." "Syria? Where is that? Is that in Africa?" On the streets of New York, people had no more notion of Syria or Lebanon than the dark side of the Moon. She was called nigger, dago, chink. Racist or not, none of the terms hit the mark. She was a no-race, a scratch of the head. Immigration records reveal her to have been one of the first thousand Arab women to enter the United States.

Soon, Nazera was an orphan. Her father — remarried briefly — like her mother died young. Shortly thereafter, her sister took off to Connecticut, notched ten children and as many miscarriages. One brother, George, hopped a merchant marine ship to China and the Boxer Rebellion; the eldest Jabaly sibling, Joseph, was trampled and killed in New York City by a horse-drawn American Express wagon. By the turn of the century, Nazera was alone with the Statue of Liberty.

Nazera went to school for a few months in the city, then skipped it. Add that to a few months of school in Lebanon and you get a life with less than a year of formal education. "Honey," she proclaimed to me in a voice born for bold print, "I went to the world school." And so she did. She hooked up with a couple of other Arab immigrant girls — among them one Sadie Dibs — hung a peddler's tray from her neck stuffed with beads, cheap necklaces, toilet water, and yes, vials of holy water, and the group was off making the circuit of the five boroughs of New York.

Imagine those olive-complected ragamuffins swinging down the brownstone street in their faded cotton dresses singing, "Holy wahtaar!" The rails of Grand Central Station pinched, the ferry boat to Staten Island tooted to their laughter! It wasn't long before Nazera and her cronies expanded business. They added new items such as cigarettes, snuff, and exotic perfumes (probably squeezed from oranges). Next they struck out from New York City. It was no longer big enough for them — they had to conquer Philadelphia, Baltimore, Washington, D.C., Pittsburgh, Cleveland, then on to New England — to New Haven, Providence, Boston. Nazera's gang implanted the East with notions wild and various.

Sadie Dibs was the leader's favorite. Nazera was the little colonel at five feet even. The two walked down the street draping their arms around each other the way true friends do — not holding the shoulder but laying the arm loosely around the friend's neck letting the wrist hang free, all the while hoisting the long trays of notions that folded and became a satchel. Once a construction worker on Washington Street spied the duo and let down his hook, snaring Nazera's case by the handle. Up in the air it went! But it fell amid the jeers of the Irish workmen, scattering her notions on the pavement. The stiffest blow came when Sadie went off and married the first man she met on their big circuit, a snuff manufacturer in Boston. Nazera never offered snuff from her tray again.

Nazera carried her hurt around for a few years; old members of her group dropped off, new ones came on. Then in Cleveland she met my future grandfather.

Aref was a Syrian making more money than were all the other Arabs in Cleveland put together. The owner of a few dry goods stores that specialized in linen, Aref dressed impeccably — a three-piece suit, a gold fob watch, a silk shirt, and a moustache trimmed with painstaking precision. His skin was powder white. His eyes had a distant, wounded, boyish look about them and he was tall, about six feet. His lips were full and he faithfully smoked Camels; three fingers of his hand were stained caramel for life. The gent was a man about town. He had fifty women after him just waiting to siphon his pockets. Beautiful women, petticoated, swirl-hair types, smitten by his gentility and mood of inner detachment. So he fell for a peddler.

If there ever was a chase in a love affair, this was it. Nazera, who should have fallen down on her knees in front of Aref and begged his acceptance, flaunted her lack of interest in him, rejected his overtures for lunch, demands for dinner, and telegrams for a midnight rendezvous. She bragged of the interest a handsome salesman named Schwartz was taking in her.

If Aref had been given to drink he would have begun drinking, but he wasn't, so he didn't. Most Arabs are not keen on alcohol and find other ways to express their disenchantment with the world, such as popping blood vessels from shouting, developing ulcers, or working themselves into an early grave. After one year of chasing Nazera through every depot, lounge, marketplace, and café in the East, Aref was worn out. Then abruptly, without so much as a "Forgive me," she did an about-face and returned one of his agonized letters with a note. Aref must have smashed the note into a thousand creases. An answer! An actual reply from this jade of the alleys!

They were married in Cleveland and there settled.

Nazera drove a four-door Chandler, and later one of the most expensive Packards of the era, a touring car complete with jump seat large enough to transport the six children who came in rapid succession — four daughters, then two sons. It was a loud, peppery brood and mischief was constant. The eldest boy, George, once plucked a goldfish from a bowl and fried it. He said he was hungry. My father, the youngest, wanted to skate, so he let the hose run all day in the backyard until the water froze, creating his own personal rink. Another time, George tied Father to his bicycle face down and prone, like some sort of human sled, and dragged him for two blocks, dislodging his nose and breaking it. Father alluded to that incident to describe the abnormally long yet unusually straight nose of his. "I had it planed down by the sidewalk," he said.

Aref Jr. as a teenager once fell asleep in a movie theater; his date left him there sleeping peacefully. He slept on while the janitors did their work. He slept through the closing of the doors and ticket booths. He was still snoring at 4 a.m. when Nazera broke down the doors with a crowbar.

How did such an independent, hot-headed woman churn out a large family in so short a time? Above anything else in the world she loved her family, was in fact idolatrous of it and extremely protective, the way one is with a possession one hasn't counted on having. But her anger was bone shattering; she could lock a child in a closet for an hour or two. She used her hand liberally and would shout till the veins in her neck bulged. She had the righteousness of Allah, Jehovah, and God combined. In some ways, her love was a cage from which only my father escaped.

It came to explode about the time her husband was losing everything in the Depression. One by one, his prosperous dry goods stores were boarded up. Still he continued to dress to the hilt and make the rounds of the fine restaurants in Cleveland. In such a place Nazera found him one noon with another woman. Dumbstruck, she went straight home, gathered up the six children, took them down to the restaurant where Grandfather was just finishing dessert, and shoved them in front of him and the strange woman. "This is the kind of man your father is!" she screeched, leaving them there with Aref holding the spoon.

Illicit lover or not — who could say? Her husband was a mild man. I never in my life heard him raise his voice, save one day over Nazera's bickering about her wayward daughter's reading habits, the way Adele would stretch for hours on a lavender divan reading pulp novels after her second divorce. "Leave her alone!" Aref shouted in such a way that the whole family turned their heads and the chandelier swayed. He shook by nature. He had Parkinson's disease most of his adult life.

Nazera's temper wasn't all of her husband's troubles. Aref also had to put up with his wife's brother, George Jabaly. I can best characterize this lively, tight-fisted, loud individual by noting that his ears almost literally smoked with hair. As a child I couldn't help spying on him behind his chair and seeing the thick ear hair. As he boomed about the Boxer Rebellion—"Tamahooda! Tamahooda!" was the call on the ships as they unfurled their sails in Shanghai—I felt sure he would blow his stack. His ears were two hairy fuses! One day it happened. He simply shook his head and rested it on Nazera's shoulder, the victim of a massive coronary.

When Nazera and George got together, they could scorch the entire planet with their judgments. This is to suggest that if Nazera's husband was cheating, he probably did it to preserve his hearing.

Judgments—Grandma had plenty of them. When I was no longer a child, she said she would love to parcel out a few for my benefit. I would turn on the tape recorder. She didn't like that and asked if it was on. I said no and she continued: "I came here in 1893. I struggled; nothing came easy. I fought for what I have. But when all is said and done, the country is run by the Yahood. They have the papers, the Congress, *yi*, they have everything! Now they want to grab the Jordan River, the Golan Heights, grab this and that. The Arabs? They are not much better. In fact, they are worse. They don't grab; they got nothing *to* grab. They don't own a thing of value so they act like dogs. [Forget the mixed blessing of oil on the Gulf states.] Farouk? *Yi!* He sleeps on the pillow and his people eat flies. Nasser—he shouts into the microphone like a hyena and when it comes time to fight, the Yahood clobber him. Honey, I am an American. I am no foreigner. I speak better English than an Englishman. And my taxes go to the Yahood and my sons go to America. I gave my sons to this country for the war." They had, in fact, survived—George a survivor of the Burma campaign, and Aref Junior one of the few back from the mangled 551st Parachute Infantry Battalion attached to the 82nd Airborne during the Battle of the Bulge. Aref Junior's feet were almost amputated after freezing in the Belgian winter; he heard about the German surrender from a hospital bed in Camp Carson, Colorado.

Despite Nazera's caustic opinions, she welcomed anyone from any race or religion into her living room and admired those who could assert their ideas with a credible argument or semblance of proof. She was not big on adornments. "If people want to see me they can come to my house," she said. "If they want to see furniture, they can go to Barker Brothers."

After the war and the discovery of "the other woman," one by one the family headed out West. Adele and Nazera were the last to come, in the Packard. Driving was Nazera's sport, her "soveraynetee," as the Wife of Bath would have put it. Husband Aref left the driving to her. He never learned to operate an automobile, never had a driver's license. In her eighties, Nazera was still twisting the large wheel of an old Pontiac, the car she bestowed on me on my sixteenth birthday.

Los Angeles more than any other American city owes its character and growth to an America flushed with victory over Germany and Japan. Before World War II, L.A. was a secret of the movie rich and citrus growers, as well as a last stop for the Dust Bowl poor. After the war, the restless, feisty drive of its young veterans pushed the country West and L.A.'s population mushroomed.

Many civilizations at their peak have worshiped the sun—the ancient Egyptians did, as did the Aztecs. As did the Americans with their need to be free, gunned like a car, circling a new-built Mecca in the sun. Voilà: the cold, concrete network of freeways that made us hot blooded, and the custom-made pools set like opals in the city's suburbs. Voilà: the post-war movies' spouting of heroes in Europe and Japan, and the orgasmic growth of a Hollywood culture that snapped neon lights down boulevards at the city's heart at the same time that Disney created the stainless park of fantasy. Los Angeles. Elbow room in the sun. It spawned a hydra-head of tolerance and intolerance unlike any metropolis in the country, and drew a squat peddler like Nazera to a house with a gabled roof. Soon she built a dollhouse in the backyard and planted near it a pomegranate tree. I call that house the House of Dreams.

Aref Senior had gone out West a year ahead of Nazera. When she arrived, they had a cool reunion in Los Angeles, but the coolness faded. The word "cool" did not exist for Nazera. She had a way of injecting life into a stone; if the stone broke from feeling, too bad. A stone was better broken than cold.

Her lean years were her fruit trees' fattest. She set to planting lemon, orange, peach, and apricot, and hooked me by the halter as I—her first grandchild—ran around, green as the fig she would take hold of. I saw her wrist's cross; I saw the swollen fig. "You were born in August," she smiled. "You came when the figs were ripe." And then she touched the clear syrup at the lip of the fig. "See? The *asil* comes off. Tell me if there is a taste like that on the earth." In the foggy winters I walked around her haphazard orchard, bewildered. "Gram," I asked. "Where is the fig tree?" And she pointed to a gnarled, gray, lifeless thing. "But it is ugly, Gram." "No," she frowned. "It is waiting to be beautiful."

In dead center of the backyard stood another plain tree with small, sharp leaves. Its fruit came slowly and every other year, scarcely. But when it came — ah! The pomegranate tree was the sacred center, and October the sacred month. All the family drew toward it for the plucking. Nazera would set out deck chairs on the grass, hoist the laundry pole off the line, and go about knocking down the highest pomegranates first. My father held the bag and chased her and the red, throbbing rain of juice. Everyone laughed and clapped and, injecting their nails into the hard rind of the fruit, squirted scarlet juice on their faces. We ate pomegranates all afternoon; her four daughters — all deep into middle age and childless — would suck the fruit till they were sick.

The time came to cart the remaining pomegranates in large sacks to the basement. In an off year, only a small bag of the fruit remained, so we didn't have to go into the dungeon. One such year was the year Nazera died.

The dollhouse. When I was a boy, tigers, elephants, and dolls lived in there — the blue ceiling was so high! When I was about thirteen, the ceiling was dangerously close to my head and I would while away afternoons alone, lying on the dollhouse floor, my head touching one wall, my feet the other, and dream of girls larger than dolls. One day the dollhouse contained only trunks of old letters. I could neither stand nor lie down inside. The place only received my head. And when I removed it and shut the blue door that now barely reached the height of my heart when I stood, I knew I was a man, and I never opened it again.

The grape arbor that fringed the entry to the dollhouse was always in use. Nazera was a superb cook, and however rough and proclaiming her voice, no one ever sounded the word "delicious" the way she did. She spent days making grape leaves, picking them off the vine, blanching them, grinding the lamb by hand, pressing chunks with her wrist, wetting the blue tattoo cross and dots. She had a running argument with her daughter, Vernice, about the "wrap."

"Vernice, your wrap is too loose. The lamb spills out."

"No, Mom. Pleeeease!"

"I'm telling you this because you must learn."

"But, Mom, I'm sixty years old!"

"It is never too late to learn the correct wrap. You must tuck the ends in. You must cover the holes eaten by the snails. If you get a leaf with a hole, plan ahead!"

Like most Arab women, Nazera did not hear refusals of food. She offered more than anyone could eat; she even offered portions of the main meal after dessert was finished. Only Father's bark would stop her from brandishing the *kibbi*, the *tabbouli*, the *khubz Arabi*, chick pea dip, *baytinjan*, peas, the pickled *lift*. She worshiped Father. Her heart quickened at the sound of his motorcycle on her driveway.

After dinner I would leave the adults chattering about the Middle East and, with a *ghrabi* cookie in hand, go stand on top of the floor heater in the hall between bedrooms. Staring down through the grate, I saw a blue flame twitching. It was my feeling when young that the entire house sat on fire — blue fire — of which that small flame was just the tip. I stood and took Communion — that is, gave myself the hoop of butter and dough that would stick to the roof of my mouth like Communion, the ghrabi — and all the while, the gas heater pressed hot air up my legs to my face. Aunts, uncles, cousins, or Nazera herself, cracking the wood floor with their heavy shoes as they passed me on their way to the toilet or to take a nap after dinner, knew never to get me off that floor heater. "It's *hiiiis* spot," sighed Aunt Vernice. "He won't budge from that grate." Once I asked Nazera if I could sleep on it overnight, but she said, "No, you'll be fried to a crisp."

In the late hours, Nazera's dining room table that had steamed with food and coffee — the widest table in my memory — became a stage and a casino. On that mahogany table I first felt an arousal for my cousin Bonnie, George's daughter. On that table Aunt Adele threatened to leave — leave the table, Los Angeles, the United States, the Northern Hemisphere, and finally step right off the globe because no one understood her, no one realized what it was like to be flattened for six years by a three-hundred-pound Chinese importer. There Aunt Bette (who had discarded her original name, her own mother's Nazera) sat with the smoke easing lazily out of her nostrils and heard her husband Jerry's jokes get dirtier by the year. There Aunt Jeannette slapped her hand down on the table so hard from laughing that it woke her husband Orville from his snooze. Around that poker table first rang the word "Hell" in my ears; there I first heard the phrases "Heavens to Betsy," "I'll coldcock you," "Pass it on," "*Immie*, you're the greatest," and "Goddamn your country," or *Yil'an baladak* in Arabic. Let's not forget *Nitshi thinishu* ("May you be pinched"), *N'tha!* ("My point!" or "Oh, point yourself!"), and *Yislamli hal wijih!* ("Bless your face!").

Marathon poker games found Father sinking below the tablecloth, pulling out his seventh card at stud; it gave him nothing, but he would jump up as if he had the game won, and smack down his cards. He never had a poker face. Grandma would say, "Here's the bitch," and lay down three queens and take all the money. She was good at poker and knew it. The table warped at the first of Uncle George's theories on race war, broke out in knots when Aunt Bette referred to her own nose as "bulbous." The aunts loved us children of the last child to excess. And I, never once thinking this was abnormal, grew up believing it must be natural to have so many people love you.

It was the House of Dreams. It was the Abode of Sorrow, where curses spilled on the oriental rugs like too-hot coffee. It was where Uncle George spouted infinite schemes to "get rich quick"—make Syrian bread to be sold in plastic bags (too bad he never did it, an idea before its time as every market in the country today has Syrian bread, if under another, less threatening name, like pita). How about selling pickled turnip, with a pair of hand-woven socks? Offer dual membership in a country club and a mausoleum. ("You move from one putting green to the other.") Through all of this sat my mother Rose, spotless and kind, uncomplicated and bewildered at such Americanized Arabs, since she came from a poorer, more traditional Arab family.

In Los Angeles all took turns bailing out of one form or another of the clothing industry. All accused Father—who reached the pinnacle of his profession on the West Coast—of working like a slave. He lost his shirt, too, or rather, dresses.

Eight years before her end, Nazera contracted cancer of the rectum. They removed the organ, as well as a large portion of her intestines. From then on she excreted through a small hole on the side of her belly. The bathroom at the Mansfield house began to take on the odors of alcohol and urine; her contraption for siphoning waste was laid discreetly behind the toilet bowl.

Gut hole or not, for a while she was her indefatigable self. She attended meetings of the Altar and Rosary Society of Saint Anne's Melkite Church, as well as meetings of the Hamasne Club, a group of ancient women who bored her to death from Hama and Homs, Syria, the latter her husband's hometown. Though she herself was from Zahleh in Lebanon, she put in some time for her husband at the Syrian club, particularly after he died of a stroke shortly before the onset of her own cancer. He had been paralyzed for three years. I remember visiting him one day and watching him struggle to speak. His neck muscles grew taut and his jaw opened but nothing came out. His head fell back on the pillow. That quiet, gentle man died without having the last say. I wonder what he would have said. Perhaps, "Nazera, stop shouting at Adele." Or, "Nazera, why didn't you marry Schwartz? Nazera, go climb in the drainpipes and give the world some peace. Nazera, I love you, stupid as I am."

There remained one last touch of glory.

On a warm spring night, Nazera bundled up her cancers to witness the fiftieth anniversary of my mother's parents at the lush Huntington Sheraton in Pasadena. There were more than five hundred people in attendance; the simple folk had done well. At the end of the dinner an oud was plucked and a tabla patted. Then one little member of the crowd stood up in the smoke-filled room.

She stood in a trance, let her eighty-eight-year-old feet take her out to the dance floor, and she began to move one foot ahead of the other, turning her hands slowly as an Arab woman does when dancing, turning and kneading the air, turning around slowly, always letting the front foot guide and draw the foot behind like a magnet, keeping the head still and kneading the air gently as if everything we breathe were dough.

The crowd was stunned when they saw Nazera's solo. They knew she was the oldest woman in the banquet room. For a few seconds, it was just Nazera and the oud and the tabla. Then the people began to clap — sharp claps to the slow glide of the ancient woman and the ancient, eggplant-shaped oud. They were riding her and she knew it. Or at least I think she did. As the claps grew louder, loud enough to tremble the chandeliers above, Nazera stopped dancing. She walked with her arms still up and hands kneading to one side of the dance floor, then the other, and her eyes went further into the trance. She was not there. She was somewhere with a beat only she could hear, for her legs had given out, and she was no longer gliding. She was plummeting sideways. Maybe that caused everyone to clap louder, holding their breath. Her eyes seemed to grow white, as if they were snowing. Her smile became the timeless, terrible expression of the Sphinx. No one dared to stop clapping, for no matter what her legs were doing, her hands were still up. Finally, Father retrieved her. Grandfather Awad, from the other side of the family, went over and kissed her even though she smiled so strangely it seemed she would bite his belt. He was crying. Her eyes were sleeting.

It was given to me to feed her that last summer when I came to visit. I could barely hold the spoon. How could one feed the Rock? Who was I to hold out food to a woman who had once laughed at the hole in her stomach and said, "I talk so much they've given me another mouth." Now she sat in silence. In her trance Nazera scorned me. That bit of applesauce stuck to her bottom lip.

Still I led her to her small porch out front, nothing like the giant L-shaped porch of Mother's parents, but Nazera always was one to make do with the minimal. As far as she was concerned, it was the length of the boardwalk in Atlantic City. Her trimmed hedge was the hedge of a king. And those tall palms on Mansfield, swishing and swaying in the breeze, were tall men like Aref, and they were not in Los Angeles. They were in Syria walking on the road from Homs to Zahleh, where her husband should have met her — tall shadows like the ones she followed across the Atlantic for a better life, the shadows she followed each day from toilet to kitchen to porch seeking a life free from scorn and fire and finding herself still under a hot sun and staring at tall, slippery shadows that contained on top — if you strained yourself enough you'd develop lesions — a sweet, brown fruit with a hard, thin nut.

In her eighty-seventh and eighty-eighth years, donning a crocheted cap, she took to writing a journal and was faithful to it. Here is one of the entries:

> February 6, 1973. it is windy Lucle was Here Vernice called chicken for supper and baked potato I had my lunch I enjoyed it and thank God for his grace Im little better my leg is not better but I am able to bare it no other way grin and bare it Im grateful it is time 12am Now a new paragraph I tried to lydown but cant find rest it is best to sit up and suffer I don't think this will ever get better this will be the end of me I called Vernice she is very discourage busissin is lousey I dont know what is happening to our country cloudy time 325pm Im waiting for Mick Douglas Show.

Invariably she started an entry with praise to the light, and somewhere down the line mentioned her pain. She never knew, or admitted, just what it was that was doing her in. She had had cobalt treatments and they were supposed to be successful. She never said the word "cancer." The entries dwindled. One of the last said, "There's a wire brush at my bones."

Even as she screamed on her deathbed, she never said what she had; the screams raised her back, turned her face red, her withered breasts green, her legs purple, her kneecaps black. She screamed, "Color! Color!" and she got her wish. Father's mouth opened wider as if it would rip at the edges, but no sound came out — until with a final huff, her body fell back, and he collapsed at the foot of her bed, crying hoarsely. Vernice covered his shoulders with Nazera's shawl of many colors and all left him there, alone.

Contact

The War, Sandlot Football, and My Father

It seems strange to me now as I think of it, but I never saw the home where my father grew up in Cleveland while he was alive. In 1990, I drove there alone to a reunion, not of his old World War II buddies — only one of whom he saw after the war, and only once — but to a reunion of his old sandlot football team, the Cleveland Olympics, which, on November 29, 1942, defeated its crosstown rival the Scarlet Hawks, 6–0, in a warm-up game at Shaw Stadium for the pro Cleveland Rams. This was the month and the year his elite wartime unit, the 551st, began to form up at Fort Benning, Georgia, exactly three months before my father, Aref Orfalea, joined the U.S. Army.

I would never have known about the Olympics if their old quarterback and captain, Bud Lank, hadn't called me three years after my father died at sixty, in a voice I did not know, with a name I vaguely caught from my father's attenuated descriptions of his childhood years. Lank had not seen Dad since the Orfalea family's trek to California a year after World War II, the great launching pad for the restless migration to the West Coast. Lank had heard of Dad's tragic death of a gunshot wound in his store in 1985, from my Aunt Margaret of Hudson, Ohio, and he wanted to talk to me.

"Come to Cleveland and see where your father spent the first twenty-three years of his life."

"But I've got three boys in diapers."

"Close your eyes and do it. You won't regret it. You can tell your boys about it someday. He had a great pair of hands."

Yes, I thought, it would be good for them to know that their grandfather had friends, good friends, and a youth. If not to know him, to know of him, and in knowing his own context, to feel the parameters of their own lives deepen. We gauge people by the hive of humanity around them, who is drawn to them, who repelled, and who sticks. My children are intrigued by friends of mine who fly into town from far away and are pleased when my wife and I make friends of the parents of their friends. But my father had taken none of his childhood friends forward with him after the war, not even through letters. The only exception was a priest, the Reverend Jay Clines, whose dour fate it was to take charge of all Catholic cemeteries in Cleveland. He had little time for the living and was dead himself, soon after my father, of a heart attack.

So in 1990, in search of friends my father had long given up for lost, I drove alone in our Ford station wagon to the Harley Hotel in Willoughby from Washington, D.C., through Maryland, Pennsylvania, past Kent, Ohio, where the car almost veered onto campus for a twenty-year memorial service for the four dead Kent State University students.

Soon I was in a cramped room at the modest Harley shaking hands with Lank, a short, husky man with a kind voice and winning smile, moving to get me a drink. Around the walls of the slender quarters were photographs of the old neighborhood crowd, mostly as teens in the prewar late '30s and early '40s. Some brave souls had volunteered contemporary photos of themselves and their families. It wasn't long before I realized that the organizing principle of this reunion was a neighborhood—a highly unlikely event inasmuch as neighborhoods tend to atomize quickly in America, their inhabitants flung geographically outward from childhood, like shards from a slow explosion.

It wasn't a high school reunion; they'd all gone to different high schools—Collinwood, Shaw, and Cathedral Latin. It wasn't a war reunion—the units were myriad. It was the regathering of a rare thing, the football team of a neighborhood, "Colonial Heights"—bounded by Ivanhoe, Belvoir, and Catalpa, sitting on a ridge overlooking Euclid Avenue as it runs downtown. It was also the final call of castaways in a sense, as the Cleveland Olympics (originally the Hilltoppers) were formed from rejection. Because of lack of weight (you had to be under 150 pounds for the sandlots), most in the Olympics could not make the high school varsity teams. On occasion, however, a player like them would make it to the big time, as did Baltimore Colts legendary quarterback Johnny Unitas, who came out of industrial leagues similar to the sandlots.

To what extent the Cleveland Olympics were kept together—raised to fever pitch of devotion—by their coach, Ross Mudler, as an inducement to stay home from war, is hard to tell. But there was little doubt in my mind, speaking with old friends of my father's, that Mudler himself was angry about the war chipping away at his starting lineup and even into his reserves. It appears that Mudler — a lifelong bachelor who stored Olympics gear and held chalkboard sessions in his mother's basement — had memories of World War I and was outraged that a second world-wide slaughter was on. He regarded the Olympics boys as his "sons in God" and made no bones about his feelings of war. He called it "the ultimate obscenity."

It was something of a specter to see Mudler stand up that night, older than the old men around him. Even though he was deep in his eighties, recovering (or not) from a broken hip, the old Olympics coach had a clear, sharp bead in his eyes and his hair had more steel gray than what hair was left to his old players. It was combed immaculately with water back from the brow as was common in the '40s. That comb of hair streaked back, angular face, and beaked nose made him resemble a woodpecker. I expected humor.

What came from the makeshift podium was a trumpet blast. Mudler's basso profundo contained the clarity of the ageless and the sobriety of someone who would soon die:

"There were no playing fields then, and most equipment was too expensive for us. You should take pride in the fact that your football organization was housed in the basement of a home. Because of my age and impairment, I think of eight kids who went to war and never came back. It is unfortunate for a father to lose his sons to that ultimate obscenity called war."

In danger of losing his emotion, Mudler paused and cleared his throat. How strange, I thought, that I am here, and that this man appears to have frozen in time. He may have lost more than many real parents: his inner life stopped in 1945. The old coach announced that he wanted to end by quoting from a poem he had found in *National Geographic*. He recited it from memory:

Sleep, my sons.
Sleep in the silent depths of the sea
or in your bed of open sod,
until you wake at dawn
to the low, clear reveille of God.

The reunion in the thin room swelled with memory and droll humor, toasts, prods, outpourings of liquor and old affections. But underneath it all I thought I heard Mudler's reveille. Rolly Reese, small and probably a speedster then, spoke of "saving everything" as a child—rags, rubber bands, yarn—the typical Depression home's hoarding. Mudler pointed to a man with a cane, gentle giant Billy Vance (my father's favorite in anecdote): "That was the greatest tackle in Cleveland." In fact, Vance was not beefy enough in high school (tackles needing two hundred pounds) to letter. Mudler was unregenerate: "There is something about a good tackle you can't duplicate."

Presumably this was the grab, not the position. *Yes*, I thought, that point of pure contact not altogether different from lovemaking—the point at which you hook the fish, you've tagged the runner at second. But no. You don't embrace a fish. And not like baseball. Baseball is flirting, elegance, barely touching the white pillow for an out. Football is, for better or worse, *contact*, with the hands, with body. From the times he would barrel into a rusher as a tight end, or knock down a runner as a defensive back, to the days he was unemployed many years later and held my mother in the kitchen long, very long, as if giving up the clinch was giving up the lifeline, my father's search for contact was a constant in his life, as constant as contact was inconstant.

Was this why he went to war?

Billy Vance moved his thick glasses and cane, and turned to me: "There was a game we played on sleet and slush. 'I'll take out the defense, you make the tackle,' I told your dad. And he did. Oh, I remember your grandmother calling him, 'Ah-Riff! Ah-Riff!' She once tried to put a blanket over his shoulders on the bench."

Was that why he went to war?

The one-woman cheering section, one-woman wrecking crew, Nazera Orfalea. The Orfalea household in Cleveland was something of a collection of magnets with too similar a charge. Some, like my father and his oldest sister Jeannette, were repelled outward. A Depression loss of wealth in the linen trade (the family had owned three Avenue Gift Shops, one at the Arcade), compounded by bickering between my proud, silent grandfather—who took his sorrow to the dark alcove in a woman's silks—and my raucous, irrepressible grandmother, had spun some of the family West before Hitler invaded Poland.

Though the Orfaleas were hardly of a military pedigree (many early Syrians such as Aref Senior came to the United States at the turn of the century to avoid fighting in the Turkish Army), by the time of the Cleveland Olympics' stunning victory in Shaw Stadium, my father's brother, George, had already gone to war and was being promoted at his

Army post in Burma. George, in fact, stayed in the Army after the war, commanded the military guard at Los Alamos during the first hydrogen bomb tests, and rose to the rank of major before retiring early, in part due to misgivings over the escalating Vietnam War.

By the winter of 1942, Aref Jr. — restless by nature, contact driven, a speed ice-skater — was feeling left behind, in an emotional maelstrom, no less.

But there was the Olympics, and its tradition to uphold. Which would win?

It is hard to understand today the excitement the sandlot football teams engendered in Midwestern cities in the '30s and early '40s. For one thing, the sandlot teams pretty much disappeared before the war was over, their ranks exhausted by the GI drain. Then men who came back crushed themselves into sex, family, and jobs.

Ross Mudler's Cleveland Olympics were the last of a proud, even loving tradition of that slop-in-the-mud sport when neighborhoods mattered more than owners and free agents. And for a time, for a boy, they held the war at bay. What few sandlot records survive show that the Olympics had remarkable predecessors in the crosstown rival Cleveland News Skippies. From 1933 to 1939, the Skippies' win-loss record was an incredible 70–2, with them winning forty-six games in a row at one point. In the first four years of the streak, the Skippies' opponents managed to score a total of three touchdowns and one safety. Little wonder that the team was dubbed football's "world amateur bantamweight champions," playing in pregame warm-ups to Red Grange's Chicago Bears, the Cleveland Rams, and the Washington Redskins when, according to one nickel program, it "nearly took the play away from the big fellows."

"Do Not Pay More Than 5 Cents for This Program" says one of the Skippies' programs in 1936. Were they so good they were scalping? A quarter a program? A *dollar?* By the time Dad was warming up for the big game in November 1942 that would decide the Cleveland sandlot championship between the Olympics and the Scarlet Hawks, the programs and games had several sponsors, among them the Fraternal Order of Eagles and the Veterans of Foreign Wars. Proceeds from the games went largely to charities such as the New Toys Shop in Cleveland, which distributed toys and clothes to poor children at Christmas or to the aging vets of World War I.

Oh to have stayed an Olympic, arms outstretched for a pass, frozen in the air forever in that November cold! To salve the wounds of a war to end all wars with your sweat. Not to break those wounds open.

I can see it all now. Father is running down the long column of steps from Mannering Road, his breath climbing the night air as he descends. At the streetcar stop on Euclid he meets Bud Lank, who promises him a breadbasket pass, and Billy Vance, who promises him a block as far as Lake Erie. The streetcar picks up passengers going to the game at the great old roundhouse that cures many an iron horse, that iron cave that will itself stand half a century later mute and empty to Aref's son.

It's not hard to place myself among the ten thousand people at Shaw Stadium (there will be more for the game to follow with the pro Rams). I like being lost in the lights. And the cheers and whoops. It's not hard to do this because Lank has sent me the official program of that Sunday night — November 29, 1942 — and staring down at it reveals that "Orf Orfalea" is playing right end next to Billy Vance at right tackle, and that he is No. 12. Amazing. His nickname is the same as mine all those school years. A kind of dog bark. He never told me. The number is unlucky: boxcars. Strange. In college-dorm football, I also played end. Never knew we were both good with our hands, though his were better with metal pipes and wood.

While I am reading the program ads, Dad is placing his helmet — not unlike the first one he will use in jumping from an airplane — in front of him as he does warm-up sit-ups. The ads read: "Christmas Cards . . . Many As Low as 50 for $1.00 . . . Carlson Printing. 4-Aces Grill, Choice Liquors, Open Until 2:30. Compliments of a Friend. Merle Owens, Funeral Director." (What's this? A Don Shalala is in reserve for St. Philomena's, a team that has played an earlier exhibition. Is he a relative of native Clevelander and President Clinton's Health and Human Services Secretary Donna Shalala?)

The Olympics wear black and white; the Scarlet Hawks, blood red. Now the teams are airborne on the ground as the crowd lifts with the first kickoff and everyone for one still moment is weightless, before the drop and the catch. Now the blood spills onto the black and white. Now there are young men sprawled on the ground. And that is how it is, bodies mauling bodies, with no score, until halftime.

Many years later, quarterback Lank, who spent his life leading those who work with their hands, bricklayers, in their union, will tell me,

"Aref and I were so tired we tripped over each other going into the locker room at halftime." Lank and my father were the only two players playing both ways—offense and defense.

Their rest is brief; soon they are back in the cold. Because the fields are slippery with new snow that is old before its time, a fleeting warm prior day has turned the field to slush and the knees to gin and the backs to Gehenna and the minds to pass, pass, somehow, Lank, get it to Orf because we can't run on this crap, don't you see?

Somewhere in the second half, the two midget titans battling it out for citywide supremacy, Lank sends Orf long, no stop-and-go, because if you stop in this mud you'll never go again, just go as best as you can toward the goal post. Lank chugs backward, tries to get a stable footing but can't, flips the ball to reserve fullback Bill Cerbin, who seems to be paddle-handing it away from frenzied tacklers. Finally, he grips it with everything he's got, throwing his shoulder out from a pass he's not used to throwing, and my father goes aloft seeing the ball block the moon for a moment. And, just at the moment, halfback Johnny Hart, who did play high school football at Shaw, smothers it right shy of Orf and slides his way to the goal line and over for the win. Not even an extra point. A bare pickin's victory, 6–0.

My father falls on his chest in the young snow and the cold of it goes straight to his heart. He is happy, make no mistake, someone got it on his team. But he is empty, he is hugging not leather but a young pile of snow.

Billy Vance turned to me that night in Willoughby, letting his cane drop to the floor. "About your father," he said, speaking about his old friend's fearful end. "Look. That is what the Lord was thinking of in the Garden of Gethsemane."

The night my father caught nothing but snow in Cleveland may very well have been the night Major Wood Joerg at Fort Benning, Georgia first ran his eyes down a list of names of young men who were good with their hands, very athletic, and ready for the sky—the future men of the 551st Parachute Infantry Battalion.

And Georgia in November is as warm as the Garden of Gethsemane.

The Messenger of the Lost Battalion

> Was it for this the clay grew tall?
> — Wilfried Owen

I

In the dark period my father was out of work after he had closed his twenty-five-year-old garment manufacturing business, he gave in to the suggestion of a friend that he take his frustration to a shooting range. He was not a lover of guns and, unlike many in the San Fernando Valley who assure intruders of an "armed response," did not own a firearm. I wouldn't say he was without fear; but he was without that kind of fear.

Nevertheless, from boredom or loneliness, he accompanied his friend — whose dress firm was still puttering along — to shoot. It was a fateful decision. It's possible that Dad hadn't shot a gun since the Second World War and, aiming at the target with a pistol, the several explosions of an afternoon bent his eardrum. From that day forward, he complained of a ringing in his ears — tinnitus, it's called. No doctor or friend could help.

As he struggled to get his work bearings, I would on occasion see him put his hand up to his ear. His own voice and the voice of others had begun to echo. I thought of him in those hard days as some kind of Beethoven trying to make music as the bustle of the world slowly ebbed out of him. Seven years after the factory closing he lay dead on the floor of his new photocopy store, a smile on his face. The ringing had stopped, the symphony begun.

On the many nights I have stayed awake thinking about him, I have wondered whether he heard that bullet coming at him for forty years without knowing it, and that the ringing from the shooting range was only the last warning. I mean forty years after a bad winter in Belgium, in which he, like tens of thousands of men, had dropped.

My father repeated only two things about his life as a paratrooper in World War II: "I ate my K-rations on a silver platter at the Hotel Negresco in Nice," and, "All my friends were killed around me." That last referred to the Battle of the Bulge. Though in retrospect I see him as the freest man I ever knew, for him the war was too painful an event to dwell on. And at sixty he was dead, the secrets of a most jarring event in his life, it would seem, buried with him.

Full of questions I had barely begun to formulate about my father, in August 1989 I was given a luminous chance to recover something of him. Members of his old battalion — a courageous and ill-fated unit — were returning to France and Belgium; my brother Mark and I didn't resist their invitation to join them. Would we find someone who knew Aref Orfalea? What really had been his war experience and how had it shaped the unusual man he was? His driven life and tragic death? Would something in the men themselves recall him? At the last minute, his seventy-nine-year-old eldest sister Jeannette, who at age five had sung "Over There!" for a World War I war bond drive, joined us, too.

Soon we were hustling down the Promenade des Anglais in Nice, halted momentarily by a visionary sight of a man in parachute tugged out to sea by speedboat, parasailing. The carmine dome of the white-washed grand old Negresco loomed. We ducked in over the plush red carpet and under a giant chandelier. Our mission was belied by our attire — bathing suits.

The floor manager's mouth pursed cynically at our story of traveling with American veterans who had run the Nazis out of Nice long ago, "Oh yes," he said. "We were captured by Italy, then Germany, and we were lib-er-a-ted by you Americans." His words were like the salad Niçoise — sour and cold.

But when I wondered aloud if the Negresco still served K-rations warm on silver plates, and mentioned my dead father had sure liked them that way, the man's face visibly changed.

"Go into the bar, please, and order whatever drink you would like — on the house."

Jean-Paul Marro later joined us, shaking his head at our gin-and-tonics. "What, no champagne?" He motioned for a mint drink himself and told us of his war experience in Algeria. His wife and he had toured the United States recently for their twentieth anniversary; Marro had found himself most moved by Arlington National Cemetery. "I realized there how many lives had been given by America for us." He bowed his head.

Seeing us off at the front of the Negresco, Marro took a green package from behind his back: "This is for your mother. Tell her France appreciates what her husband did for our freedom." It was a bottle of French perfume. That was a moment of beauty and linkage across time, continents, and generations I will never forget, brought by joining our search with that of the few survivors of one of the most unusual units in U.S. military history—the 551st Parachute Infantry Battalion.

Why, exactly, was the 551st unique? One of only two independent U.S. parachute battalions that fought in the war, it evolved into a highly individualistic, cantankerous band of outsiders welded together in a national emergency. One of them was among the first U.S. soldiers to jump out of planes in 1940 at Fort Benning, Georgia, as part of the original paratrooper Test Platoon. The battalion was the first (and last) to hazard test jumps out of gliders. Two months after D-Day in Normandy, General Eisenhower overruled Churchill, who wanted an invasion of the Balkans, by opening up a second front in southern France. On August 15, 1944, the 551st executed a near perfect jump into the foothills behind Nice as part of Operation Dragoon—one of the first daylight combat drops in U.S. history.

The 551st was the first American unit to capture a Nazi general (in Draguignan), the first U.S. force to reach Cannes and Nice. For a job that normally would have required a division (fifteen thousand men), the six-hundred-man battalion patrolled a forty-five-mile stretch of the France-Italy border in harsh winter conditions under Nazi shelling in the Maritime Alps. Finally, on December 27, 1944, Major General James Gavin gave the 551st the signal honor of spearheading the Allied counterattack against the terrifying German "Bulge" in Belgium, on its northern shoulder in the 82nd Airborne sector. The battalion's heroic push came at great cost—on January 7 only 110 of its 643 men walked out of the decisive battle at Rochelinval; many of those were walking wounded. Other than the wipeout of the 509th, the other independent parachute battalion, at Anzio, Italy, and later in Belgium, the 551st probably sustained the worst casualty rate of any U.S. battalion on the European front, between 84 and 94 percent.

Strangely, shortly after Rochelinval, the 551st was disbanded, its records destroyed, its valor undecorated, and its existence forgotten—a fate more akin to Vietnam, it would seem, than the so-called good war.

It didn't take long to realize that the reunion in Europe carried a great deal of emotional weight for all. There was familial weight, as well. With the twenty returning veterans were twelve spouses, thirteen children, and seven grandchildren. Phil Hand of Georgia, who had first begun to piece the few survivors of the 551st together in the late seventies, brought a son whose mind, he said, had been destroyed by glue-sniffing in the sixties. "He thinks he's a paratrooper," "Bubbles" Hand, a pink-faced man with sad, Irish setter eyes, said to me one afternoon on a veranda in Nice. Ralph Burns of Lake View Terrace, California—no youngster at sixty-nine with a Parkinson's shake—did not leave behind his crippled wife Ruth, but wheeled her everywhere we went, up and down war memorial steps, over the lawns of the graves at Henri Chapelle. A wealthy California developer with a taste for alcohol had brought his two feisty daughters—or they had brought him. Jack Leaf took sick in Nice and would be confined much of the trip to his hotel room. Leaf was no wet blanket, though. Early on in the trip I asked if he had married a French girl. "Every time I met one," he quipped.

Even Aunt Jeannette, to whom Dad had sent most of his war correspondence, would not let a black-and-blue knee bashed the week of our departure stop her. The flame of war is terrible and magnetic, especially for those whose youth was brought to a climax in it. For our journey Aunt Jeannette became the older sister many of the men had written to during the war.

I never asked my mother to accompany us. I knew what her answer would be—silence. Dad had promised her a trip to Europe someday, but the rigors of raising three children, the crazy fashion industry, and his subsequent financial decline prevented it. When she finally went to Europe, it was with her brother and his wife on their invitation. Dad minded the store. It was given to me to reach her that dim August night; she was in London. I instructed my uncle not to tell her that her husband had been shot, nor by whom. I had to get her home, after all, so I concocted a lie. "Car accident, bad shape" was all I said.

For her I am sure as she flew home the whole continent of Europe sank to a bottomless Sargasso Sea.

II

In addition to the about-face at the Negresco, three moments stood out in our twelve-day journey: the visit to the Dragoon drop-zone at La Motte, a troubled vet's hike to a machine-gun nest site at La Turbie, and Rochelinval itself, the site of the destruction of the 551st.

The men seemed in a trance as they moved out—now in their sixties and seventies—across the Valbourges estate at La Motte, France, trying to remember just which bush or plot of earth had taken their falling bodies forty-five years ago. Their maroon berets, navy blue blazers, white shirts and hair flickered among the grapevines, raspberries, and apple and pear trees.

"There it is!" Will Marks of Pennsylvania pointed to a lone poplar in the distance fronting a pond. "All my life I dreamed of falling into a tree by itself. You guys have been telling me we fell in the woods. And there it is—my tree!"

Harry Renick, a retired machinist from Detroit who took to making wishing wells, commented drily, "I made a three-point landing here: feet, butt, and helmet." Others had been seriously injured, impaled on stakes in the vineyard.

Approaching Valbourges to dedicate a plaque at the Stevens family chapel, Otto Schultz of West Virginia spied the tiled roof of a barn and remembered banging down on the tiles, riding his still-inflated chute to the ground. One of the Stevens family joked, "The broken tiles—they are still there. You may fix them!"

In the courtyard of the old, worn chateau sat an apparition in a wheelchair, ninety-one-year-old Mme. Henriette Stevens, who had bound up the first wounds of the 551st. The men spoke to her in low, hoarse English; she followed their eyes, hugged them. As I approached, someone said, "But you are too young to be one of the paratroopers, no?" I looked at Mrs. Stevens—she resembled my father's irascible Lebanese immigrant mother who had peddled on the streets of New York at the turn of the century. "I am here for my father, Madame," I said in basic French, tipping my beret. "He is dead now, but I give you his thanks." She clasped my hand in two of hers.

I wore that maroon beret the whole trip, some admission for an old Vietnam War protester. Retired Colonel Doug Dillard, then president of the 551st Association, had given the beret to me earlier in the day for a wreath-laying ceremony at the U.S. Rhone cemetery at Draguignan. It was cocked correctly for me by one of the *vielles suspentes* ("old risers" literally, what the surviving French resistance paratroopers call themselves) who'd come all the way from Paris for the ceremony. When I heard the "Star Spangled Banner," the "Marseillaise," and taps, my hand instinctively moved from heart to forehead to join the men.

On our bus that night back to Nice, I asked Harry Renick what the 551st motto—GOYA—meant. "Get Off Your Ass," Harry said mildly.

That smacked of Dad's favorite "Go get 'em!" which he cried out whenever he was happy, challenged, or off on his beloved motorcycle into the Mojave Desert. My brother's Freebird's Restaurant in Santa Barbara, in fact, commemorates both the motto and the motorcycle, where one hangs from the ceiling above the diners. Hearing that, Otto ventured, "You know, we requisitioned a motorcycle from the Germans at Cannes. One guy was fond as hell of that thing. It could have been your father."

Slowly, the gray canvas of my father's life in the war gained an oval of color here, there, and the anger and gaiety we knew as he was raising us began to dovetail with the verve in darkness that got him through the war, or indeed, was caused by it. My father was a life-messenger of sorts. He always seemed to want to urge life along; left to its own means, life could atrophy or destroy or worst of all end up meaningless. GOYA! "Go get 'em!" "Rise and shine!" "Up and at 'em!" "We're off and running!" "Zing 'em!" For Dad, reveille was a constant requirement in civilian life — at all hours, I might add.

How many childhood car trips to the Sierras began with his lusty version of "Blood on the Risers" (sung to the tune of "The Battle Hymn of the Republic" with all the irony of Paul Fussell's "chickenshit" intact):

> "Is everybody happy?" cried the sergeant looking up,
> Our Hero feebly answered, "Yes," and then they stood
>   him up,
> He leaped right out into the blast, his static line
>   unhooked,
> AND HE AIN'T GONNA JUMP NO MORE!
> GORY, GORY, WHAT A HELLUVA WAY TO DIE!

I had one last question about the La Motte drop. Dad once vaguely mentioned his most fearful moment in the service as a night jump. But the 551st had dropped in southern France on a late summer afternoon. Instead of fear of the night, there was fear of German guns, which could sight them. So when was the night jump? The men figured it wasn't in France but in training in Sicily or at Camp Mackall, North Carolina, where they participated in dangerous, innovative airborne tests, such as the first live parachute jumps from gliders. There on the foggy night of February 16, 1944, eight GIs were misdropped in lakes; they parachuted with one hundred pounds of equipment straight to the bottom and drowned. The disaster jolted the bereaved relatives of drop victim Benjamin Prezotti of Brooklyn to contact columnist Drew Pearson. An angry piece by Pearson prompted the Army to adopt the British "quick release" harness.

The only quick release the horrific event engendered in the men was of jets of anxiety. Restless by nature (their first mission to drop on a Vichy-leaning Martinique was aborted), the 551st rebelled. At one point, two hundred of its men were in the guardhouse. I remember Dad once telling me, only half-jokingly, that he spent more time jumping in between two warring servicemen than in combat against the Nazis. When one is pumped up for war and the climax is withdrawn, or worse, one's own men are wasted in training, something in the muscles either goes limp or very taut. To blur training and combat, as Paul Fussell has noted, is "so wrong as to be unmentionable."

Only the return of their charismatic, youthful commander, Colonel Wood Joerg, calmed them somewhat. After a hearing, the older Colonel Rupert Graves, who had overseen the tragic Mackall night jump, was transferred, but not before shouting at the 551st from his balcony, "You're not going to ruin my career! You're not soldiers! You're all rabble!"

In one of the ironies of war, Colonel Graves ended up commanding the 551st again when it was attached at the Battle of the Bulge to his 517th Parachute Regimental Combat Team. A day after its attachment to Graves, it was the 551st that got the nod to enter the meat grinder. Several of the men wondered if they were the victims of a clash of personalities at the top, if not outright vengefulness, that traced itself to their training days.

III

Maybe the rebellion was inbred.

What, in fact, makes a man want to jump out of a plane? And not just that, but to be one of the first to do it in battle? It's a bit like running away to the circus, but worse — no one shoots at the acrobat on the high wire.

I can't imagine doing it myself. I am a born acrophobe. My wife, who thought nothing of waterskiing in the ninth month of pregnancy, was ordered to grip my hand when, on our honeymoon, we ascended to the apex of the Eiffel Tower. I distracted myself by focusing on the stripes of her sweater. There is something about terra firma that is very dear to me, and I am being literal.

I queried the men about being "airborne." Otto Shultz, retired from Union Carbide (he had worked on the Bhopal project and shook his head about it) thought back to childhood, "I'd run along a wall to leap into sand as a kid—always the farthest one back." Charles Fairlamb, at seventy-four retired from Boeing in Seattle, joined the 551st in Panama where he was working with the phone company repairing lines. "I figured I liked to keep climbing poles!" he grinned. There seemed in the men an excess of energy, a critical mass of sorts, that had made them a chancy bunch. There was an almost cherished restlessness about them. "Most people who became paratroopers were dissatisfied where they were," Phil Hand said. "A bunch of malcontents," Ed Hartman put it bluntly.

Parachuting attracted the romantic, no doubt. Dan Morgan of Washington joined the 551st after being disappointed to discover that there was no horse cavalry mounted to fight the Japanese: "They had replaced horses with halftracks." There was also the matter of status. "If you could see it lightning and hear it thunder you could get into the Army," said Charles Austin of Texas. "Not everyone could be a paratrooper." It wasn't so much a question of being fearless. "After jumping thirteen times, I had never landed in a plane in my life, so the first time I landed it was like a screw propeller going into the ground—I was scared as hell," a grizzled, trim Max Bryan from Yorktown, Virginia, admitted. "But you say to yourself, I was a man."

As for my father, I can only guess the motive. He was the last of six children, after four sisters and a brother already stationed in Burma. He'd certainly had plenty of babying and something to prove. Unlike his siblings who had grown up in wealth, by the time Aref was coming of age in Cleveland, Ohio, his millionaire linen merchant father had lost it all in the Depression. He watched his father move from being a gent with a gold fob at the cash register to operating a lathe, and he witnessed the ensuing rancor between my grandmother and grandfather. A life of grandeur and wealth slipping into penury—what else to do but jump? A good war is a good place to jump.

Like all rebels, the men of the 551st seemed to be acutely skeptical of authority—not the best attitude for those involved in that hierarchical penultimate, the U.S. Army. (The murderous blunder at Camp Mackall only reinforced their attitude.) Their very "551" was assigned out of sequence (battalions of its sort being numbered 501 to 517) so that the Germans would think there were more U.S. paratroopers than actually existed. They savored their independent status, and relished it when their commanding officer, Colonel Wood Joerg, told them, "Each of you is worth five other men."

If one person appears to have epitomized the spirit of the 551st, it was Joerg himself. Ebullient, charming, an unreconstructed rebel "Jaw-Jaw" (Georgia) boy at West Point, he was not a great student. The 1937 USMA yearbook lists him as 230th out of 298 in class ranking. But it also credits him as a "Rabble Rouser" who pumped up the stands during ball games and had "a heart a yard long and a smile a mile wide." By the time of the offensive at the Bulge, that smile and that heart would have to change places.

He liked to root, work his deep southern accent on the girls in a way that was both shy and confident, and dance. He was not, according to one classmate, "a hive (bookworm)" but a "hopoid." Joerg was hop manager for the Point. He was not a "make" (cadet officer) but a "clean sleeve" (no chevrons to denote rank of authority). He was also an "area bird"—someone who spent many hours walking punishment tours around the Point with a rifle because of his horsing around.

A classmate who outlived him long enough to become a brigadier general said Joerg was "full of the milk of human kindness." He had a weakness for plebes who took a terrible beating as he had from upper-classmen, a sympathy he later exhibited—enough to be warned—for men under his command.

The line soldiers of the 551st loved him, it seems, and he returned the sentiment; some remember him on the phone in a frenzy to get the suicidal mission at Rochelinval canceled. It appears that the man from "Jaw-Jaw" saw death at an early age, and it made him dance. Joerg's first roommate at West Point died as a cadet, sending him into great inner turmoil. The first Pointer killed in World War II was from Joerg's cadet company.

It fit the dark irony surrounding the 551st like a hard chute that one Major General C.S. O'Malley would remember Wood Joerg's "heroic death at Bastogne." When the hot shrapnel pierced his helmet and killed him, Joerg and the men who fell around him in the snow were twenty-five miles north of where McAuliffe gave his famous "Nuts!" reply to a German order to surrender. Brigadier General McAuliffe was rescued by Patton, but there would be no rescue at a snow-clamped, obscure knoll called Rochelinval.

IV

My father was not a physical fitness nut. His generation as a whole found nothing particularly worth worshiping about the body. Those who fought World War II worked like dogs to end up with a kidney-shaped pool and a circular drive, daily ate bacon and eggs, drank coffee not decaf, smoked Lucky Strikes or Marlboros, had affairs instead of relationships, and took up, if anything, bowling, or the somnolent game of golf. Dad vehemently refused to be a golfer.

As a teenager in Cleveland, he played football and ice hockey. A split end for a rather accomplished neighborhood football team, the Cleveland Olympics, just before he entered the war, he hit a peak when the Olympics copped a citywide championship.

His quarterback friend, Bud Lank, and he were the only ones who played both offense and defense and on both first- and second-string teams. They were never out of the Olympics lineup. Muscular in a lean way, five feet ten inches, Aref was pound-for-pound the best tackler and blocker on the team, Lank thought. He recalled fondly, "Your father was a contact kind of guy."

That he was. He would hold your shoulder to make a point, touch a finger to knee to underscore it, bear hug with a grip that was not afraid to last. Lank said Aref was always slapping the players on the back in the huddle, spurring them on a quicker stop-and-go, a blunter block. He was, in short, a Wood Joerg type.

Los Angeles was not the best place for an excellent ice skater to bring up a family. As much as he loved Mother, it was clearly a disappointment to him that she never learned to skate (and abhorred his motorcycle). I became his partner on ice as a boy, as did my sister, Leslie. But most of the time he skated alone with the slight crouch of a speed skater, crossing over smoothly on turns, weaving gently, swiftly, in and out of the fumbling Angelenos, an anonymous messenger of grace. He loved skating music; if he heard "Frenesi" or anything by Glenn Miller, he immediately took off. An evening at the small Valley rink would end with him unlacing our boots and wistfully blowing over his hot chocolate as he confided that that ultimate female skating partner had eluded him.

If he had found her, earlier, would any of us children have existed? Perhaps a son would not have been afraid of heights.

I tried. I skated pretty well for a native Angeleno—I had a good teacher. But I never learned to stop on a dime as my father, who barreled toward the wall, pivoted at the last second, and bit his blades sideways into the ice with a *shuusssh*, ice shavings spraying on my sister and me. I suppose if you know how to stop, you're not so afraid of speed. If I speed-skate anywhere it's on the page, or else I parachute to its bottom. It's not a bad substitute for innate, physical grace, which my father—unconscious of his own body—had in spades.

The jogging-and-health mania that began with my generation and Jane Fonda'd into a multibillion-dollar industry seemed stupid and pointless to him even when he discovered, as did everyone, cholesterol. "I'm going puffing," he would announce to my mother's exhortations, exhaling smoke. He smoked seriously—inhales and exhales were dramatic billowing caesuras, smoke signals of dilemma or pain. Strangely enough, smoke for him was a life force. Toward the end he tried to quit for Mom, even adopted lower-tar cigarettes. But his heart wasn't in it.

I say all this to note the paradox of that generation of Americans which spent its childhood in the Depression, fought the Second War as teenagers, and built as adults the country we are today, for better or worse, richer or polluted, in plutonium and in health. That paradox is one of excess and selflessness. It was a generation that acted first, thought later. Ours, on the other hand, thinks most everything into oblivion. Ours projects all, yet seems at a loss to do anything that will substantially alter what we so brilliantly project, most of which is payment for sixty years of excess since the war—chemical water, dying forests, rising seas from melting ice caps themselves the result of our love of cars, soaring deficits, clogged arteries, radioactive bombs like hardened foam from a million panting mouths.

I can't blame my father or his generation for the Age of Excess any more than I blame my own for its Age of Informed Narcissism. History and time create us more than we fathom. I only note the ironies—Dad's excess was generous, selfless, and dealt the future some mortal blows. Our touted social consciousness seems drained to a pittance of the grand protest era that gave us "our" war crucible, Vietnam—how else could the Iraq war have continued unchecked for so long? We became late, curiously cranky parents. And we are not so hot with the future, either, sinking in the mire of the present, saving nothing but the bills from our credit cards.

Our sin is presbyopia; his generation's—myopia. Even then by the day we escape from the immediate, from *contact*. We are all learning to draw in our wagons quite well from the teeming hordes of the ghetto, the homeless, drug wars (though there are enough of us and our children to provide the drug lords a steady market). We become kinder, gentler Republicans, "concerned" Democrats, at a fair remove from what needs our kindness and gentleness and concern less than our ability to act. To *act*? That might entail uncertainty, even heartache.

Perfectly healthy as I was in my twenties—a bicycler, basketball player, swimmer—I once prodded Dad that he needed exercise. He snapped, "I got my exercise hauling fifty dresses at a clip over my shoulders up and down Ninth and Los Angeles streets. I got my exercise lugging an eighty-pound radio over the Maritime Alps." It was the closest he ever came to bravado. It was as out of character as it was for him to be out of work.

I used to dream about the Maritime Alps, unable ever to find them on the map. They held a lofty, Tibetan image in my mind. After the 551st came down from the Provence foothills of its parachute drop, taking Cannes, Nice, and other towns of the Cote d'Azur, it was ordered to go up into the high mountains separating France from Italy, where the retreating Germans fled. This was September 1944. These were the Maritime Alps. (Three months after serving one of the longest uninterrupted combat stints in Europe, the 551st was relieved in the Alps by the heralded Japanese-American battalion, the 100th.)

On some bright August days in 1989, we veterans and family ascended the Maritimes. I had my eye out for old Army radios. His had probably been an SCR-300 backpack version, good practice for hauling a garment bag stuffed with samples. German pillboxes still squatted in the crags of the mountain. Chuck Fairlamb remembered boulders the Germans had rolled into the dry riverbed of the Var River so that gliders couldn't land there. As the road narrowed and steepened, and the clear green Var flowed in a lazy late summer fall past islets and cottonwoods, Harry seemed dreamy.

"What a place to come at night with a girl!" he mused, his dull blue eyes brightening at the sight. "You lie down on a towel with the rocks and the water rushing by. And boy, the wind over you! After you're done, you go dip it in the cold water. Downstream it gets warmer!"

I asked Harry, a tall man who looked like he might hunt, if the 551st ever saw bears or other animals in the Alps.

"Animals?" he dropped. "We were too concerned with the two-legged animals."

At St. Martin–Vesubie, a good-sized crowd swarmed us in the town square where, *tilleuls* rippling in a mountain breeze, we had a wreath-laying ceremony with the mayor and town council and *vin d'honneur*. One gap-toothed woman, eyes sparkling in a leathery face, insisted I translate for her that she had done the men's laundry during the war. Another with eyeglasses had given them gum; she nodded shyly. Everywhere we went were townspeople clutching forty-year-old photos, trying to compare the burnished boyish GI faces with the men whose skin had turned to many dry rivers, but whose eyes were searching for that one person who knew them then, who bound a bullet wound or even sold them baguettes.

Swerving up the steep, narrow mountain road to the next village of their Alpine duty—tiny Isola—I could just imagine Dad in his glory on the motorcycle bending to the precipice as he distributed messages to the battalion. A chapel from the Middle Ages thrust its steeple above the green valley.

"Helluva nice place to live—I wouldn't want to fight a war here," Max Bryan mused.

Phil Hand recalled that after the war his insomnia and bad nerves from the Bulge were relieved only by imagining the period the 551st had spent in the snow-covered Alps, "one of the most beautiful and peaceful things I'd ever known." It was arduous duty, as well. Many of the men had to learn cross-country skiing for their patrols. Some were picked off in the snow by German snipers. Some did the picking.

In November 1944, Dad wrote his sister Jeannette that he helped "serve Mass," avoiding in the V-mail tradition of saying where he was. It was the Alps period. Attending Mass in a little chapel in Isola, my brother and I lit a candle and thought of him pouring the cruets as a nineteen-year-old in fatigues. For all his passion, he had a deep well of humility and faith that began to ebb only with the onset of my sister's mental illness in the late 1970s. A rosary taken from a bombed shrine in 1944 by scout Joe Cicchinelli of Arizona—miraculously unhurt—was worn by a statue of the Blessed Mother at Isola chapel. Outside the chapel, Bob Van Horssen of Grand Haven, Michigan—father of ten—gave his wings to a crippled girl.

Before having lunch at the Hotel de France (which had been badly shelled during the war), we found ourselves made part of a procession for St. Roch, the local patron, through whose intercession the Black Plague of the Middle Ages bypassed Isola. Down the cobblestones we walked behind a wooden statue of St. Roch. Someone pointed up a building's high wall. Bullet holes from the war still peppered it. St. Roch had not spared the village that. And some mute collective protest bone in Isola had kept that evidence from being repaired.

Higher we went, up to seven thousand feet and the last Alpine town patrolled by the 551st — St. Etienne de Tinée. We were mobbed. It seemed the entire town of one thousand had turned out to greet us. There was another French Army band and a company of French troops for the ceremonies. A gaggle of French generals and an admiral stood pointing, nodding.

Chuck Miller of Rancho Cucamonga, California, remembered the long, arduous hikes up and down the mountain slope, playing a kind of hide-and-seek with the Germans above: "At St. Etienne we'd switch places with the Germans. We'd look up with our binoculars at them, and then they would go down and look up at us." As Melville said of the American Civil War: "All wars are boyish, and are fought by boys."

By midnight we were beautifully beat and traveling down the mountain. In the dark, Glenn Miller tunes bathed us in memory, like a warm tide. Doug Dillard had put a tape on:

Hy-a Mister Jackson! everything's O K-A-L-A-M-A-Z-O-O
Oh what a gal, a real pipperoo
I'll make my bid for that freckle-faced kid I'm
hurrying to.
I'm going to Michigan to see the sweetest gal in
Kalamazoo.

Wishing-well Harry, who really had taken to the willowy brunette waitress in St. Etienne ("Tell her she's got class. Tell her she's beautiful"), saw in the dimness Aunt Jeannette drink some spring water from a bottle.

"Don't drink that water, it'll rust your pipes," Harry said, having a last beer.

"I'm not going to worry about that now!" squawked near-octogenarian Aunt Jen.

Harry leaned over and flicked on my reading light as I was taking out my notebook. "You gotta put a little life in this life." He made us laugh, garbling "light" for "life." Considering the 551st, perhaps that was not a garble.

At La Turbie, Joe Cicchinelli took me on a forced march up a hillside to a disturbing memory. In advance of the battalion and with the help of a French civilian, Charles Calori, Cicchinelli and two other GIs had lobbed grenades into the machine-gun nest in a shack, killing the gunner.

But it was at the shadowy hutch out back—where two more Germans were surprised with bullets—that Cicchinelli jumped back and forth in the underbrush, squeezing his jaw. "One of them didn't die," he shook his head. It was that one, Joe said, lowering his voice, that he shot in the head and watched, agog, as the youth's brains spilled in a stream on the floor.

"What could I do?" Joe raised his head up to the sky. There was no answer—not from the bracken he was breaking as he paced, not from the bleached wood of the shack, not from us.

A shorter version of our father with his weathered tan, mustache, taut strength, and share of ghosts—Cicchinelli had spent three years in psychotherapy working on that moment in La Turbie, a bayonet attack at the Bulge, and months as a German POW. Now Joe counsels Vietnam and Iraq veterans. He still possesses the ID photos of the three young blond Germans, taken off their bodies sixty years ago.

That shack. That hutch. It was the first time he had faced it again since the war. And though Cicchinelli had returned three times to Europe and was staying with a Maquis veteran rather than at our hotel, he admitted, "The reason I come back—I hope by coming I can forget it."

On the dirt path back, I came upon the incongruous rusted guts of a piano. My father had met Mother while playing his patented single piano tune at a party. Had he ever killed someone face-to-face in the war? Mark said he has asked him that question once, and that Dad had said, no, he hadn't.

He lied.

Some months after we returned from Europe, his old football-playing buddy Bud Lank sent me a revealing tape of his childhood memories of my father.

After the war, and after some months' stay at various Army hospitals for his frozen feet, my father came back to Cleveland. One night he, Lank, and two other ex-GIs (including Tommy Stampfl of the 551st) went out drinking. By midnight, they were fairly well loosened up in a bar and began to tell what many GIs would never tell again—their darkest moment in the war.

Danny Polamski's moment was his body, or what was left of it—he'd lost both legs and an arm to a mine. Lank had broken his leg in a jeep accident. Dad's dark moment was not his injury, however.

He said about forty German soldiers had holed up in a bakery. The 551st opened up with machine guns and rifles. As two Germans tried to escape out the side window, my father shot them both. Later, walking with a squad along a hedgerow, some Germans jumped up, and at point-blank range he shot one of them.

At the Battle of the Bulge the 551st fought through farmland, for the most part. The towns they went through were barely a cluster of stone houses — Dairomont, Odrimont. It's probable that the hedgerow incident was in Belgium. But the bakery?

One day I took a close look at an old photo of Joe Cicchinelli crouching with townspeople in Draguignan just after he had helped capture the Nazi general there and torn down the Nazi flag from the mayor's office. I squinted at the store window behind him. There it said: *Patisserie.*

It is likely that my father killed two men whose faces he could see all too well only a day into battle, a day after the jump into France. It must have stunned him. After 1945, he told no one about it.

In childhood games of cowboys and Indians, Aref was the only kid who always played the Indian, Lank said. It must have jarred the young man who had always been the Indian suddenly to have the lethal upper hand, if only for a few seconds, the way Cicchinelli was shocked enough at LaTurbie to seize the photos of the boys he had killed, as if that would somehow resuscitate them.

Phil Hand spoke of "emptying into" a German soldier at La Motte. "Fifty others emptied into him," Hand thought, the pure fear of the first day in battle. The idea of killing being an emptying of self — a draining of one, violently, into another — there is something pathetically sexual about it, something utterly forlorn. You are emptying more than bullets. Your soul is switched in the kill. You become the dead one. In killing him, in "emptying into" him, his deadness, by implication, invades you. In death he is full of you; in life you are a vacuum.

The day before we left Nice for Belgium I sat with Cicchinelli on the roof of the Hotel Pullman. The sun glared off the mirror sunglasses of some topless women lounging by the rooftop pool. Around us the great bowl of Nice sparkled — its steeples, clay-tiled roofs, mottled, hazy hills. California by another name.

After a while we stopped talking. Joe fingered a napkin and looked up at me.

"How did your father die?"

"He was shot." I startled myself. Few who ask get the truth, and no one else in the 551st asked.

"Who shot him?"

"My sister."

He clamped my hand. His grip was hard, as if he were squeezing the handle of an elevator cut loose in a shaft. His head bent, ticking slightly.

"Oh, ooh."

There was less oxygen in Nice that afternoon, and much less sun, and no topless women. That languid roof shrank into a lonely hutch in back of a photocopy store—a place where people are put out of their misery.

V

"I know him."

Phil Hand held up a black-and-white photo of my father—the dashing GI home from the war, his airborne patch captured on his shoulder, his thick back hair pleasantly awry at the widow's peak, "ears lowered." A slight mustache. He looks like Richard Gere. There's a gal nuzzled alongside him, someone who didn't become my mother.

His feet are unfrozen, healed, and though they hurt in the cold, tonight is not cold, the liquor is flowing. He's at a club in Cleveland or some family shindig. He's manly, confident. But not too confident. He isn't smiling. His eyes are tree-bark in snow.

"I know him."

Phil Hand didn't nod, looking at the photo as we sat on the veranda of our Nice hotel. He was staring steadily through thick glasses. He knows the man's soul, I think, but not the man. That may be better than the man, but that is not what I want. I want damn physical recognition.

I'd been showing the photo to the men of the 551st from the day we began the journey. No one knew him or recognized him. Most wanted to recognize him, no doubt, for our sake. But recognition of buddies they knew then takes a while for the old vets, even with flesh-and-blood partners before them.

Over the next decade that non-recognition would change, to my wonder. The disappointment then was real but no surprise. A battalion is 600 to 800 men; a company is 150 men; a platoon, 40. Only four men from Dad's Headquarters Company were on the trip. One of them, Chuck Bernard, who had been Dad's boss at the message center, drew a blank. Six years later, just before he died, it hit him. He took out a photo he had kept in his wallet all his life of himself and a dark-skinned man— it was my father.

But at Nice, in only one of hundreds of Phil Hand's photos was there a face so darkened, so inscrutable, I could pour my hope of recognition into it, one among fifteen grease-smeared men waiting to take off from Italy for the drop into southern France.

"It's yours. Take it." Phil gave the shade-man to me. I had thought the trip might lessen, not lengthen, the shadows I had come to live with.

Our Nice farewell speaker that night at dinner was Rear Admiral H. G. (Hank) Chiles, Jr., then commander of a submarine group with the U.S. Sixth Fleet. Only about fifty people, we were hardly a big enough group to draw an admiral, not to mention one on active duty in the midst of another hostage-crisis (Colonel Higgins of the United Nations Truce Supervision Organization had just been hanged on videotape in south Lebanon).

"I and many of my generation stand in awe of you and the sacrifice of your generation during World War II," Chiles told the men. "You must know it's a humbling experience for a fifty-one-year-old rear admiral to stand here. I've asked myself over the past few days what I could possibly say that would be meaningful to people such as you. You see, you are *legends*."

The men, most of whom were privates during the war, looked stunned. To be praised by an admiral in such an intimate setting for feats long ago forgotten by the high brass was disorienting, to say the least.

Pointing to successful fleet exchange visits to Norfolk and Sebastopol under perestroika (the Soviet Union was to dissolve into fifteen states in two years with hardly a shot fired), Chiles told the vets, "There are signs of a more peaceful world, signs that perhaps future generations of Americans might know a world less disposed to violence than what you saw and fought for."

Who of us doesn't want to believe that? Yet I saw in my mind's eye the hot muzzle of my sister's gun—the wreckage it wreaked in a few seconds. That had nothing to do with Communism, perestroika, or external enemies of any kind. If all the wars in the world suddenly stopped, the impossible time bomb of our waste would have to be dismantled; two hundred million guns, sixty-five million of them handguns, would remain marking time in their American drawers, closets, beds, hands. And two million as sick as my sister was sick. No. There is another war. It is in front of us every day. It stems from who we are, what we are—it is a war of being, of being fractured. And now with the Iraq war dragging on, a war of betrayal of our most cherished principles and the commonweal. Drugs, AIDS, maimed Iraq vets home from an absurd war, the homeless, the insane — as they grow, the war grows. As do the guns. We are at war with ourselves. We very much need — with the economy now collapsing — a second American revolution.

A poet of Russia's Silver Age, Valery Bruysov, noted that there are those who are freedom's "captives." Precisely.

Admiral Chiles ended with a surprisingly pacifistic reference to a soldier at Verdun, tipped his cap once again to the 551st for its "great contribution to freedom," and asked the men and their families to pray "for an America strong in peace so we don't have to be strong in war."

I couldn't have agreed more. Two hundred million guns on our streets and in homes is not strength.

VI

"I didn't want to live it," Chuck Miller said, feeling the old sap on a pine's bark. "I didn't have to relive it. Maybe it's better to keep it cloudy. But I seem strong-willed enough not to be torn up by the past. I've been called cold-hearted. I knew we'd taken a horrible beating. But until I went to my first reunion in Chicago, I was under the impression we only had three people left."

It was Chuck Miller, an un-cold retired air conditioner repairman, looking out at the silent green hills of the Ardennes where, in a bitter two weeks at the turn of 1945, the 551st came to its end. Miller was talking about memory, the dread of it and its strange allure. There were few of the returning veterans who approached the killing field "with tranquil restoration," as Wordsworth would have it.

Memory. Drawn like moths to the flame of it, worried as to what it might contain, avid to share it with loved ones who might believe the otherwise unbelievable, or in Cicchinelli's case, to burn it so hot in the soul it would finally cool and come off like a scab. Something awe-full and awful to confront. What else but memory makes us human? As if preparing for the original battle, however difficult, the old men seemed to say: *We are what we remember*. Not the half of it we nurse or suppress, but the whole of it we find, usually, with others.

The community of memory — the only community that lasts — quickened in the men when by train and bus following the route the 551st took in December 1944 as it rushed to the Ardennes to help stop Hitler's last onslaught, we arrived in Belgium.

Five facts: Ardennes horses, more nervous and quick than most, are exported to the United States. Belgians are the largest per capita drinkers of beer in the world. The towns of eastern Belgium in the Ardennes have been crushed three times this century by invading Germans. The world's largest mushroom industry based here uses the cool, damp, old Nazi bunkers for growth. And lastly, according to our host and former Belgian resistance leader Leo Carlier, Belgians are obstinately independent, each wanting "his house to be different." This sounded like 551st territory. It was also the scene of Hitler's last stand.

More than six hundred thousand Americans fought in the six weeks after December 16, 1944, the fiercest clash of the war in Western Europe — the Battle of the Bulge. They took most of the eighty-one thousand Allied casualties in that battle. No one thought Hitler would attack in the dense Ardennes forest, or would intensify the attack in the midst of the worst European winter recorded in the century. He did both.

Pine shadows dappled the men on the bus while Carlier related, "You have been the 'unknown soldiers,' the 551st. I met Colonel Dillard in 1985 and heard for the first time about your story and your destruction. I promised him we would make a memorial and I vowed you would never be forgotten. Tomorrow you will be invaded."

He wasn't kidding. Hundreds of people, some from as far as Brussels, showed up for the dedication. Their fervor was moving, even for one as skeptical of American foreign policy as I am. A poster inside the town hall at Lierneux still warned children not to touch live bullets and shells in the fields, destructive relics of two world wars.

Now in the village of Rochelinval, a monument to the 551st exists. Not the Americans, not the U.S. Army, but the Belgians themselves built the stone memorial; it took them two years. A young construction equipment operator, Claude Orban, did much of the spade work. We watched in hushed silence as Heide and Bo Wilson, grandchildren of Lieutenant Colonel Joerg, who was killed in an artillery treeburst nearby, unveiled the memorial.

The next day, our last, the men roamed the fields and the woods. "Can you imagine the enormous sound then, and how quiet it is now?" mused Chuck Miller as he hiked, shaking off a question about his heart condition.

I stood with Chuck Fairlamb, who fired the first mortar in the December 27, 1944, raid on Noirefontaine ordered by General Gavin that commenced the Allied rollback on the northern tier of the Bulge. We stood together on the green turf where that mortar round was lobbed so long ago. Only the buzz of gnats disturbed our ears.

From January 3 to January 7, 1945, over a snow-filled, forested area near Trois Ponts, the 551st pushed the Germans back three miles in five days — very slow, agonized fighting, often hand-to-hand combat. "It's always easier to defend, as at Bastogne, than to attack, as we did toward Rochelinval," explained Phil Hand. "We had to swing over the area like a gate."

"By God, did we take that many casualties in that small area?" wondered Doug Dillard, who feels closer to the 551st than to battalions he himself commanded in Korea and Vietnam. Dillard pointed out a creek where the men soaked their boots, the beginning of their battle with frostbitten feet and trenchfoot in the subzero weather. My father's feet froze up; he was evacuated to Liège. When I leapt over a barbed-wire fence to photograph the creek, the men smiled. Airborne, if for only a second.

It was not easy to picture in the green, silent farmland, but many froze to death, too. No overshoes were issued. The men were under a merciless order not to wear overcoats so that they would be distinguishable from Germans and could supposedly move faster. Cicchinelli remembered firing ("We were so pissed") at overcoat-clad 517th Regiment GIs. Hand recalled soldiers "circling a little sapling which they gripped," trying to stay both awake and warm. Sleep was death. After three days of no sleep or food some slept.

On January 4, 1945, one of the few fixed bayonet attacks in the European theater occurred, carried out by Company A of the 551st. It's an order given in a desperate situation to strike up a soldier's adrenalin, but also to avoid shooting your own people circling behind in the fog. The Germans stood up in their gun depressions, stunned. Sixty-four of them were killed by gun butts and blades. "I could very well have blocked it all out because of this day," Miller admitted. "And you know I'm German. It's such a dirty shame that someone like Hitler could change people's psyches the way he did."

"We were going a little mad, you know," Cicchinelli confessed. Company A stabbed and mutilated corpses until Lieutenant Dick Durkee stopped them. They were breaking the stocks of their rifles off on the dead bodies. Durkee named it cruelty. But few of Company A survived, either. Three days later attacking Rochelinval, when Durkee ordered Private Pat Casanova to get the rest of the men, Casanova of New Jersey shouted, "I can't, sir." "Why not?" Durkee yelled. "Because they're all dead, sir," was the reply.

Shortly after the bayonet attack Cicchinelli was taken prisoner by a Nazi patrol probably as lost in the snow as he was. Seventeen years later, working as a mail carrier he came to a wooded area near Flagstaff, Arizona, that resembled the Ardennes of Belgium. "I relived it all," he said, and had to rearrange his route before quitting altogether.

Finally we faced the five-hundred-yard meadow sloping down from a hill then abruptly up to Rochelinval, now green, but covered on January 7, 1945, with a foot and a half of snow. Of the thousand rounds of artillery available to the 551st for its attack on Rochelinval, only four were shot off at dawn. Joerg tried to get the half-crazed unit relieved, to get the attack called off. He got neither. Only an order to take the hill, which was topped by dug-in Germans and their machine guns.

"He saved my life by giving me an order," Joe Thibault of Massachusetts said in choked voice, recalling Joerg's last moments. " 'Go get the self-propelled [gun]!' I saw it in his eyes. He knew." Charles Fairlamb also saw Joerg rise out of the protection of his foxhole and say, "Isn't the smell of mortars sweet, Chuck?" Fairlamb opined, "I think he knew he was doomed and we all were doomed. He just sort of stood up to take his fate."

Incredibly, with their commander killed by an artillery treeburst, down to less than a hundred men and a dozen officers, the 551st crested the hill and took Rochelinval, pushing the Germans back across the Salm River.

In late January 1945, General Gavin told the 551st that they had been disbanded by the Department of the Army. Survivors filtered elsewhere. As Harry Renick put it, "I was disintegrated into the 82nd Airborne."

For all the "firsts" they notched, the 551st lost not only its existence, but its history. The National Archives hold twelve cubic feet of official records for the other independent parachute battalion, which was also disbanded—the heavily decorated 509th. For the 551st, when I first called up the records, there was a folder less than an inch thick. At Fort Benning's McCarthy Hall, every parachute unit that ever fought for the U.S. Army had its insignia emblazoned on the walls—except for the 551st.

Over the years, the men chewed on several theories: that Gavin was embarrassed enough by the losses to wipe out all records; that they were so heartbroken at their disbandment after Rochelinval, they themselves burned the records in the fields; that the 551st was just snake-bitten from the beginning; that the death of their commander deprived them of their most credible advocate for honors; that their "impossible" objective at Rochelinval was punishment for being a maverick unit. But they had no answers. Some thought the unit's final humiliation lay with General Matthew Ridgway, in whose massive XVIII Airborne Corps they formed a small part; Ridgway apparently disliked the independent paratroop units and was on the verge of disbanding them anyway before the Bulge hit. At the age of ninety-four, however, Ridgway wrote Colonel Dillard that the blotting out of the 551st was "a grave error and injustice to as gallant a combat battalion as any in World War II in Europe." The paratrooper icon also wrote me shortly afterward that he was aware of "serious efforts" under way to bring the "full record" of the 551st's heroism and tragic fate to public light. Little did I know I would devote eight years of my life to that effort.

After the few survivors were broken apart and stripped of their history together, thirty years went by. In 1977, Phil Hand determined "to find whatever buddies I had left before I died." He used telephone directories, ads in *Static Line*, the airborne newsletter, his wife's government WATS line. The first reunion in August 1977 brought eighteen members. At one point, about one hundred and fifty men had been found and more than one hundred people came to reunions. By 2006, however, the last reunion in Seattle drew only seven men. The GOYAs were dying out.

How strange it was that these precious men could receive the French Croix de Guerre personally from General Charles DeGaulle and many years afterward see a monument erected to their sacrifice in Belgium but for so long be completely ignored by their own country.*

Lieutenant General (Ret.) William Yarborough, then commander of the 509th, their brother unit laden with honors denied the 551st, called the independent units' disbandment "a crime of the first order." Speaking

---

*A late Presidential Unit Citation for the 551st proposed around the time of the fiftieth anniversary of World War II was twice denied by the Pentagon's Center for Military History. However, after the publication of *Messengers of the Lost Battalion*, a tougher effort was launched with the determined help of Lieutenant General (Retired) John Norton, General Gavin's G-3 at the Battle of the Bulge. Finally, under President Clinton, the Secretary of the Army approved the PUC for the 551st and it was awarded in solemn ceremony by Army Chief of Staff General Eric Shinseki at the Pentagon on April 6, 2001.

of the extraordinary intangibles that go into making an elite unit, he said, "For the Army as a whole to forget this, or to sublimate it to the degree that it is considered less important than bullets and bayonets, is to break faith with the real meaning of what it portends to be a soldier."

Or a man.

VII

One night in Liège, Fred Hilgardner of Missouri made me realize my brother Mark and I were not alone in our own search.

"I'm retracing my father's steps, just like you," he said, taking a good pull of his cigarette. The elder Hilgardner had lost a leg during the First World War at the nearby Meuse-Argonne, and had died when his son was barely a year old. "Everybody loved him." Fred crushed his cigarette, and in the furl of smoke I saw emerge one last time in Belgium the phoenix-genie of our father. How a father can pull the wagon of a son's life, even from the grave!

Whether or not flag-burning should be unlawful, sentiments such as Fred Hilgardner's should never be taken lightly: "They'll play the national anthem at a ballgame — ball players will scratch their nuts, chew gum. Men in the stands sucking their beer, not taking off their caps. Flags on the Fourth — some drag the ground. The flag means more to me than a piece of cloth. It represents men's lives." There is no blind patriotism in the 551st — quite the contrary. Becoming "a shadow battalion," as Dan Morgan called it, ensured that. Medals were not what the 551st was after.

Truth is medal enough. "Setting the record straight" for a handful of children and grandchildren as to what their fathers did in history's near-suicide was really the purpose of going back, as Doug Dillard intimated one night.

Suddenly Hilgardner had a vision, and tapped me on the shoulder, "You get around these guys and you don't seem so damn old. You know, there were two guys that last night in Nice who'd swing a gal around so well. They topped everybody. They danced jitterbug. Maybe your dad was one of them."

Did he love to dance! *That* my mother handled well, to the point that when they danced they seemed to fuse. They never looked at each other, but a quick touch at fingertip would trigger a whirl, a twist, a sidestep, a clinch. Different as they were, they were rhythm personified, *In the*

Mood. And they taught us children to dance, plugging in the photograph, scattering sand on the garage floor.

Maybe one of those hopoids was Dad, Fred. Maybe Wood Joerg was clapping. That last night before Belgium . . .

It became clear to me. From the first day of the trip when Joe Thibault, whose son died of a drug overdose at thirty-nine, came over with tears in his eyes, gripping me on the shoulder, to Otto's sequestered motorcycle, to Phil Hand's shadowy photo, to Hilgardner's last dancer, that the men of the 551st were looking for their messenger. He was unknown. That made him all the more sought after. He was their youth. He was the cipher of their strange, long-delayed coming together. He had something to say to them in the form of two sons. Just as we sought our father in them, they sought him in us.

My brother Mark said it best with a spontaneous toast at our Liège farewell dinner, palpable in candlelight: "It's been painful to realize that none of you knew Dad personally. But I must tell you extraordinary men that in these short days I found a piece of my father in every one of you. Here's to the men of the 551st! May their memory live forever!"

From the troubled exuberance of Joe Cicchinelli to the stoic avoidance of Chuck Miller, which spared others pain—they all had our father stamped on them. Each was the kind of man—gracious, wry, self-abnegating—in whose care you would place your life. My sister placed her life in my father's hands. He did not drop it, though it killed him. During her sometimes frightening ten-year struggle with schizophrenia, my sister did plenty to scare off the most devoted person. By neither him nor my mother was she abandoned.

In his old factory, Dad gave employ to a black with a cleft palate, a French dress designer with a hunchback, a Jewish bookkeeper who, at seventy, supported an invalid brother. At home, he brought in for help with housekeeping a wonderful human being named Margarita Cruz, whose son was killed by death squads in El Salvador. He was the Indian. He dropped from planes for others.

That inkling he had during the war intensified toward the end in his ear's ringing—of a war closer to home. He didn't see a way out of it. For one of his disposition, there wasn't any. Maybe this is why he clung so to life, with such abandon, knowing what a lucky gift a moment of joy was, knowing its duration, how a landscape could be green with friends and suddenly snow-covered with their bodies.

A few months before he died, he sat in front of me and said softly, looking up, "Life is hell."

I suppose I will think about that statement till I die. How out of character it was.

But maybe not. Maybe, for a GOYA, it was a compliment. I have come to see my father's fate as akin to the fate of the men with whom he served in battle so long ago. They became in their sacrifice what he became: lost in a bottomless war, but a messenger of life at all costs.

In Eugene O'Neill's *The Iceman Cometh*, Hickey speaks of his doomed wife: "I could see disgust having a battle in her eyes with love. Love always won." Staring down the barrel of the past, I think the 551st saw the same thing my father saw that terrible day in Belgium and in Los Angeles: ultimate love.

An Act of Forgiveness

The whole purpose of forgiveness is to become free. Whatever you don't forgive, imprisons you.

— Marco Pardo

Sixteen years before the nation's black day, our family met its own September 11, but with no one to hunt down or indict. In the days following our catastrophe, local newspapers printed a few accounts ("Family Argument Turns to Tragedy"), but we were soon left alone to begin our years of sadness.

We buried my father and sister at Holy Cross Cemetery in Culver City in August 1985. Aref and Leslie. So much of their lives were intertwined: their dancing, the garments that he manufactured and she wore, their long, parallel falls from grace — and their deaths.

For most of those sixteen years, forgiveness for the person who sealed their fate was the last thing on my mind, despite advice to the contrary. "People who are unable to forgive create cutoffs and these can be lethal," a family therapist once told me. "It affects your children and grandchildren." But I could not hear him.

Forgiveness, as our family physician reminded me, is not only central to a healthy life, it is "one of the only ways we can approach God." He went on to say that whatever man endeavors to do, God does one better. We make a building, He makes a flower. But in forgiving, we engage in something god-like.

We have a general sense of forgiveness as caving in. But forgiveness is central to the Judaeo-Christian-Islamic tradition. In the Old Testament, fire-breathing Jeremiah hears his Maker declare, "I will forgive their iniquity and I will remember their sin no more" (31:34). Forgiveness is the very lodestone of the New Testament, from the prodigal son to the Lord's Prayer itself (whose only repeated verb is "forgive") right up to the Cross, where Christ exonerates his murderers: "Father, forgive them, for they know not what they do" (Luke 23:24). My old childhood school-mate and substance-abuse counselor Marco Pardo comments, "Christ does not want to die with a poisoned heart." And the Koran makes it clear: "God is much-forgiving, a dispenser of grace" (Sura al-Imran, 3:86–91).

Still, the years did not soften my resolve. But the agony of a nation did. Whether the al-Qaeda terrorists are hunted down completely, whether the last bandit is snuffed out, the survivors of those who died in the World Trade Center and the Pentagon and the fields of Pennsylvania may arrive, if they haven't already, where I arrived in 2002.

For the first time since the deaths of my father and sister, I found myself cresting a hill at Holy Cross Cemetery, amid the drum of the cars below on the San Diego Freeway and the sound of my own feet avoiding the graves of strangers. I weighed the enormity of my family's loss and finally allowed myself to wonder about what can be forgiven—and what cannot.

August 2, 1985. It was a Friday. I had just gotten home after work, looking forward to playing with our newborn boy, who was lolling with his mother on our bed in a small brick row house in Washington, D.C. The phone rang. My first reaction to what my brother said ("Greg, I'll need you now for the rest of my life") was to laugh. That sort of senti-mentality did not seem like him. I even laughed when he spat out that our sister had shot and killed our father at the family store, and then killed herself. A co-worker and a customer had managed to crawl out through the front door, he said. I assumed it was one of his attempts to catch me off guard, so I waited for the punch line. There was none, only the silence and heavy breathing of someone who is pricing each inhale for the first time in his life.

Just days before, I had stood shoulder to shoulder with my sister before the baptismal font at St. Matthew's Cathedral, the site of Presi-dent Kennedy's funeral mass. My wife and I had asked Leslie to be our first son's godmother, and she had flown with my mother from Los Angeles to attend. My father, who stayed behind to man the family store, had sent along a little note of joy to his first grandchild, Matthew: "You are a dream come true and I long to hold you in my arms." We thought being part of the ceremony would bolster my sister's spirits. We also thought we could detect evidence that she was emerging from her long bout with mental illness. It was only after Leslie was dead that I discovered that her hospital records suggested schizophrenia. No one ever used that word as far as I can remember while she was alive. It was always "troubled," "down," "low," "depressed."

Soon after my brother's call, I was on a late flight to Los Angeles. My wife followed two days later with the baby, her milk suddenly dried up from shock. My father-in-law, who drove me to National Airport, said, "You are now the patriarch of your family." "So soon?" I asked.

My mother Rose was in England, visiting her youngest brother and his family, so I was greeted by five stunned aunts. After they left, my brother and I stayed up for a while; as if hardness were a blessing, we finally fell asleep on the floor.

The next morning, my oldest friend, John ("Juan") Millsfield, whose father-in-law had just died, called and said there was much to do; he would walk me through it. Our first stop was the funeral home, where we were greeted by a sallow young man in rumpled shirt and brown pants. He led us into the casket room, and after a stilted introduction to the various models, I selected two caskets—one of oak for my sister and one of mahogany for Dad. The latter was more expensive, and I resisted the subtle pressure of the mortician's assistant to put them in the same wood, to show equality in death. I wanted my sister to be buried in something cheaper than oak. Maybe pine would do, or, for all I cared, cement.

Juan kept urging, "To hold on is to do," and sometimes I think the whole country of America is founded on that principle. Do, do, do! Or fall forever. We drove down the San Diego Freeway to Holy Cross Cemetery where I surveyed the family plot under an elm. There was my grandmother Nazera's injunction on a metal plate: "Keep Up the Courage and Don't Get Discouraged." (An irrepressible peddler, she had also insisted, "Don't stack me.") A St. Joseph statue stood close by, and I thought that fair, as my father's middle name was Joseph, the patron saint of—among other things—a happy death.

Was my father happy? In spite of the gruesome way he was felled, he had been smiling. At least this is what the detective first on the scene had said.

Detective Joe Diglio was my next stop. He looked to be in his early forties with a born tan similar to mine, and kind, light brown eyes. Just under six feet, trim and strong, he had my father's ageless build, and he moved with care and silence to sit at his desk. Before opening a folder, he looked at me and said quietly, "I am very sorry." He was shaken. I did not expect this, and it helped brace me.

The detective pulled out a pad of paper and began to draw a crude schematic of the store. He placed my father at a copy machine in an open space behind the counter. He wasn't absolutely certain where my sister was standing as she began shooting, but the trajectories and damage appeared to place her firing from the very back of the store outward, probably in the back corridor with its stacks of supplies.

Then Diglio showed me where the bullets hit. He found two in the spiral jacket spines hanging on the wall to the left, one in the frame of the door to the back corridor, and one in my father's back.

"Back?"

"Yes. From the scuff marks I could tell he was trying to get away."

I couldn't believe it. Aref Orfalea almost had a foot amputated because of feverish work as a paratrooper messenger at the Battle of the Bulge. I'd seen my father risk limb, if not life, in breaking up fights between men at baseball games or in traffic. I thought his first instinct would be to tackle her.

"There wasn't time," Diglio took out a cigarette and offered me one. He thought my father was about eight feet from my sister — close, but not close enough when someone is firing point blank.

Diglio pulled a drawer out, took something in hand, and placed it on his desk in front of me. The iron slug, slightly tarnished, gleamed in the light of the desk lamp. Attached to it — I don't know if Diglio saw this — was a small hair. The bullet had been found in the ceiling of the back corridor where it had punctured an overhead neon light. By Diglio's gestures I was made to understand that she had pointed the gun at her temple.

But I wanted to ask about the first shots. "Was she aiming?"

Diglio nodded. No one could know for sure, but the scuff marks and the trajectories pointed toward that conclusion.

"I don't think she'd ever fired a real gun before," I said. "How could anyone be that accurate?"

"When you're not used to firearms or you're angry or unstable, or worse, both, the gun pretty much fires itself," Diglio said.

He stood up and paced, as if looking for something. He had been collected and sympathetic, but suddenly, he let himself go for a few seconds. *I've seen it all, but not this*, he told me. *A daughter and a father. Gone in an instant. And for what?* One news report had described an argument over a salary advance; another, a disagreement over the price of a photocopying service, but what really got Joe Diglio was the gun.

"What kind of gun was it?" I asked.

"A .38-caliber Smith & Wesson. It's not a cheap gun. She paid $234 for it right up the road here — National Gun Sales. That's the kind of gun that's standard issue for a police force."

"When did she buy it?"

Diglio fished for the receipt. "March 15. Five months ago."

I was home that day when my father gave my sister a tongue-lashing for being late to open the store. Leslie had flipped out. She had smashed a bathroom mirror at work and had driven herself to an emergency room to have her bloody hand bandaged. She returned home after visiting my father's sister Jeannette, who told her to calm down. But Leslie didn't calm down. Two hours after trashing the store's bathroom, her dark brown eyes were dilated, her speech was staccato and she was hyperventilating. After her outburst, I paced the floor of our family den in front of my parents and told them of another eerie incident. During a previous visit home to Los Angeles, my edgy sleep had been broken by my sister's screams from her bedroom; it was as if she were fighting somebody off. I got up, opened my bedroom door intending to walk down the hallway to her room, but instead I found myself facing my sister, who had stalked down the hallway to my room. Her eyes were wide and wild, she was breathing fast, and I saw her hide something behind her back.

"Leslie, you go to bed now and stop that shouting," I croaked. She stalked back to her room and slammed the door. I pulled the bed in front of my bedroom door. For the only time in my life, I was terrified of someone I loved.

"I'm not coming home until you commit her again to the asylum or do something to get her away from this family," I told my parents the night after the bathroom trashing at the store. My mother thought I was overreacting; I don't think my father said anything. After a long unemployment, he was trying to get a new business off the ground, to hold onto the family home, and himself, all the while giving employ to an unstable person who happened to be his daughter. I imagine he was driven by his natural instinct as a father to love her and protect her before himself.

"She shouldn't have gotten that gun," I said to Diglio.

His eyes grew large and reddened. Moving to leave, he touched a photograph of his daughters — smiling, sparkling in the backyard — and said, "Can I walk you out?"

"Which way is the gun shop?" I asked.

A gun disaster urges fiction. You "develop" scenarios and settings to offset the concern or morbid curiosity of others. The truth is too hard to spit out — and you don't want to alienate people. So you dodge.

It was not pretty.

Intruder at the store.

We lost two.

Even if a gun is mentioned, it's a murky loss — if it's a robber, or a carjacker, or an accidental shooting (as my mother still believes it was). By dodging, you convert the whole thing into story because it's a way of negotiating the bottom of a well, because it's a way of shouting: *Don't equate me with this insanity.*

On the evening of that Saturday, the first day after the shooting, I called my uncle's home in London. I figured correctly that Mother would be asleep, that Uncle Gary would answer the phone. When I told him what had happened, there was a lot of silence across the Atlantic Ocean in that fiber-optic nerve.

"Are you sure?"

"Dead sure."

"My God, what do we tell your mom?"

"You can't tell her the truth. Remember? She had to be hospitalized for an irregular heartbeat when her father died. But we have to get her here for the funeral. We have to concoct a story."

"Yeah."

"Let her sleep. But at breakfast, tell her there has been an accident, a car accident, and Dad is in bad shape. Don't tell he is dead. Hold out a thread of hope that he might make it. That will get her moving fast."

"What about Leslie?"

"Don't mention her. If she asks, just say she's at home. For all I know, that's no lie."

That ramp at the LAX international terminal is ramped into my brain. My grandmother came off first, tired, but ready for the worst, then my mother, followed by Uncle Gary. My mother did not look tired. She was alert, her onyx eyes bright.

"Where is your sister?" were the first words off her lips, and then, "How is Dad?"

"Come here, Mom. Let's go this way." My doctor cousin George Ajalat and I moved her toward the elevator, which would take us to the second-floor first aid station. I coughed and made ridiculous, empty gestures, saying only "It's hard, Mom, it's hard," until we got in the large elevator. She grabbed me, demanding to know where my sister was. I told her. She screamed and flung herself back and forth against the elevator. For a second, I feared she would jar it loose. Her eyes were wide and crowded with sudden wrinkles. She hyperventilated.

We ushered her quickly to the aid station, where my cousin gave her smelling salts to keep her from blacking out and then a tranquilizing shot. She lay back on the cot, moaning, turning her head from side to side.

Later, Gary told me that all the way across the Atlantic, Mom had asked him for the truth. Each time, he leaned away from her and faked a conversation with the stranger next to him, nodding his head up and down, his eyes moistening, a courageous pantomime.

Father John Columba Fogarty, my former high school literature teacher, the man who officiated at my wedding as well as the funeral of my grandmother Nazera, who also baptized one of our boys, came from Chicago to lead the double funeral at St. Mel's in Woodland Hills. At times in the ceremony, I heard his voice crack.

I see it now: As Mother spots the two caskets wheeled to the front, one draped with the American flag, she swoons and looks close to passing out. I recall the little verbal clues learned in birth class that I spoke to my wife to keep her oxygen flowing during labor: "Pant, pant, puff!" I whisper them to my mother and get her doing the inhale-exhale of a mother giving birth. Birth to grief lifelong. But she rallies. That day at the funeral of her husband and daughter, Rose begins the hard habits of a survivor, paradoxically learned in relation to the struggle of a first grandson to see the light.

"Leslie and Aref are dancing with the angels," Father John said, and then he wept. It was an incomprehensible image. Yes, my sister and father had liked to dance together, but on this day a suggestion of joy seemed profane. It was too early and too raw to suggest mercy.

My overriding concern at the cemetery was to get someone to speak for my father and sister. A cousin of my father's from Dallas, Mike Hamrah, slipped me an elegiac note he wrote to Aref that ended fittingly: "You did well, friend." But he wouldn't read it aloud. I tried several people, but everyone was tongue-tied. Finally, an adopted "cousin,"

Dr. Nicholas Habib, did the honors. After long silence, stubbing out a cigarette on the freshly dug earth near the caskets, he spoke eloquently of my father's feel for those down on their luck or lonely, of his own informal "adoption" into our family. He saluted my mother and asked all to help her in the years to come.

But no one volunteered to speak for my sister. Finally, the silence was unbearable, and two stepped forward. Not family. Two workers at the family store, one of whom had crawled out during the shooting with his life. I cannot remember what they said.

After I fell into the roses heaped on my sister's casket, cutting my face, a good, strong man, Victor George, helped me up. I saw him fourteen years later, at the mercy meal for one of the last original immigrants in our family. "You held me up long ago," I said as I looked at him, as if the fourteen years had never been. "Yes," Victor said quickly. "And I always will."

Thus, in the tall shaft created by the shooting, I grasped a slender thread, and am doing so now, weaving it as I go into a strong rope.

We filed a lawsuit against the gun store in 1986, a year after the tragedy, barely inside the statute of limitations. In those days, it took some time to secure a lawyer who would even take on such a case. Gloria Allred's firm refused us, saying we didn't have a chance. Her firm had reached an out-of-court settlement for the family of a young woman named Tara Ann Katona, who had killed herself with a gun sold by the same store that had sold my sister her gun—National Gun Sales in Northridge. Katona's mother had called the shop and begged the store not to sell a gun to her daughter, who was getting out of a psychiatric hospital and had been talking suicide to an inmate. The store sold it to her anyway. Katona lost her life; her family received $175,000. Allred declared a victory for gun control, lost in the back pages of the *Los Angeles Times*.

"Did your mother tell the store not to sell the gun to your sister?" the Allred lawyer asked.

"No," I said. "She was living at home at the time, but no one could possibly guess she'd buy a gun."

I found out some years later that this was not entirely true. We took our case to another firm, Windle Turley in Dallas, and deep into our lawsuit, my mother told me that my sister had bought another pistol from National Gun Sales in 1982, three years before the shooting. She had told my father the gun gave her a "sense of power." But somehow he had coaxed her to turn it in to him, and it was disposed of through a neighbor. As far as I know, my mother and father told no one in the family about it. That gun purchase, like her mental illness, was so horrid they pushed it out of their minds.

In the lawsuit, we argued that the gun store, in selling the second pistol to my sister while she was having a "psychotic event," was negligent. We hoped to have testimony from those who witnessed her severe agitation on the day of the gun purchase — me, my mother, others at the gun store, family store, and the hospital emergency room. We planned to argue that the gun store clerk should have called the phone number on the purchase form to get some information about her visibly disturbed behavior, which, by law, should prevent such a sale. (That phone number turned out to be my parents'.) After four years of answering hundreds of questions sent by the lawyers for the defense — Haight, Brown, and Bonesteel, an upscale Beverly Hills law firm that played hardball — dozens of depositions and affidavits, listening to expert witnesses during depositions, and having my sister's records and writings combed and recombed, we found ourselves totally exhausted. Haight, Brown and Bonesteel filed a cross-complaint on behalf of the gun store — subsequently dropped — that accused my parents of failing to adequately supervise Leslie.

Finally, in 1990, our case was thrown out of court, by the cryptic one-and-a-half page summary judgment of Judge Richard Adler of the Van Nuys District Court. The gun store not only won the case by the stroke of a pen. The code-like judgment document ("i.e., see section 4, par. B, col. 7") suppressed that there was ever anything at stake. Our Dallas attorneys, who had been catalyzed into their lonely interest in gun violence cases after Kennedy's assassination in their hometown, explained: "The judge [Adler] was of the opinion there was no evidence to indicate Leslie displayed bizarre behavior at the time she purchased the gun. The judge was not willing to impose any greater duty upon a gun seller than those required by the existing statutes and regulations." The fact that my mother and I signed a written affidavit that we saw her out-of-control state and bandaged hand just after the purchase and that the hospital personnel had testified that they witnessed her distressed state while bandaging her hand did not seem to matter.

Frustrated in the courts, we took our grief elsewhere. Shortly after the August shooting, my mother and I were welcomed into the Washington office of Pete Shields, who had founded a gun violence public interest group, then called Handgun Control, after his son had been shot to death in 1975 in San Francisco by the so-called Zebra Killers. Shields was very empathetic, the all-too-rare "real article" in a city with hired guns for one industry or another. He put his arms around my mother and they both shook with their tears. A few months later, she opened a memorial fund at Handgun Control in the name of her husband and daughter.

In 1992, our family helped lobby for the Brady Bill—named for Shields' tireless successor Sarah Brady, the wife of a former presidential press secretary paralyzed for life by gunshot in an assassination attempt on President Reagan. My mother met with her then L.A. congressman, Democrat Anthony Beilenson of Woodland Hills, a pivotal vote on 1994's Brady Law and the assault weapons ban. Though at times the sorrow seemed endless, these modest victories for sanity brought our family some measure of relief.

According to the Brady Campaign to Prevent Gun Violence (formerly Handgun Control), firearm deaths declined nationwide 27 percent from the time the Brady Law was passed to the end of the nineties (38,000 to 28,874), when a so-called computerized "instant" background check (called "NICS"), went into effect. NICS was demanded by Republicans who reluctantly approved the Brady Law. Because the "instant" computer check is significantly flawed, murders and suicides with guns began to tick upward. Though the computer can show a "red flag" warning for certain purchasers, giving the FBI up to three days to report back to a gun dealer, oftentimes the system gets clogged and a bad sale goes through. In practice, 90 percent of gun background checks are processed in minutes, though large amounts of important data are not in the system even a decade later—such as 20 percent of felons and 90 percent of those adjudicated as mentally ill. Cho Seung-Hui, the deranged student who shot and killed 32 of his fellow students at Virginia Tech in 2007, was one such case. Rogue gun shops, like National Gun Sales, are woefully slow in being prosecuted by authorities. Fifty-seven percent of all guns used in crimes come from 1 percent of dealers, yet because of weak laws and lack of enforcement, it takes on average eleven years to shut a rogue shop down. Only in 2006—after forty years of investigation!—were authorities able to shut down Trader Sports of San Leandro, California, which had sold an incredible 1,424 guns used in crimes in its last three years alone.

The carnage continues. In 2004, 29,569 Americans shot and killed each other and themselves—nine times those killed on September 11.

Many in Congress have resisted passing new legislation — such as the return of a waiting-period background check for all purchases, gun registration, and ballistic fingerprinting — that might further curb those deaths. By June 2008, the U.S. Supreme Court ruled against the District of Columbia's ban on handguns. From the 1930s on, the highest court in the land has struck down the notion that the Second Amendment gives a "right to bear arms," finding it applies rather to a "well-regulated militia" or national guard. In the paranoia following September 11 and the Patriot Act, gun control advocates worried that, far from assuring that gun violence would be cut, the Supreme Court overturning the D.C. ban with a pro-gun interpretation of the 2nd amendment opens the floodgate to firearms. A pistol in every pot.

Since 1970, firearm mass violence has significantly increased. Grant Duwe's landmark 2007 study found 215 mass gun murders (four or more killed within 24 hours) for the nineties — a 22 percent increase from the eighties (176 incidents). The Brady Campaign lists 157 major shootings (three or more people shot in succession) from 2000 to June 1, 2008. U.S. school shootings alone numbered almost a hundred from 2000 to April 30, 2008, triple the number (28) the Brady Campaign counted for the nineties. Bullet spraying has become a kind of anti-personnel bomb, and President Bush's diffidence in 2004 that allowed the assault weapons ban to sunset didn't help matters. We seem to be in reverse in domestic as well as foreign policy; one American safe zone after another has fallen to darkness.

Some years after our dark day in August, I walked alone into National Gun Sales off by itself in the dust on a dry stretch of Parthenia Boulevard along the railroad tracks. What hits you in a gun shop right off is the sheer number of the weapons. Shotguns and assault rifles spread along the walls like wings of a forbidding flock. I dawdled for a while at one of the racks of magazines and books dealing with hunting, shooting, explosives, soldiers of fortune — "men without women," as Hemingway once called them.

What did my sister feel, coming into this dark den? Did she know she was entering her death? Did she think the gun would melt and enwrap her like a protective cloak?

From the ammo boxes the clerk came, seeing me staring at a .38 Smith & Wesson. "Nice piece of equipment," he said quietly.

"Uh huh."

"You want to see it?"

"All right."

He brought it out of the light and laid it slowly on the glass. Just enough for the trigger guard to tick. It was cool, the butt pocked for a good grip. Not light.

"Feel good?"

"Yeah."

I wanted to buy a gun. For the first time in my life.

"You'll like it. No one ever brings one back."

"Uh huh."

Something in the way he spoke and moved, back toward the ammo, under the gun wings, arms folded like the director of the universe, made me touch the box of cartridges. He moved directions on an orange card in front of me like a draw card to an inside straight. "Here's a shooting range down the block. If you want to try it out. They've got 'em there."

"Sure."

The door opened on the light, the light shined in the darkness, and the darkness grasped it.

Who was my sister?

For twenty years, Leslie Orfalea was a healthy, balanced, playful person who loved acting and dancing. There is a family picture of us as kids both holding up foam, smiling in the tub. Even in the eleven years of her bizarre descent into mental illness, she had many stretches of sanity, pleasantness, and cheer. The week after the tragedy, a customer came into the family store wondering what happened to the sweet girl behind the counter.

Perhaps my seniority didn't help. I was born ten months after my parents wed. By the time my sister Leslie came along, I had had the rule of the roost for four years. I was also the first-born male of ten grandchildren, and that was a place of high honor to chin up to.

Then there were the dirt clods. That great novel of boyhood friendship, A Separate Peace, hangs on one verb: "jounced." In the key passage marking the descent of a golden friendship into guilt, sadness, and inner torture, Gene "jounces" with his feet the limb of a tree on which his best friend Finny is standing. A consummate athlete, Finny falls from this jouncing and is crippled for life, in fact, dies young from the injuries sustained in the fateful fall, just after giving Gene an extraordinary absolution.

My sister was not in a tree. She was walking down Nutwood Street in Anaheim one bright spring Saturday in 1958 bouncing a rubber ball, the sun bouncing off her glasses when dirt clods hit her in the face, knocking her glasses to the street. A friend and I threw them; the clods scratched the corneas of Leslie's eyes.

As a teenager, my sister struggled to live up to or even surpass my hyper-involved school performance. But in her own eyes, she always came up short. After I copped the presidency of my high school, she lost a run at her school's vice presidency. I went to Georgetown for four years; she went to the University of Portland (Oregon) and left after a year and a bad relationship. Even before her mind snapped, she would tell me, "I have lived so long in your shadow," and I wondered how on earth I could trim it.

After transferring to the University of Denver, she began to hear voices. It was her ears, we thought, and so she went to a specialist. But there was nothing wrong with her ears. It was her sleep. And a doctor gave her sedatives, but more sleep didn't quiet the voices. It was her diet, but no concoction of rice, sprouts, yogurt, and vitamins dulled what was calling at her. Perhaps it was a tumor, but a CAT scan showed nothing abnormal.

Ironically, during the onset of her illness at twenty, she had some success on the college stage. A klatch of talented and concerned friends surrounded her, including the granddaughter of Helen Hayes. She had what seemed like a sweetheart of a boyfriend. In fact, he introduced her to psychedelic drugs — pure poison for someone with a predisposition to mental illness.

Two years after graduation, she traveled to Oklahoma with a dinner theater company and things took a turn for the worse. The story is still sketchy, but she fell into an affair with the director, who constantly berated her during rehearsals to the point of a nervous breakdown. How she ever managed to drive herself back to Los Angeles is beyond me.

All of this was bad enough, but 1977 also saw the demise of my father's once prosperous garment business and the beginning of his five-year battle with unemployment. After being vice president of another firm, he took part-time work in advertising and sales. In slow horror, the family watched my sister coil into a dance with my tottering father; she was pulling him into an abyss. It was a bewildering time for him, at best. I remember him walking in the late morning back and forth on the circular drive of the family home in his bathrobe.

In the fall of 1977, my sister was referred by a psychiatrist who drove a candy-apple red Cadillac to Del Amo psychiatric hospital in

Torrance, "the town that slept with the lights on." There she remained for eight months, enduring, among other things, a knife attack by an inmate and the dosage of the wrong drug that nearly did her in. Alarmed, my parents pulled her out, but when she emerged, the Leslie we once knew was gone, and in her place was a bottomless stare.

Upon entry to the hospital, she had been diagnosed with psycho-neurotic depressive reaction, which quickly changed to psychotic depressive reaction. She admitted not only hearing voices but seeing "funny lights in front of her." But it wasn't until after seven months that the word "schizophrenic" entered her psychiatrist's bimonthly summary. If Leslie hadn't been hospitalized, he wrote, she "may have ended up in a severe schizophrenic break."

Reviewing her records today, a team of psychiatric professionals tell me it's very likely my sister was suffering from schizophrenia before she entered the hospital—and after she left. Since schizophrenia is known as a genetic disease, I searched our family's history, but came up with no one that fit the description of the illness. About as close as I could come was a great-aunt who was said to have had a breakdown after having ten children. A Spokane, Washington nurse once told me that in 1953, the year of my sister's birth in that cold northwestern city, a virulent strain of flu had taken several lives in the city and could have caused brain lesions in utero enough to manifest schizophrenia in my sister's teen years.

Leslie's drug usage didn't help. Her hospital records say that the "patient has admitted to massive psychedelic drug use of several years' duration." Her desire to take illicit drugs "outside" as she got closer to release "is an increasingly important issue . . . otherwise she will have a psychotic decompensation since she is extremely sensitive to marijuana or psychedelic drugs."

In its "Diagnostic and Statistical Manual of Mental Disorders—Fourth Edition," the American Psychiatric Association suggests that the use of LSD can precipitate schizophrenia. A 2002 report in the *American Journal of Epidemiology* indicates that marijuana use can lead to "psychosis in psychosis-free subjects," and other studies suggest that the symptoms can worsen if a patient is taking antidepressants and smoking marijuana at the same time.

The record continued, "The patient needs a great deal of work in terms of the ways she sets herself up with very destructive people who will exploit and take advantage of her. This includes many boyfriends and associates in the industry." Presumably, this was the entertainment industry. Whether she would have benefited from further hospitalization elsewhere, her time at the facility was literally life threatening, the diagnoses spotty at best, and my parents got her out of there, with no other concrete help in sight. Over the next seven years, she was treated by other therapists but never entered another psychiatric institution.

In 1983, my father opened and became a partner in a photocopy shop in my cousin's well-known chain. He set about fixing it up and put in place a business that posthumously became a bigger success than his dress firm. There he gave Leslie work, thinking, as any son of an immigrant would, that a little work cures a lot of woe. That was the store where it happened.

It came to me one day, thinking of the shadows my sister lived in. The gun not only took the voices away, it not only brought her center stage and onto the front page of the newspaper and final release from craven boyfriends and the furrowed brows of loved ones. In taking my father with her, in some sort of twisted logic, she was saying to the one person who could not resist her, "Come. I don't want to be alone anymore."

Some years after the shooting, I regarded the slumping figure of my friend Dan Hill as he entered a Georgetown University reunion. A strapping six-foot-three Robert Redford lookalike in our college years, Dan was using a cane and had aged drastically. He soon told me how. He and his wife had been out driving down a long stretch of Arizona roadway when a vehicle suddenly plowed straight into them. They barely survived; his wife's face was severely disfigured and Dan himself was in a coma for more than a week. One knee was pretty much destroyed.

At the end of the reunion, Dan looked at me as he took his cane and said, "Forgiveness is where it's at." That magnanimity was startling, coming from a man who had been robbed of his athleticism and good health. It was like a stone thrown into the pool of my soul. The ripples would not be denied.

It's hard to admit—it may be the hardest thing of all—but some good came from the shootings long ago. It was as if Dylan Thomas's words "And death shall have no dominion" were taken in deep. My heartbroken mother took over running the family photocopy shop and was so good at it she grew two more stores. At a company meeting, she was lauded by my cousin Paul as his own role model. My mother, primarily a homemaker before the tragedy, made a better income as a retail businesswoman than my manufacturer father. Score one for tenacity.

She fought back in other ways: art classes, reading to seniors, championing gun control, hosting classic July Fourth swim parties for family and friends, giving herself totally to her sons and grandsons. All in all, a miraculous resilience that spoke to many.

My father died more or less in the line of duty. Score one for courage and a quick death. Thank God there would be no cancer or slow rotting for a man of such vitality.

My relationships with loved ones deepened after the tragedy. My marriage endured and grew precious. My wife and I had another boy the year after the shooting, and then another. Would we have been so urgent to breed had Death not come calling so loudly? My father's oldest sister, Jeannette, and I became extremely close. We traveled together to southern France and Belgium, representing my father at the first return to the killing fields of World War II by members of his lost battalion. I ended up writing a book about them.

For every friendship that withered from the shootings, another grew tighter or was born. One old school friend I hadn't seen for fifteen years, Philip Pictaggi, literally emerged from the crowd at the double funeral and became a great supporter of my work on the battalion and of me.

Unchartable good out of evil. It seems to be one of the strangest, but truest, lessons of life.

But the parallel reality, and the more obvious one, is that our family, and to some extent, our friends, lost too much. All the resilience in the world will not stop some things from being irretrievable. Our three boys never knew their grandfather. My mother, successful as she became, grew a tough crust to survive those years and worked herself so hard she had little time for romantic love. She lived the prime years of her life alone. My father's brother and sisters, except Jeannette, became more inward than ever, living behind shuttered windows, hardly ever going out, except for Sunday Mass. For a time, my wife saw California as a dark place, and she curled away from the pain of the shootings and other shadows. And me? I hunkered down in Washington, D.C., hiding myself in bureaucracy.

Imagine a country-in-hiding. From itself.

The rind of a decade and half cracked first at the library shootings at Littleton, Colorado, and then was shattered by September 11. An inner wall had been hit by the ax of mass violence. Kafka took such violence metaphorically as the purpose of literature—an ax at the frozen heart.

That's how I came to be threading my way through the lids of the dead at Holy Cross cemetery in 2002. On that gusty, bright February morning, the wind was a hand.

For all the justifiable outrage over bin Laden and his henchmen, the hew and cry had begun to make me wonder about the nature of revenge. Yes, they need to be brought to justice. But more than half the battle in staving off a recurrence of such heinous acts is to try and understand why they happen in the first place and to do something about the milieu of deprivation, injustice, and hatred that brings people to such an abyss. We need to look at the history of the region and our poorer part in it; slamming the door on terror through force is not nearly enough and may in itself reap a bitter harvest.

I finally realized that I couldn't begin to think of forgiveness until I looked closely at the human face that took my loved ones, the history of that face, and the depths of despair that mental illness brought to it. I had to face my sister, in the way I have been given to confront such things: through writing.

At the cemetery, my mother filled a jug of water at the tap by the road and handed it to me. It was my first time there since our loved ones were killed seventeen years before. Mother carried with her two miniature rose bushes — one yellow, one fire-engine red. It took a while to find the graves. "I always get lost," she said, angling from the grotto of St. Joseph down through the gravestones, searching for her marker sycamore. We passed a replica of the Pieta and I thought: Did my sister hold my father in her arms?

When she spotted the tree, Mother walked straight to their graves, two black stone markers side by side like a table setting for two. She knelt and with a cloth wiped the markings of snails, dead insects, and dirt. Soon the darkness shone below her knotted hand.

I busied myself, uprooting the shaggy grass along the edges of the black stones just as my father used to do for his parents' graves here — as if you could tidy sorrow itself. The crabgrass was thicker on Leslie's grave. Mom gave me her scissors, but I said I needed a spade, and she produced one. We placed the two small pots side by side — red for Dad, yellow for Les — and watered this bridge between them before arching our backs to pray.

My father's grave reads: "Aref Joseph Orfalea, Beloved Father and Husband, 1924–1985. Go Get Em." That last was his favorite imperative to all who would truly live, and I was glad to see it. Then I caught the figure on Leslie's grave: an angel kneeling, hands clasped, wings drawn up. The prayer etched there startled me: *May you be dancing in the light of God.* It was a less profane, more redemptive version of Father Columba's eulogy — "Leslie and Aref are dancing with the angels" — that had struck me back then as impossible, even absurd. Mother had produced a spiritual upgrade, a sign of her instinctive forgiveness, and she had done it very early on.

I hadn't. I had held onto my anger like a stone as black as their graves. But that day the words fell out of me: "I forgive you, sister. Forgive me." The grades. The anger. The judgment. The distance. *The dirt.* I also said to myself, "Forgive God."

When I stood up facing west, it was colder. A cloud had covered the sun. I looked straight ahead. There, downhill through a hole in a stand of eucalyptus, past the San Diego Freeway and the town of Inglewood, was the sea. It shined like a melted coin. If I moved slightly to the left or right of either of their graves, it disappeared.

I pointed this out to Mother, who smiled and said she'd never seen it before, had never looked beyond their graves that way. We both agreed it was a great vantage point, and almost worth seventeen years of heartache to discover. She muttered something about poets seeing beauty everyone else misses.

A shaft of light came through the cloud. It touched on the St. Joseph statue and slowly crept across the grass. I thought, of course, that it was leading to us. Then I took my shadow off and walked with Mother back to the road.

Taps for a Broken Soldier

The body had come a long way. It had fought in Burma along the Burma Road in the Second World War. It had fought in Korea during the Inchon landing. It had done time at NATO headquarters in Germany and in Military Intelligence at the start of the Vietnam War at Fort Holabird. It was my uncle, Major George Orfalea, flown all the way from his humble apartment in Los Angeles for burial in Arlington National Cemetery.

I was the only family member greeting the hearse. It was a hot day, July 27, 2006. Uncle George was one of four soldiers scheduled for burial at 10 a.m. He was to be buried in Lot 60, where the turf is being turned daily for soldiers dead in Iraq.

I stood clutching two dozen store-bought roses wrapped in cellophane with a bar code for price. It was the best I could do, hustled into duty at the last minute when it became obvious no one else could make it. My own family is almost entirely in Los Angeles. My uncle's wife is up in years and couldn't make the cross-country trip; his one daughter in Georgia had been battling cancer and demurred.

"Arlington was his last wish, Greg," my cousin Bonnie told me over the phone. "You be there and represent us all."

Evidently, Arlington itself thought no one was coming, because a volunteer from a ladies' veterans society showed up and was going to do the honors of receiving the flag. I hope she wasn't disappointed.

A chaplain greeted me at the administration center in full dress uniform, a friendly man who went through a brief exercise of jotting down notes about my uncle's life, none of which he used while reading, quite beautifully from memory, the 23rd Psalm, "The Lord is my shepherd, I shall not want."

What did my uncle want?

It seems every family has a sphinx-like figure, and ours was Uncle George. Though he was my godfather, I saw him rarely — once or twice a decade. However, his service in the Army was as distinguished as his subsequent hermetic civilian life was not. In the early fifties, he was named Captain of the Guard at Los Alamos. He once told me he ordered all rifles trained on a man who approached the cyclotron without a white smock, standard operating procedure at the time. That man was Edward Teller, the father of the hydrogen bomb!

"Too bad you didn't open fire," I grumbled, and my uncle smiled.

"I saw the bones in my hands at Alamagordo when the H-bomb exploded," he told me, lifting his hands.

While stationed in Mannheim in Germany, my uncle was one of NATO chief of staff General Bernard Rogers' top aides. He was being groomed, my father thought, for a generalship himself. Soon George was named to the Military Intelligence group at Fort Holabird, which was tasked by Secretary Robert McNamara to study the impact on our military of an American escalation in the Vietnam War. Uncle George concentrated on casualties. As early as 1961, he estimated U.S. dead would reach fifty thousand.

"Pretty close," he said in retirement. "We lost fifty-eight thousand."

The study went up the chute to McNamara, where it was promptly buried. More quickly than my Uncle George at Arlington.

Major Orfalea was then told he could make colonel only by commanding a battalion in Vietnam or Alaska. With no taste for wasted blood or ice, my uncle declined, and he retired sooner than he had ever thought he would — after twenty years of service, in 1963. He took himself in bewilderment to his sister's Los Angeles dress shop at the corner of Hollywood and Highland boulevards. Half his life was spent in seclusion; he was never the same man again.

Eight young soldiers in full dress eased the casket out of its cream-white hearse. It was common pine. My uncle died poor. With no honor and little money, he had given a final order: a wooden box was enough for him.

To the men, it was gold, or at least they handled it that way, easing it out, taking it reverently up the grassy slope to the gravesite, depositing it on slats over the freshly dug grave.

A fly buzzed in the roses. My cousin had told me to forget flowers, George didn't like them. But I had to put something on his casket besides my hand. Something others would do.

Alongside me was Douglas Dillard, a retired Army colonel and close friend. His stalwart wife Virginia, wheelchair bound, sat dutifully in the car at the curb on Eisenhower Avenue. Both had answered my somewhat desperate early-morning call for someone to be with me at that grave.

Doug sat next to me in silence, as we occupied two of the six green felt–lined folding chairs. Hardly a bleeding-heart liberal, Colonel Dillard did not whisper when he said, "Look down there. Those boys back from Iraq are dead because of Bush's war." It was almost as if he wanted the chaplain to hear. And the honor guard. And his old fellow World War II GI, George Orfalea, lying, I wanted to think, in some final peace.

What did he die of? It seemed hardly to matter. He had refused to go to a doctor for five years, in spite of a bleeding ulcer. He was determined at the end to suffer with no respite.

"Please, Uncle George," I had pleaded over the phone. "Please go to the hospital."

"I don't want to," he said repeatedly.

The autopsy revealed that he had had two massive heart attacks in a row at home.

The chaplain handed me the flag, carefully folded into a triangle by the honor guard. I trembled and kissed it, out of sheer love for my poor country and uncle.

How can we honor the individuality of a man, the importance of the human soul, and carry on this mindless war? Are we in the "cradle of civilization," or the cradle of the end of civilization?

Seven soldiers in a line of graves off in the distance shot three times — an abbreviated version of the 21-gun salute. I entrusted the wrapped flag to Colonel Dillard, unwrapped the old cheap roses, and placed them on the casket's pine.

"I love you, Uncle George," my voice box barely squeezed out. "I know you are with Dad." The two of them were as different as Burma and France. I began to shake uncontrollably. Memories crowded in: Uncle George marching me in Los Angeles as a little boy down from Grandma's house to Wilshire Boulevard, drilling me in the manual-of-arms. Uncle George calling out in his elided speech, as if all the world were troops to be trained: "It'saworldfullofyesmen."

Yes, it's a world full of yes men. In Iraq. Israel. Palestine. And Washington.

Now taps.

As I listened to the dirge of the single trumpet played out across the dead of 250 years of war, I prayed a moment for a No. An honest and sincere no. From the jellied spines of our Congress or the go-along-to-get-along newsmen or our metronomic judges. Someone to counter the murderous ideals of our president and resurrect the Constitution. A no like the one my poor uncle spoke so long ago that cost him his career and buried his life far from this Arlington sea of graves.

Angeleno Days

It isn't the beach, it's the mountain. It isn't the sand sun surf of the advertisements and the Beach Boys' bushy bushy blonde hairdo or the poetry
in the sand or even the little surfer little one makes my heart come all
undone, it's the shadowy mountain looming over all this sun that makes
California California. Otherwise it's Florida and plain deterioration.

I am traveling a road that wasn't there when I was a boy, the 210
freeway that girds the San Gabriels and the San Bernadinos behind Los
Angeles, a late-in-the-life-of-the-city road that clings to the foothills of
these mountains as if they might erupt and kick it away. What is it about
upsurges of the earth — they make up half of L.A. County's land mass —
that holds, that brings me a strange calm in the midst of a year of
monumental changes in my family? It's January 2004; I've arrived back
after twenty years' exile to teach at a fine college in the midst of California winter. The San Gabriels glow like green felt. The shadows compress
the green and conspire with the sunlight to make the escarpments seem
to move, an extinct animal come to life in spring before everything goes
brown, gold, then to fire. Is it the sense that the mountains remain when
all else in California changes? Is it the illusion of softness in those felt
hills, as if you could put your pained head there like a pillow? Much of
my hometown appeals from afar, but up close pierces your heart like a
burr. Or becomes tinder.

Carey McWilliams, the dean of L.A. historians who had migrated to
Los Angeles from a decidedly mountainous Colorado, in 1946 saw the
sea and light transform the mountains in startling ways: "But let the light
turn soft with ocean mist, and miraculous changes occur. The bare mountain ranges, appallingly harsh in contour, suddenly become enwrapped in
an entrancing ever-changing loveliness of light and shadow . . . and
the land itself becomes a thing of beauty." It is not just the mountains
that surround, but the light, that unique, brilliantly white, life-starting,

eye-bending L.A. light that art essayist Lawrence Weschler found himself "pining for every day of the nearly two decades since I left Southern California." Weschler grew up near me in the San Fernando Valley
and found himself midlife like me East ensconced in the bowels of the
enemy — New York.

I am back after twenty years in Washington, D.C., twenty years of
emptying my blood into the gutter with the federal government, here to
do the work of the lord of literature, excited, hopeful like Father Serra
himself when he first set foot on the bay of San Diego at 56, an old man in
1769, as I return not much younger yet thinking with that great California sin that I am young in some socket of my bones. I did it. I did a
California thing — changed in midlife for new work in a new place — and
challenged God and Thomas Wolfe to see if, indeed, you could buck the
odds, you could go home. Of course *you* can. But what about everyone
else? Home doesn't exactly sit still.

Or go with you. With a terrible congruence, just as I am given my
heart's dream — to return to teach in my hometown — my wife gets, after
dedicating herself to raising our three children, her first full-time job
outside the home. I've taken a pay cut to teach, and her salary is larger.
Her attachment to Washington can be divined from the following: except for two years in college in Colorado, she has spent her life in or near
the Capital; she is fond of pointing out around the city the cement foun-
dations poured by her great-grandfather, including that under the classic
Marriot Wardman Hotel, where we spent our first night as man and
wife; she takes understandable pride in an artistic knack for restoring old
homes. When an untoward tornado threw a tree on our Depression-era
garage, she observed, "There's your new study," which I dutifully entered and in which I wrote a book.

I am in Los Angeles, the city of my birth and spirit, alone. It's winter
in California — clarity after a torrential downpour. But my wife prefers
a winter of plain old snow. I can see her right now, opening up our
bedroom window on sub-freezing air, cooing over it! And me closing it
after she goes to sleep because I'm freezing. I once pointed out snow on
the San Bernardinos, but snow and ice need to be right there in front of
you ready to crack your skull. And the coup de grace — in a lovely,
sparkling beach neighborhood, she drops, "How come the garages are
all in front?" Dry heat that makes me linger makes her wonder. And
palms and eucalyptus are not real trees. Nineteenth-century live oak-,
carob-, and pepper tree–laden neighborhoods such as Pasadena aren't

old enough, for some reason. And when I fan my arms towards the desert in Joshua Tree, or the Pacific off Zuma, or the wintergreen of the San Gabriels, she croaks, "Who needs more nature than Rock Creek Park?" And off she jogs in Rock Creek Park with one of two girlfriends who live a stone's throw away.

All my family and friends, and her family, as well, encourage me to follow my calling to teach, and pray. My wife herself, in a telling moment as we do dishes in the kitchen, looks hard into the sink and says, "Take it," hinting she might change her mind over time. It's a big gamble, but one I know I must take or watch the marriage die of my own bitterness. So here I am, living out of a small apartment, traveling, exhilarated at the mountains so shortly green, rolling the manual window down of the little red car of my aunt who lies, half paralyzed, in a rest home.

From the day I signed on to teach three years in California, I took over the little red hardly driven Geo Prizm of my aunt, Jeannette Orfalea Graham, and thus in a way my homecoming became wedded to her story of coming West during the Great Depression and her final decline at ninety-five. The ocean wind and great sunlight that filled her with excitement in 1935 did the same thing to her nephew seventy years later. By then, though, she was felled. One of the great malapropisms in our language — there's no rest in a rest home, save a drug-fed stupor — Aunt Jen's was called the Woodland Care Center, and though it was in Woodland Hills it was not in the hills of that suburban town but the flat plain of the San Fernando Valley, and any woodlands that might have been were long ago chopped down for farms and orchards, which in turn were ploughed under for a million people to rest their heads in the first huge suburb of the West. It is hard to turn the corner of the gas station at Corbin and Sherman Way, right past the rest home, and follow the colonnade of tall palms to her modest yellow home with the walnut tree. The trees front and back are gone, and the little artist studio her husband with the bum leg built for her out back — I hadn't the heart to find out what happened to it. I can't imagine anyone painting in it. The best I can do is situate someone's tractor-like lawnmower wedged where once Jeannette Graham painted her landscapes of rural Ohio where she was born in 1910, one year after her fellow midwesterner turned lover of the West, Wallace Stegner. In her artist studio, where once were oils of old barns, combines in the snow, a weathervane, would have to be something artless and useful, run by gas. This was, after all, Los Angeles.

These stereotypes of L.A. They die hard even for a writer determined to slay them once and for all. The old saw—a damn dram of truth lurks in the gallons of stereotype, keeping it alive in spite of what we know. Not to say L.A. is car-free!

In her twenties, and appearing to be fleeing something, Jeannette Orfalea drove out to California around 1935 alone; she was probably pregnant or recently pregnant. She was a vibrant, chesty, throat-full-of-laughter woman with a pile of chestnut hair, the same color of hair as my sister's. Jeannette had great dimples; she seized you with her laughter and her arms. I don't think I ever met anyone as hungry for life as my Aunt Jen, the oldest of six children, with the possible exception of the sixth, my father. She had their father's elegance and style and her mother Nazera's nonstop energy, sans the grating judgments. It was said men just glommed onto her. A first cousin was in love with her till the day he died in California. Albert Orfalea, my Kinko-founding cousin's father, still called her to go for coffee into their seventies and eighties.

Jeannette was married, briefly, to Bob Federly, in Cleveland, Ohio, where she had been working at her father's Avenue Gift Shop in the old arcade, and later—after her father went bankrupt—the drafting unit of an aircraft company and, finally, the women's clothing section of a department store. I imagine she must have sold more than one man a wifely dress trying it on with her hourglass figure. I also imagine her bored with a dead-end job in a large entity, latching onto Bob Federly for some excitement. It's interesting to me that someone who was as conversant as Jen revealed so little of her intimate life, even to me, who was her adoring and son-like nephew. She was a good listener with a good listener's self-confident reserve. I can't recall who told me Jen was the only one of the four Orfalea sisters ever to come close to having a child, but I think it plausible that she fled Cleveland and her marriage after some apocryphal choice over the baby. Did Federly get her pregnant before the marriage? Did she promise to abort the child for Buffalo Bob in some desperate ploy to hold onto him and discover after a trip to the abortionist that he wasn't worth hanging onto, her Catholic conscience a vortex flinging her outward, as far as the Pacific? Or was it a simpler tragedy—the baby miscarried or was stillborn and Federly left her?

There's no way of knowing now. All six of the original Orfalea children of my immigrant grandparents are dead—all of them dying in Los Angeles—and although Jeannette herself was the last to go in 2007,

for the three years of my exile's return to California, her vocal chords
were paralyzed. She could barely manage a muffled "I wuv u."

So sexual tragedy may be the root of my father's family coming
West. Ten years after Jen's hegira, the rest of the Cleveland family pulled
up roots, relations between my grandfather and grandmother so frigid
they traveled a year apart in separate cars, and drove into L.A. just after
World War II, two GI boys in tow. To add to the sexual aspect of all this,
my father, pictured with a leggy blonde woman at the beach at Lake Erie
just after coming home from the war, had given up on her, or she him. He
had failed to make love to her in the back seat of his car, whether from a
physical misfiring or religious conviction. A paratrooper barely surviving the Battle of the Bulge takes such a thing particularly hard, I would
think. No surprise that within a year of coming West he met my Syrian
mother, with jet black hair and short legs, and he married that non-
blonde beauty without looking back. (I am being literal; I think he traveled back to Cleveland only once after that in forty years.) He was also
the only one of six kids to marry his own ethnicity.

It's hard to say if race figured into the Orfaleas coming West, but it
might have. Cleveland had an old Syrian community and the Orfaleas
had, in fact, been one of its pioneers in the late nineteenth century. Was it
hard to get ahead in the Midwest with dark skin and your father gone
broke? It is known that my grandmother was working in the cafeteria of
the aircraft company during the war to make ends meet, and Aref Junior,
my father, with his heavy equipment skills as a paratrooper, landed a
postwar Cleveland job with John Deere Tractors. But it doesn't take too
much to see young Aref giving up on the sea of Midwest blondes and
seeking not blondes but soothing darkies out West. For the rest of his
siblings, moving West was just the opposite ethnically; they waded completely into larger gene pools with German, Dutch, Irish and Chinese
spouses — no Arabs — and at the same time, turned inward. The Orfaleas
were known as Americanized loners. "Why don't they ever get out?"
my father would ask rhetorically about his sisters and brother, opening
blinds as sure as they would close theirs. But I think the answer simple, if
tragic: they had no children (excepting my Uncle George's one daughter
Bonnie). Children draw you out. They hid themselves in various aspects
of the garment industry. The only daughter of four who knew briefly
what it meant to be pregnant, Jeannette took her lonely pleasure to
the canvas. "If I hadn't painted, I would have gone crazy," she once

confessed to me, the only other wayward artist soul in a family of businesspeople. In some ways, with the exception of my father, her siblings, ever more isolated in Los Angeles, which fairly begs you to get in your car or be lost, did go crazy, mildly, behind shuttered windows in homes smelling of oriental rugs but too rarely of grape leaves and *kibbi*. Slowly they were lost to any world but the one of their own original family and in that the urge to Americanize had an ironic, and hard, joke on them: they ended up in the dead end of their own clan.

My mother's family came West from Brooklyn, New York, in 1947, about the same time the last of the solitudinous Orfaleas drove out from Cleveland, but the Awads journeyed for a fresher, less shadowy reason: health and sunshine. My grandfather Kamel's emphysema begged for a warmer climate; his doctor told him it was a matter of life and death. For a time, they considered Florida, even bought property there; but as my grandmother Matile once said, "Honey, in Florida, they only have sun and no business; in California, they have sun and business." It was a pretty accurate summary of the advantages of the far western edge of the continent. As for the sun, it was plentiful in Pasadena, where they settled into a small, turn-of-the-century bungalow bought without having gone inside. Kamel saw the sizable L-shaped porch — as big as the insides of the house — and said that was home. It was years later before I discovered that the porch in Pasadena approximated the outdoor courtyard world he grew up in at the center of clay dwellings in Arbeen, Syria, the little farming village from which he emigrated in 1920. Nestling against the San Gabriel Mountains, Pasadena also recalled the high mountain village of Mheiti in Lebanon, where my grandmother had managed to survive the deprivations of the Great War — and two siblings who starved to death — before coming with her mother, father, and three other brothers to America at about the same time as her soon-to-be husband. (One of those two émigré brothers died shortly after crossing the ocean of wounds sustained in the Great War, and another succumbed in his forties in New York to leukemia, itself generated by bad bouts of malaria he caught while serving as a U.S. medic on Guadalcanal. If her husband was running to sun, Thatee Matile was clearly running as far as she could from every possible war.)

At first, when I returned to California after years in the East, I took refuge in my cousins and aunts and uncles of my mother's family in Pasadena, many of whom now lived in the town across the arroyo further back in the foothills, La Canada. I truly relished visiting them, having been flung outside the "cousin net" for two decades, and for a time it siphoned off an internal spring of loneliness that would seep into me every time I gestured to a wife who was not there. Another cruel joke of sorts did not escape me: in order to enjoy the extended family I had sorely missed, moored in Washington all those years, I had had to give up the comfort of my immediate family, though two of the boys were entering college. I used to ask my wife, "Why do these two worlds, these two ways of having family, have to be mutually exclusive? Why can't we share my family out there for some years as we have yours?" The feminist dream of parity or even reciprocity in marriage took a nose dive on that one; sometimes she'd point out it was I who had come East for school and work, not vice versa, and my intentions to make it temporary were irrelevant or brushed away by time and settlement. Sometimes she'd say her small extended D.C. family of about eight good people wasn't what held her, and I began to think: D.C., now the putative center of the world, is her identity and the neighborhood that gave her her familiar, invariable habits. And I began to wonder, despite years away from it, if perhaps mine is L.A. On the other hand, couldn't one have two homes, as Edward Hoagland once said of his dual residence of New York and Vermont? Doesn't the very fact of marriage make one live in two worlds?

The first RAM reunion I went to in Sierra Madre (for the Roum, Awad and Malouf clans, all of whom intermarried in the West) numbered two hundred people. It was delightful and disorienting, as most of the RAM children and grandchildren I didn't recognize. They were born after I left for college in the East.

California's native writers have extraordinarily different takes on their home state, often based on their different childhood experiences, the variety of regions the state presents to an imagination that shape a particular kind of spirit, and, of course, the inevitable pulls away from it for all kinds of reasons ranging from job to family to war. The same holds true of native Angelenos vis a vis Los Angeles. Joan Didion's vision of California in *Where I Was From* — and it is one of great foreboding if not rapaciousness — is that of an American "blue blood" who descends from Englishmen coming West after the Revolutionary War to fight the Indians and stake some land, who travel partway to California with the infamous Donner Party, barely missing its cannibalism in the snows of 1846–47, veering off to Oregon, before finally coming to the mining camps of the Sierra Nevadas, a bit late to cash in on the Gold Rush of 1848. Her ancestors settled 150 years ago in Sacramento, not as dull then as now, along a river that was soon to be choked with dams to supply water to places less dull, like Hollywood, places Didion and her husband were drawn to for, one must think, some celluloid gold, with disappointment equal to if not greater than that of her forefathers.

As deep as her roots go back in time in California — further back than those of any writer I know, certainly further than my own — she views the "clinically radical" women of her Western ancestors as evidence of "a tendency, which I came to see as endemic, towards slight and major derangements, apparently eccentric pronouncements, opaque bewilderment, and moves to places not quite on schedule." In short, the slow lunacy of people with the affectations of "first settlers" (forget, of course, the Spaniards and the Indians) living in a dreary place in the dead hot center of the state along a river that is slowly strangled. No wonder Hollywood, and the Hollywood colony in Malibu, is the place she chose to live as an adult (after fleeing as a young adult to New York and the publishing world, a place she would flee to more than once). Life had become unreal in its degradation of the bountiful beauty of California, at least to a child of early settlers. If courting unreality, why not go all the way?

I'm being coy. I have enormous respect for Joan Didion's writing and nod a great deal over what she says about the contradictions of a state, for example, so subservient to federal money for agriculture, hydro-electric power, land reclamation, highways, park preservation, oil depletion allowances, etc., while at the same time touting itself as the last great testimony to rugged individualism in America. She is right that much about the deeply tarnished gold of our home state "doesn't add up" and may be meant for fools. But if California for her is "a wearying enigma," it has remained for me an invigorating one, an enigma still able to inspire awe like no other place I know on earth despite the suffering my own family has sustained in the state, a suffering directly related to one of the great myths of the West, the freedom-empowering gun. I can say from brute experience that the gun frees nothing and enchains a great deal before you have time to think.

Though it inherited the corrosive Western myth of the properly out-fitted law-unto-oneself one sees in easterner Owen Wister's *The Virginian*, California is hardly the only state with pistols aplenty and, in fact, has among the most restrictive gun laws in the nation. This is part of the frustrating doubleness of a state that has probably more social con-

science and forward-thinking public policy, certainly about the environment, than any other, and at the same time continues to stuff its roads
with more internal combustion engines than any other U.S. metropolis. I
just mean to say that my own family's post–World War II hejira to
California, and Los Angeles in particular, came on the heels of the thiev-
ing burst of water out of the Owens Valley that made L.A. possible, and
that if, in retrospect, I have questioned time and again whether my life
and those of my family were founded literally on a chimera, that sense of
hope, of creating something out of nothing—the life of a writer—has
never left me and is directly related to the ungodly energy that my family
brought to and found in California after the worst war in history. It did
not come to Hollywood. It came to make things that can hold you—
children and clothes.

I also think coming to Los Angeles as an Arab within the last fifty
years launches a fundamentally different attitude towards the society of
the Far West than that of descendants of white pioneers five generations
ago who cannot help but see everything tainted, exploited, defiled, and
ruined. I have never felt out of place in an essentially brown city; the
Hispanic origins of Los Angeles, even the horde of so-called "illegal"
immigrant Mexicans tilling the farms and the gardens that the spoiled
americanos won't, have never felt threatening or alienating to me. Quite
the contrary. We have intermarried with Latinos, with whom, of course,
Arabs share literal blood dating back to the conquest of Spain by Tariq
ibn-Ziyad in 711 A.D. The sun, a plain malevolent orb in Didion, found
so strongly in Southern California, was nothing short of talismanic to
Arab immigrants, whose number in Los Angeles is now the largest in the
country.

It's fascinating that Didion admits to having eyes like her grandmother, "Reese eyes," ones that "reddened and watered at the first pre-
monition of sun or primroses or raised voices." This is a highly delicate
sensibility for a razor-sharp mind such as Didion's. I can't imagine what it
would have been like if our family's eyes teared up at "raised voices." Life
would have been a constant blur! As for the sun, we just got darker and
darker; I have never worn sunglasses in my life. Perhaps I am fated for skin
cancer or blindness, but there it is. The sun is perfectly welcome to do anything it wants to me (provided, of course, good Angeleno that I am, there
is something shady or cool nearby, like an ocean). In truth, my mother,
who had the whitest complexion of her tribe, always wore a hat outside
and drenched herself in creams, lambasting me for my brazen attitude
towards the direct sun, UV rays and all. And yes, she was a bit miffed by a

childhood summer picture of herself at Coney Island dark as a "black girl." This from the most colorblind individual I have ever known.

Mike Davis' Los Angeles is even more spectral than Didion's, and one must believe that his provocative, landmark study *City of Quartz* had birth in its author's blue collar–worker family, which migrated from the Midwest in the Depression-era Dust Bowl, looking for factories and water-fed farms. Davis was born in hardscrabble Fontana, a place of stifling heat and not just smog, but belching smoke forty miles east of Los Angeles on the rim of the desert. The motorcycle gang, the Hell's Angels, was also born in Fontana. Davis's people worked in the aluminum smelting plants of Kaiser there — a remnant of which still makes steel for the Chinese — and if Didion's L.A. is unreal, Davis's L.A. is too real, a city of heavy and polluting industry, the West Coast version of Elizabeth, New Jersey, with a surrounding, sulfurous stink to match. Though his family eventually settled east of San Diego, in El Cajon, where his father was a meat-cutter and started a union, Davis, a truck driver for some years, saw family and friends lose health, if not life, to the smelting plants and other factories that produced steel, rubber tires, gasoline, gypsum, and manure in and around the city. This was no orange grove idyll. "A radical absence of personal security has always been a condition of my life," Davis has said. My own family and community had closer connections to L.A.'s manufacturing world, as I've noted, than to Didion's Hollywood, though we made less destructive things, such as clothes, handbags, and potatoes. I still see hope of organic life in L.A., as much as it struggles against and is beaten down by the inorganic.

Even Didion, in secret moments, one must feel, lifts her head to the organic life that once entranced her ancestors. Declining an invitation to speak at my college due to a heavy schedule, she was glad I caught something of that life hiding in her quietly devastating, stunning paean to minute elements of grief in *The Year of Magical Thinking*. "Ah, the jacarandas!" she exclaimed in her lovely handwritten postcard. She was referring to my catch of her memory of the horn-like, delicate flower at her wedding to John Gregory Dunne at Mission San Juan Bautista in the northern San Joaquin Valley. The same jacarandas I grew up holding my palms to in Anaheim, as they snowed lilac. The pavement, alas, caught more than I, a mauve, hard road through my youth.

Walking to work in Los Angeles — in any American city — is a gift of the gods. On my return to the place where a song once proclaimed, "No One

Walks in L.A," I was glad to buck the trend. On my morning walk for milk to the local market I would pass a lovely restored California Crafts- man home painted mint green and covered with the egg-shaped granite. The white picket fence fringed with star jasmine lifted an aroma, mixed with an orphan orange tree across the street and the tang of sweet alys- sum that said to me "home." The nostrils, not the eyes, bring us home. Ahead, beyond two tall palms, the mountains took a dust and then thick cover of snow. It was the very vision of nineteenth-century California!

However, between the palms and the snow, the jasmine and the hard blue sky, was a gas station, a leg of the famous Route 66. One had to look hard to avoid it. And the smell was not the smell of jasmine. Soon, relentless sun shrank the snow.

For a city just beginning to come to grips with the costs of its insa- tiable urge to change and remake, much had changed since I left at twenty-seven. For starters, in the past quarter-century (1980–2007), Los Angeles City had grown from roughly 3 million to 4 million people, and LA County went from 7.4 to 10.7 million. The 2000 census showed the Hispanic-Latino population to be 47 percent of the city, and most de- mographers feel that L.A. was, by 2008, a majority Latino city, the only one other than Miami north of Mexico. Since I was a boy in 1960, the city had tripled both its Hispanic-Latino and Asian population, while the black sector — devastated by riots, joblessness, and gang wars — had shrunk by half. By 2000, 36 percent of the city was foreign-born, triple that in 1970. Los Angeles was now the country's Ellis Island, usurping the immigration role traditionally claimed by New York.

Naturally, there were environmental costs for this dynamic, explo- sive growth. The City of the Angels had little buildable land left, and the only place to grow was toward the desert, before which lay a tinder-box of brush and flammable woodlands. When I first arrived back West, a colleague of mine took me on a drive up the canyons of the San Gabriels to point out the charred shacks and blackened eucalyptus from the vi- cious fires of 2003, the worst in the state's history in terms of damage ($1 billion), homes and buildings destroyed (more than six thousand), and the worst to that date in acreage burned since the 1940s. Nothing much was left of homes but the chimneys, a blackened, crumbling car in the charred drive a testament to the futile dream of mobility. The hot "devil winds" of the Santa Anas had blown especially long in especially bad heat, and the Southern California version of leaf fall — cinders — fell over much of the southern half of the state, flaring up badly in the tumbleweed hills of the suburbs around San Diego, Calabassas, Malibu, Ventura, as well as the Inland Empire east of Los Angeles where I was now living. The October 2003 fires alone killed twenty-one people. At the root of two of the worst fires — in San Diego and the San Bernardino Mountains — was human error, a campfire, someone trying to rough it, and a careless match.

If there was any doubt of the effects of overcrowding and global warming on Southern California, the fourteen 2007 fall fires, together with the massive Zaca fire in Santa Barbara County that poured a grey smoke over the gorgeous coastline for most of the summer, brought the year's total to the largest amount of California acreage burned since records began in 1932. More than half a million people were evacuated in the October 2007 fires. What was worse to contemplate was the so-called "firebug" phenomenon, people who get some kind of high, even a sexual kick, over lighting fires, or making them worse, including some seriously twisted firemen. You might call these the "interior" Santa Anas, the gusty nervousness Raymond Chandler captured in his classic short story, "Red Wind."

My friend and colleague showed me where the 2003 fire had roared towards million-dollar new homes built in the last slivers of land before the desert, as well as confronting an old community meeting house that dates from the 1920s. A small number of firefighters stood with their hoses and masks between the homes and the meeting house and quickly determined that they didn't have enough manpower to save both. They chose — and in this showed the late-maturing Southern California community consciousness — to protect the old Padua, and let the expensive homes, which had been evacuated, be consumed. It was not a popular decision with the homeowners, needless to say, but for the community at large it was a statement: We are here to protect what is common to us, not what separates us, especially if that commonplace is old and irreplaceable. As I say, respecting the old — something new for SoCal.

We helped save Johnson's Pastures, a hiker's paradise, from developers. Other civic measures showed simple but unmistakably positive changes concerning the always endangered L.A. environment: for example, the City provides seven free trees per household to develop shade and freshen the air; purchasing a high-efficiency clothes washer to save up to thirty gallons of water per load qualifies for a $250 rebate and tax breaks; the City will buy back your gas-powered lawnmower, which pollutes as much as forty-three new cars, for $300 to put towards an electric mower ($400). In 2006, Los Angeles became the first city in the world to adopt specific, punishable standards to combat global warming.

The notoriously cemented, drivable L.A. River, in which I hunted polliwogs and frogs as a child in one of its few isolated moats, became in 2001 a sort of 9/11 in reverse, as community groups in concert with the City began to unbuckle "the Wash" of its concrete, buy up adjacent land, and swath the banks with a park that could replace, yes, Rock Creek Park in D.C. as the largest and longest park in an American city. D.J. Waldie called an unbound, greening L.A. River "the anti-freeway—not dispersing L.A. but pulling it together." A 32-acre site alongside the railyards downtown—the largest undeveloped plot of land left in the central city—was planted with corn and became known as the Cornfields, commemorating the *zanja madre*, or mother ditch, that the eighteenth-century Spaniards created for crops with water diverted from the once healthy L.A. River. When the corn grew nine feet, "Reinventing L.A." leader Robert Gottlieb saw it "providing a landscape of improvisation, [where] visitors could look at the City Hall skyline through the rows of corn and envision a type of reconstructed nature in the city."

Granting that L.A. still has air pollution, the distance it has come could not be caught by anyone who hadn't been born a half-century back and raised in the city. When I hiked the pastures, slowly my lung capacity expanded and I began to go further and further into the foothills. Winded as I finally got, my lungs never hurt. But they had. When I was a boy, smog levels were so high that if I spent an hour outside playing tennis or basketball my lungs felt like they would explode. It hurt simply to breathe, and I contracted bad asthma. Ozone was first identified chemically when I was three, in 1952; it wasn't even being measured in the air until I was sixteen; when I left for college in the East, L.A. was registering ozone levels nearly five times higher than the national standards for healthy air. Painful breathing I experienced in the fifties and sixties in L.A. replicates itself in other world cities that suffer horrendous air pollution today, such as Beijing, Cairo, and Mexico City, which tumbled in one generation from one of the cleanest (Carlos Fuentes' first novel mentions that clean air in its title!) to the dirtiest in the world.

However, with the advent of smog devices on cars, scrubbers on industrial stacks, cleaner-burning gasoline eliminating sulfur and lead, and now hybrid and electric cars (which California requires manufacturers to make in order to sell cars at all in the state), the number of Stage One "red alert" smog days went from 118 in 1975—so bad you were warned not to go outside—to none in 2000. This precipitous drop in air pollution has been duplicated in no other American city. Granting that in no other American city was the problem so pronounced, it's still an achievement of magnitude for a people so often seen as enchained by excess.

Another welcome sight was something that quickly disappeared in the Los Angeles of my youth—rapid transit trains and subways. The City of the Angels did once have such transportation, trolley lines I remember by criss-crossings in the sky of overhead electrical wires, but these were finally uprooted by pressure of the highway lobby in 1961, when the Pacific Railway's Red Car System pulled up its last silver slots in the road. A recurrent nightmare for years was my trying to fly up and reach the sky through electrical wires that would narrow. I'd never make it. My dream of flying freedom came true on the road—cut loose by Eisenhower's Interstate Highway of 1956, born the same year a "killer fog" of pollution took the lives of one thousand people in London. A decidedly mixed blessing, the anointing of the highways.

Alarmed at the cumulative health costs of the smog, shamed into thinking maybe the Red Cars weren't a bad idea, in 1990, L.A. put in the first tentative light rail ("Blue") line from Seventh Street downtown close to my father's old dress factory twenty-two miles to Long Beach, and the car owners were put on notice: You do not own the road. You might even want to consider alternatives to three hours of a traffic jam during rush hour. I spied the cars, rode in the double-decker train through El Monte to Union Station downtown with my students on "bring 'em back alive" writing assignments to discover Olvera Street and the Latino heart of the city at First and Grand. It was hardly standing room only—and the "honor system" of no turnstiles has made 5 percent of riders free-loaders—but it was a start. Now there are five light-rail and subway lines covering seventy-three miles, with a weekday average ridership of 276,900 (compared to 772,826 for Washington, D.C., and 339,359 for San Francisco, cities whose populations are much smaller than L.A.'s but that came to subways sooner—1976 and 1972, respectively—with more track miles: 103 and 101 miles). Even the latest line, the 2005-vintage Orange Busway, which traverses 14 miles of the entire bedroom community of the San Fernando Valley to North Hollywood, shows tangible, though modest, increase in ridership (from 18,767 per weekday in its first year of operation to 25,475 per weekday by April 2007). With gas prices approaching $5 a gallon—it was 80 cents a gallon when I left L.A.

in 1978 — riders may be forced to take Metro to work, if the dreary bumper-to-bumper doesn't finally take its toll on human patience. Of course now we have the infinite cell phone to blot the traffic out. That isn't peculiar to L.A., but it was truly a vision of hell to watch people sitting in their steel cages in an endless row from mountain to sea babbling like characters out of Samuel Beckett.

Some things are certainly worse in L.A., not the least, traffic. Until the real L.A. River comes back to life, we are left with freeways writer Mike Anton compares to "raging rivers," where one out of ten deaths is a pedestrian who has had to pull over for a flat or overheating — "falling out of the raft." The 101 freeway to and from Mother's home in Tarzana was thick most of the day. It was one of the only freeways in the city without a "diamond" lane for carpoolers, and it suffered for it. In fact, there was now the phenomenon of reverse traffic, especially in evening rush hour, where there were more cars going back into the city than coming out, a phenomenon I also noted in Washington, D.C. when I commuted back to our city home from Rockville. This means that the so-called "edge cities," the suburbs, are spawning places to work, and the cities are becoming more attractive places to live. As my realtor wife says, people are more willing to pay higher prices to live close in or, as the case may be, lower prices in tougher areas whose "charm" is being slowly unearthed — gentrification.

But as someone with Angeleno genes, I see traffic as a puzzle to solve, a maze in which to find the little-known cut-out. I remember my father zipping with vigor up the slow lane between Lankershim and Highland on his way to work downtown with me, knowing exactly when the gap in traffic would occur, passing dozens if not hundreds of drivers he'd call "cattle" before curving back in time to catch the faster lanes loosening up. It was masterful. His skill came from years of misery studying traffic patterns, the way a Babylonian slave may have created the sundial while cutting stone for the Hanging Gardens.

Call this "Rhapsody in Traffic."

And then one day I find myself lost late at night on Fifth Street downtown coming back from a wedding at USC. I think I can game it, remembering my life in the garment district as a teenage bundler, cutter, shipper. I can find the roads that will avoid the grapevine. And what I find is a road of humans lying on the ground. In novelist John Fante's 1930s, Fifth Street had cheap one-night hotels and bars; in the 1960s, Fifth Street had a few panhandlers, jobbers selling off-price goods; now, in the first decade of the twenty-first century, Fifth Street's sidewalks aren't visible. They are covered with bodies and human filth. Rows and rows of dirty blankets and cardboard shipping boxes used as homes. Your backyard a pool of urine. Your bar the gutter. Your girlfriend the needle. Your car a cane.

Miles of bodies, cop cars, colored lights a-twirl, a miserable out-of-season Christmas. Fifth Street brought fully to its fate, where Fante spotted Camilla and her stretched top and tanned legs eighty years before. This phenomenon of the permanently homeless — what Mike Davis in his recent book *Planet of Slums* calls "surplus humanity" or "the warehousing of people" without work, housing, or land, comprising one-third of urban residents worldwide — was now a fixture in Los Angeles, within blocks of Kobe Bryant's mega-million-dollar stage for throwing balls in a basket at the Staples Center.

That this sick juxtaposition of poverty and wealth can be seen the world over didn't soften its blow to one hungry for any awakening in his home city. Angels do fear to tread in many parts of the City of Angels. Drug use and violent crime rates in L.A. are actually back down to the levels of my childhood; the proliferation of gangs now accounts for most homicides. However, L.A. syphilis rates are twice the national average. In the San Fernando Valley when I go for a meal to take out for my mother, I see sixteen-year-old girls with breasts pushed up unnaturally like pastels from See's, their eyes marked for battle as sure as a tight end's in football — black — their bodies tattooed, their hair colored crimson. And I discover that the Valley is now the pornography capital of America, that any one of these — whose dishabille isn't too different from that of some college students, including the pajama-in-public fellows — may be carting the burrito to a blackened suburban garage, the new stage set of our time. And I know, like those lining Fifth Street, these too-soon women are poor, poor of mind and poor of pocket, and that for all that has improved, the poor have grown like an army in Iraq, though still they are invisible, unless you stumble on them, lost, where you once ran racks of dresses as a teenager or perhaps right next door to your own mother's suburban home, entering a blackened garage.

In my first semester, I was told by a student that my questioning her use of the f-word twenty-five times was stifling her voice; another student agreed, and she used the f-word fifteen times to prove it, falling conspicuously asleep on our seminar table, throwing her head down. Since I was new at the school, I pulled my punches, but what I should have done is gone over to her and whispered in her ear, "You do that again and you can get the f— out of my class." When she handed in an embarrassing final paper that was an indulgent love letter to a boyfriend, there was no time left for revision.

The student with the twenty-five f-words turned out to be a good writer after absorbing the concept of overkill. (I'm reminded by my old Alaska buddy John Hildebrand that for many youth today, the f-word is "filler," what you say when you don't know what else to say.) After several difficult and testy sessions, and many more drafts, she produced a moving "magnum opus" final about spousal abuse and the courage of a mother.

I gave three Ds that first semester and was told I was the first professor there to give Ds in more than a decade. (I'm sure that is an exaggeration, but grade inflation is a part of everyday life at campuses today. You have to work hard in my classes to get a D — that is, not at all.) There were three or so blistering teacher evaluations that roughly tracked the bad grades, although I figure the lady who slept in class got in a good rabbit punch eval before graduating.

The other class that first semester — a freshman composition course — ran smoothly.

I took stock. It was probably a bad idea to assign one's own book in the class with dyspeptic seniors in their last semester.

Some wanted me to trim my sizable reading lists and personal anecdote — though as many felt the benefits of these things. Teacher evaluations over the next three years climbed to the point that after that rough first class, seven of my next eight classes registered an average student rating of 9 (out of 10). Many gifted student writers came to my classes and it was a wonder watching them work, grow, and inspire. The "Autobiography and Memoir" class seemed to draw several young women suffering from anorexia or "cutting" habits. One student, who wrote an exceptional paper entitled "N + 1" — the mathematical notation, she said, for an individual — explained why a progressive like herself, who opposed Bush in almost every way, was voting for him in 2004. She was against abortion. Shy of sticking out in a class of Kerryites, after several weeks she got up the courage to put her essay "on the pan" for critique. A group reading of it met with silence. Then a resounding, spontaneous round of applause. And this from her deeply liberal, even radical, fellows. I wasn't the only one reduced to tears.

There were other such days I will never forget — the paper of the young man from Seattle who wrote obsessively of his hometown, until he noticed on our field trip to the Watts Towers (in the "Writing Los Angeles" course) that they were shaped like mizzen masts. "It's a ship," he proclaimed. "And it's facing East." His final paper expanded on the notion of home, as Simon Rodia, the creator of the Watts Towers, was Italian and figuratively was sailing for home. Another member of that class wrote a moving self-indictment called "Work the Room," which also skewered the country club ethic, or lack of ethic, in which he grew up, a sense of entitlement that falsely sheathed him, so that when he got caught for dealing marijuana, the consequences and wisdom of a father took time to grab him. A brave coming-of-age story, whose ending he is still perfecting.

In my Creative Nonfiction class, students gave us harrowing, touching character studies of family members battling mental illness. One student's independent study novel of Zimbabwean refugee maids in a St. Louis motel was amazing. In "The Art and Craft of the Short Story," a young woman wowed us with a story about love and an unwanted pregnancy. Another modeled her "Letters from Baghdad," on Henry James' "A Bundle of Letters," interlacing letters from an American female GI, an Iraqi mother, and an Iraqi insurgent who hides a bomb on the mother's unsuspecting young boy. It was a stunner, as good—even better than—James.

For all this fruitfulness, I'd hear from time to time a nagging inner whisper as if home held forbidden fruit.

One quite troubling incident left many of us wondering about the parameters of political correctness. A teacher at a nearby college revealed that her car had been attacked, its windows smashed, and hateful epithets smeared on it, such as "Nigger Lover," "Kike Whore," and "Shut Up, Bitch." Within a day of the revelations, my college shut down in solidarity protest for the first time since the Vietnam War. The Black Student Union asked that students wear black; it was one of the hottest days of the year. One of my students later wrote, "I remember sweating an embarrassing amount. I hoped no one would notice. That's one of my most vivid memories of the day." She also remembered that as she went to a rally, "I was quite conflicted about what my away-message on AOL Instant Messenger should say. . . . Some people's away messages were blank, in honor of the tragedy, I guess. Would leaving it blank show enough feeling?" Several on our campus spoke eloquently about the

hankering evidence of racial and sexual hatred in society, even and especially in a top academic community, that had to be eradicated by every
means possible — by statute, by example, and in our hearts.

Although I had been on campus for only two months, the incident
was shocking to me for personal reasons. I went to the Black Student
Union rally, but when one of my African American students spotted me
and encouraged me to say something, I almost turned and walked away,
a little nervous to be outspoken so soon in my new position. Yet speak I
did. I recounted an incident when I was young bicycling along in Anaheim, a community founded by German Americans in the nineteenth
century, which as late as the forties had a branch of the Ku Klux Klan
within its city limits. I was eleven and had done a diorama for my history
project that year on the Klan in Anaheim. I remember my mother had
helped me put it together, using burnt toothpicks for crosses and white
cotton swabs — fitting! — to anchor the paper mache Klansmen. I can't
remember what I used for the black men who were hung, though I think I
used a metal miniature noose borrowed from a "Clue" board game.

In any case, as I churned away on my red Schwinn one day after the
project, one of the bigger kids in the neighborhood biked alongside me,
rammed my handlebars with his and shouted, "Go home, nigger!" I
didn't fall, but I shimmied near the gutter before hopping off my bike,
rubbing my arm. I didn't miss his drift, though I had never heard that
word. Even in researching my project, I had never seen the n-word written or heard it uttered. When I returned home and told my mother what
had happened, she cringed. "Don't you ever say that word, *ever*," she
spat out.

At a later mass rally, many registered the best sentiments intelligent
people can about racial and religious and sexual tolerance. Administra-
tors and professors milled in the crowd on a long green field before the
parapet of one of the dormitories, from where people were speaking, a
place that was, according to my observant student, "a popular weekend
party spot . . . the exact location where on a previous Saturday night I'd
seen mud wrestling pits turn into massive pseudo-orgies. Helicopters
circled above and their spotlights galvanized the crowd, which was eager
to show the nation how much (we) cared."

And then the abused professor spoke. No surprise she was pretty
ticked. Her voice was shrill and reminded me of the indignant monotone
you would hear from our supposed leaders during the Vietnam pro-

test moratoriums. We used to call them "Radical Ricks." Yet, I said to myself, perhaps she is so wounded by what happened that she is hiding her anger and embarrassment in cant. But the way she ended her speech really made me wonder: "And to those who did this to me: Go to hell!!"

Even for a response to a hate crime, that was a bit over the top. Still, no one, myself included, suspected anything weird. No one had been arrested. We wondered if the vandals were students, but we assumed, and wanted to assume, that the crime had been done by the hoi polloi of the surrounding white, conservative neighborhood.

It had been done by neither.

It was the professor herself.

She was arrested on charges of insurance fraud, convicted, and sentenced to a year in jail, for what the judge likened to calling in a fake bomb threat. She had literally graffitied herself.

Why would someone do such a thing?

Not too many of my colleagues asked that question in conversations with me. Most seemed a little stunned by it all and wanted to put it away as soon as possible, as if it were an aberration of nature. It had made national news, and what had been righteous embarrassment, and a positive referendum on our academic community's conscience, ended up not so righteous. It was now in the realm of the bizarre. My gutsy, self-critical student admitted, "There is something disconcerting about my behavior that day," wondering why her chief concerns were her e-mail message and what to wear. "There was a certain sense that no one knew what they were fighting for," she related. "My peers seemed lost. Everyone had a reason to be offended, even scared, I suppose. But no one was." After spring break, students seemed to have forgotten what had happened: "No one said, 'Hey wait, we just got played.'" She asked herself why: "Has the sun and the Abercrombie and Fitch student body and country club atmosphere sucked away our social consciences? Are our minds numbed by watching too much TV? Or is the apathy characteristic of college students in general? Are we just a lazy and self-absorbed age group?" She concluded: "We should have been embarrassed . . . the 'hate crime' was not real, but neither was our reaction. We came together because we had to. We rallied because they told us to. We were sad because that's how you're supposed to act . . . [The professor] spray-painted her own car and [our college] came to an unprecedented stand-still. But to mourn what? Her artistry, her skill at deception, her ability to play a role better than we could?"

Granting that powerful, astringent assessment, I still wanted to know: what kind of person does such a thing? And more—how does a community leave itself open to such a fraud? As it turned out, the professor was disturbed, had a history of arrests for shoplifting, using fictitious license plates, refusing to comply with police. She herself was not a minority, at least not a protected or official one, though it appears she was a recent convert from Catholicism to Judaism. It was hard to know what to conclude, though anti-Semitic Web sites had some twisted ideas. Perhaps the day off speaking about race was not a wasted one, I thought. Was the troubled prof angling for just that in her crazy way? Is there sometimes a need behind a farce, and not just her need for recognition? Perhaps. But it wasn't only our sensitive nerves about race that her violent charade touched, but, as my student divined, our rush to be counted, our need to be checked off as correct—in short, our sensitivity about status.

In the rest home there is no status. The smell of it takes care of any of those pretensions the minute you walk in. Everyone is a buck private before God. The halls are lined with people in worse shape than my Aunt Jen. One woman, hunchbacked in her wheelchair, calls out to each passer-by, nurse, doctor, and bottlewasher, "Help! Help!" No one helps her. I go to an aid station and ask why no one helps her. Because, I am told by a taciturn nurse, flipping her clipboard, she never stops.

There's one lady who shakes with Parkinson's and has bright eyes, to whom my mother bestows a flower every time she visits Jeannette. "They just want someone to stop," she says. "This one has no children or relatives at all. At least Jen has us."

Sometimes we catch Jen around lunchtime. It's torture, perhaps more for us than for her, because she has had a feeding tube since her series of strokes, and she can't eat and everyone else is eating, or at least trying. Her neck and mouth muscles are pretty much gone. The feeding tube is the subject of some controversy in the family—Jen herself did not want it and said so in her will. She refused any life support and signed her body over to science after death. However, in the initial days of her paralysis, her sister Bette, who had power of attorney, said, "I can't let my own sister starve to death," and thus countermanded Jen's own wishes, sticking her with a feeding tube that gave her five more years of life.

What did she do with them? Well, she tried to talk, occasionally coughing out her love for us, or repeating some semblance of a word. She saw the sun come up and go down on a three-by-four-foot window, she listened to the rants of a succession of patients worse off than her, all of whom died, she watched thousands of hours of crazy-ass television, patiently, hearing almost none of it. A complete waste, it would seem. Except for one thing.

When we wheel her out after her cleaning to the corridor and place a drawing pad in front of her, with her only moving limb — her left arm — she begins to copy the image on a holy card, over and over again — the Blessed Mother in every colored pencil. None of the drawings show Mary's eyes — only, and in detail, her left hand.

I take to the Dodgers like dope. Perhaps I am the dope and not the Dodgers, but I hold onto the Blue for dear life, like the restless Pacific, the one always-changing Unchangeable Element in Southern California. Let the Angels try and decide if they are from Anaheim, or Los Angeles, or Timbuktu. The Dodgers were Brooklyn and became Los Angeles and they will never be anywhere else, of that and little else I am certain. They are as much a part of this widespread cockeyed humanity prostrate in the sun as they were dodging trolleys in New York's first suburb a century ago. Artful they are not; in 2007, the finest physical specimen on the team, rookie Matt Kemp, was caught off base or overrunning a base no less than six times in a week. This is like Errol Flynn subbing for one of the Marx Brothers. But the Dodgers will always be akin to the klutzy Brooklyn-based Dead End Kids, if not Chico and Zeppo, and they are a perfect team for a city that seems doomed to be number two to New York forever. In 2006, two of the most accomplished veterans on the team — Jeff Kent and J.D. Drew — ended up smashing into each other at home! *Both* of them tagged out!

As changeable as professional baseball teams are today, when a Cal Ripkin staying with one team through his whole career is an aberration, something other than the individuals themselves holds you to a team. In the Dodgers' case, I think it has to do with the uniforms. They're simple and beautiful, a combination of the sea and sky — that L.A. light — the blue and white, and whoever enters them enters the embattled hope and heart of Los Angeles itself. As well as a whole against-the-grain tradition of trolley dodgers. Life becomes a fugue of "dem Bums" — a realization and refutation of bad fate, day in, day out, often in the same day, if not inning. One hopes Brooklynite Joe Torre understands this, coming West to take over the reins of the hated team of his youth (he was a Giants fan!) dodging sunstroke.

It's no surprise that coming home from a fine, draining day teaching, after a little chat with my Latino neighbors Tony and Molly downstairs, or the lady next door with the parrot, and then a phone call to our eldest son Matt in college at Santa Fe, I'd plop on the couch with a salad or potato and flick on the Blue Crew. Their stumbling antics were transformed into the near operatic by the mellifluous voice of the finest sports announcer ever to clap on earphones, Vincent G. Scully, known to all Angelenos as Vinny or Vin, as if he were a wine without the article. I hear Vin, and I hear wine. And I hear my childhood and anything else good in this world. On more than one night at five and fifty I have gone to sleep to the voice of Vin Scully. It is a kind of lullaby, punctuated with bat cracks, and the cricket-like hush of the crowd.

But it's not just Vin's voice, it's his love of the language — he's a fellow English major — his knowledge of the game, and his sheer delight in doing what he does, in being where he is. Sampling just one fall game against the Diamondbacks gives the flavor. Let's take Scully verbs. A ground ball that's weak doesn't roll slowly, it's "going to die on the grass." A similar weak hit that gets through is a "squib single." Juan Pierre isn't just thrown out stealing second, he's "erased." A well-hit ball is "whacked into the gap." There are classic Scully euphemisms: an easily caught fly ball is a "room-service fly." Finally, there is the signature Scully onomatopoeia, his voice's way of traveling with the undulations of the ball itself. A signature strike out makes him hit four stresses, "SWUNG-ON-AND-MISSED." No poet was ever more certain of the end. And his classic home run call, the same today as fifty years ago when I barely understood the words, "Young goes back, A-WAY back, to the WAAALL, SHE IS . . . GAWN!" Naturally, a home run is a "she."

Tired of going to games alone, watching them alone, I call up a friend whom I shall name Pat, a recently divorced teacher who had come West from Indiana for college at Berkeley where she met her husband-to-be, with whom she had two wonderful kids. She invites me several times to her high school to hold a writing workshop, encouraging me to hang in there with my marriage; though she feels relieved, she confides that her divorce is a deep loss, especially for her children.

"I'm with you for the Dodgers!" she lilts over the phone in a bird-voice. When she jumps up after a hit, her puff of short blonde hair shakes like a pom-pom. She dances around. Her calf muscles shine in the stadium lights. She's a hiker. The muscles remind me of my wife, a devoted runner. But the dancing almost hurts to watch.

I fly home once a month trying to hold on to both coasts. I get familiar with the little Long Beach Airport, its quaint upstairs "Prop Room," which dates from the 1920s and the first planes to fly commercial routes. I spend long hours reading the paper in the morning darkness, having left early enough to avoid the Orange Crush. A Jet Blue stewardess sees me on so many flights, she asks what's wrong, and I tell her I'm trying to hold my family together while I teach out West. She frowns and gives me three free roundtrip tickets. I thank her with a lunch at Seal Beach; she laughs while I dunk in the ocean on a day of whipping wind. A grey-haired wind-surfer almost cuts my windpipe zipping by on his small catamaran; his huge red kite falls down between us in the shallow water like a matador's cape as if to say: *Try it, buddy. You'll be about as successful as you are with that stew up there.* Who's covering her eyes from the glare.

At first, the distance my wife and I have set between us magnetizes us when I return. We seem to snatch each other from a great void. In a crowded dorm room at Boston College where we are visiting one of our sons for Parents Weekend — I'm in from the West, she's come with youngest son Luke driving from D.C. — we fly into each others' arms to cheers. I feel our sons' hopes for us and of course my own. But I don't know if she does, if she has registered what I have in that sweeping embrace. You build a relationship on shared memories, and we are creating fewer. Being so far away, she gets harder to read than normal and that's pretty hard. She's always appeared even-keeled, tamping down strong emotion; I'm the fool with his emotions on his sleeve, who carries handkerchiefs for every occasion. In our twenty-three years together, I've seen her cry twice, both times at a talent show for autistic and other disabled kids at Luke's school. Luke was in the chorus. It made me happy to see her so moved, vulnerable.

And it's wonderful to feel her foot angle toward mine. It's great to hear her humming in the morning, to eat at her masterful table. In the first year of our separate lives, my wife holds out hope — she "might" make the move. "You have nothing permanent there," she insists. "If it were tenure, that might be different." There's a killer subjunctive — Might makes wrong! She dismisses my shaky disquisition on the importance of mates being present to schmooze with the mighty by a wave of her hand and notes that the trash needs to be taken out.

I fly back and forth; the worlds meld. The sycamores on Thirty-third Street in Chevy Chase, D.C., smell sour as the sycamores on the way to my mother's in Tarzana, or lining the street of my grandmother Nazera's old home in the Wilshire district. Sycamores are sycamores; I once was told that "sycamore" has been established as one of the most euphonious words in the English language. Is it more so in the East or West? It smells of sex to me in either place.

Okay, Stones. Not what you want, what you need. And what I need, even before sex, is community, and when I'm back home in Washington, I go to the homes of our neighborhood friends with whom we have raised our children, and we laugh, and play the Name Game, and get soused, and even dance at a New Year's Eve party. And back in Los Angeles I go out to art openings with my writing colleague and her husband, and I meet several other colleagues for lunches or dinner. Poet Garrett Hongo and I become fast friends touring our native town, religiously following the Dodger blue and Laker purple. I take Pat to a Dodgers game, or she takes me to dinner with her kids. And soon the Potomac begins to empty into the Pacific. And the plane ramp at Dulles is the plane ramp in Long Beach or LAX. And when I go to Mass at Blessed Sacrament in D.C., I am at Mass at Our Lady of the Assumption out West, or escorting my mother to her home parish in Encino, Our Lady of Grace, where we sing, "You shall not fear the terror of the night," that line from "On Eagles' Wings"—a song beloved by my paratrooper father before he was spread-eagled in his store, shot by someone he loved more than himself. The song also makes me think of Andy, our middle son, whose high school and now college sports teams are Eagles and who sang this as his graduation song. My eyes well up at "bear you on the breath of dawn, make you shine like the sun," while I hold old oak pews East and West, as if propping myself up to walk. As if my faith—strained as it is—is my only walker.

Where is home? It is hard to tell anymore. People ask me, and I tend to say, "Los Angeles." But then what is Washington? Even loathing its politics and sclerotic government, it's still familiar, at least the neighborhood around Chevy Chase Circle. And when I leave, the ache in my chest is barely dispelled by the buoyant warm air coming down the movable stairs in Long Beach, entering Aunt Jen's red car, zooming to meet my doctor cousin Mike Malouf for lunch near the clinic he runs for poor Mexicans in Orange, reaching class breathless, having crossed a continent to speak with my students, who have just barely crossed the green of our school, rubbing their eyes from sleep.

In truth, I feel at sea. My world has become the Pacific Ocean and my airplane a little dinghy in the sky above that sea. Perhaps the continent is only a large island between the seas of my life.

Luke, our youngest, comes to visit me. We tour a good special education class and a junior college, which he's interested in attending to be with Daddy (Mom, too, I put my palms together). With his disabilities, he has more emotional intelligence, I think, than the entire family. Not to mention pure heart. It is he who calls me every night, handing the phone to his mother. It is he who plugs in "my wife" for our D.C. number when I finally get a cell phone.

I take him to Disneyland. We meet some students and staff from my school. It's a good, clear spring day. All my life I seem to have been in dialogue with Disneyland, enraptured at first, later at odds, here laughing, there scornful of its falseness. When I was growing up in Anaheim, I watched over the horizon of shrinking dairy farms, withering orange groves, and burgeoning tract homes, a mountain being built — the Matterhorn. Though it was hardly pied beauty, perhaps Hopkins had such a strange mountain in mind — its slopes shone like shook foil. I took pleasure as a child flying down in the toboggans, getting an eagle's eye view of the place in an aerial bucket on a cable, enjoying the Jungleland ride with the hippo's mouth showing you its dental work. As for the great "new" ride of those early days, Pirates of the Caribbean, it's now one of the oldest, and unfortunately closed for Luke and me that day. But my sharpest memory of it is still clear — laughing and singing with my high school graduating class during "Grad Night at Disneyland," our phony boat getting stuck on a cable's rise under one of the pirates, whose hairy leg hung over us for an hour. The motorized pirate winked and endlessly blared, "Yo ho, yo ho, a pirates life for me!" My high school girlfriend finally pulled out of our necking session under that hairy leg and the mind-numbing song, wondering aloud if we were ever going to be let out.

"Let's try Mr. Toad's Wild Ride, Luke."

"Sure!" he chimes, *sure* being one of Luke's favorite words.

Disneyland crowds still swell near a ride, but something has changed: You don't need tickets anymore. You pay up front — a pirate's ransom — and you can go on any ride in the house. The lines are still long, but they move quicker. In fact, everything moves quicker. It seems everyone in Disneyland today is moving fast, anxious to get to the next ride — if you don't get in as many rides as you can, you've been gypped. There's no strolling, one of the things I liked about the place in the old days. The children in line are pulling on their parents' arms, "Pleeze! Take me to Space Mountain!" "But we aren't through Mr. Toad yet!" a father exclaims, exasperated. "But get me there! Get me there!" begs the little girl, clearly fearing that Mr. Toad, one of Disneyland's earliest rides and showing some wear of paint, won't be fast enough.

She's right; it isn't. Which is one of the reasons I always liked it. But today even it seems hokier than ever. I have to juice up the suspense.

"Look, Luke, a train is coming!"

It's the non-threatening sound of a freight train blaring behind an engine light hanging from an obvious wire. I can tell by Luke's laugh he sees the wire.

As we pass the various cardboard gates and characters from *Wind in the Willows* glow-painted — the 1920s cop blowing his whistle, Toad in a frenzy — and land in hell with the little red devils jumping on the wall like hinged Post-Its, a scene that terrified me as a child — we realize nothing on the ride is exciting, fearful, or even funny. And Luke's somewhat querulous smile registers that. The hypnotized stare of the teenage attendant at the end of the road doesn't help.

"Not so good, Dad," he says. "Let's eat."

Another teen worker in white hat and uniform stabs at a napkin, spears it, and eats it with his dustpan-on-a-pole. We eat, and the refuse practically screams to be tossed in a pastel can. We eat quickly, as the mobs are constantly moving in and out of the theme eateries so that finally there is no theme but speed. Disneyland has become speed, a computer game writ large.

We enjoy the Matterhorn ride, though Luke inspects the guts of the Styrofoam mountain as I once did; I remember writing a poem in graduate school, "The Disney Matterhorn Confronts the Alaska Range," which Robert Bly himself wrote me about favorably. "My God / my life's a sacrilege," it went, a bit much, early-twenties angst, but an indication of how far I was living out in the woods in Fairbanks from the worst make-believe of the Southland.

Luke and I do the Matterhorn. But even better is the Calico Gold Mine ride with its steeper splashes and dips and surges. Luke likes the ups and downs. He also likes one of the college girls and calls her a "dawl" and I think: How will he date, if he does date? Or marry? But why not, I think, when so many smarties never make it.

On the classic old teacup ride out of Alice in Wonderland, we both nearly throw up. We've eaten too soon before the teacups, and we are dizzy and sick. He wants to go. I almost force him into Monstro's whale mouth for a final ride—the one in the slow canal boat that passes the same *Wind in the Willows* characters now out along riverbanks, Moley's little home, Toad Hall two feet tall, the quietness of the ride pleasant, a touch of classical music—Luke's favorite—calming us. This oldest of all rides at Disneyland is one we both like and a good place to end.

As we leave through the diminutive castle in Fantasyland, I hear the faint song of Jiminy Cricket that never failed, even in my most dismissive Alaska days, to touch me with its plaintive "When you wish upon a star, makes no difference who you are." Many times as I got older, I would be brought to secret tears by it, counting off the wishes that had fallen into the sea. But now, with one of my best wishes attained, a beautiful live boy, as Gepetto would say, and two more in my quiver, the song does not move me. The place has been too clean, too fast, and too predictable. Luke's assessment of the Magic Kingdom, "It's okay," is about right, and no more. We put our arms around each other's shoulders. I'm glad life is slowing down to normal again. The best thing about Disneyland was Luke.

When Luke leaves, I feel less at home. I go down to Laguna Beach alone, with snorkel and fins. And I swim in the shimmering water toward Bird Rock where my father took me from Anaheim long ago, my first spear-fishing trip. Below, the golden garibaldi flits in and out of the coral reef, begging me to dive deeper, where my father once lanced a halibut that I carried proudly by his spear out of the water, trailing blood on the sand.

Now I have no spear for fish. The garibaldi taunts me. I circle Bird Rock, now drawn to the rock by the current, now swimming hard away, pulled behind it facing the shadowy outline of Catalina across the inlet, and soon the shore is receding, swelling above the water. When I swim back with adrenalin-mad arms, I'm washed up on a bed of mussels.

Try standing on a bed of mussels. It's like a bicoastal marriage.

As the second year of my exile's return stretches into the third, my wife's "maybe" hardens into a "no." She is not going to move. She is doing well professionally. Real estate in Washington resists recession because every two years the politicos and their entourages come and go, needing or shedding houses, and the lobbyists only grow. "California is a woman," she says one night, sipping a beer.

Our family doctor in D.C., a wise man who is concerned for us, tells me one day, "Adaptability is the one thing you can say for sure decreases with age." He also says it is not uncommon for some women to "be married to a zip code." He also speculates about a realtor's penchant for endless motion, "We're told people who can't stop are angry about something. They keep in constant activity so they don't expose their anger."

Perhaps I am angry, too; I keep in motion, teaching, swimming, hiking, zooming my Aunt Jen's little red car all over Los Angeles visiting family and friends. Perhaps the whole city is angry, tying itself in knots of concrete clover. But more than anger at terrorists — anger at Washington, an old Western anger, at starting a needless and foolishly crippling war, one that has sent gas prices soaring, perhaps an even bigger problem to Angelenos than the slow appearance of our boys and girls in body bags from the Middle East. Killed in the same desert camouflage fatigues they wore training in the Mojave.

Could these be the Western ripples of 9/11? In reality, Los Angeles seems little affected by the terrorist attacks on Washington and New York. It is almost as if we are in another country, that the Rockies, not to mention the Sierra Nevadas, are an imposing barrier to that threat, though we know a 2000 attack on LAX was foiled at the last minute, and a plan to ram an airliner 9/11–style into the U.S. Bank Tower, the tallest building on the West Coast, was apparently quashed in February 2002. When I return to Washington each month, the evidence of 9/11 is everywhere: more concrete barriers like extracted wisdom teeth all over downtown, the increased *thwop thwop thwopping* of helicopters at night in our neighborhood, cameras on intersection stoplights, the serpentine lines at Dulles Airport at all hours (at least two hours are needed in advance at Dulles to clear security, the worst of any airport in the country). Even more telling evidence of 9/11's effect on the Capital is the psychological wear and tear. My friends, mostly lawyers and lobbyists, seem beaten down, defeated, almost firing squad material. One of them, who is a managing partner at one of the top firms in Washington, tells me during a round of golf out near Frederick, "I have it on good sources that Bush is seriously addicted to substances." When I venture that he's almost destroyed the country, my friend, who is anything but an alarmist, the epitome of professionalism, balance, and principle, returns, "He already has."

Though fear in the Capital is palpable, there's a "deer-in-the-headlights" feeling about the place — most are too stunned or worn out to act or ask themselves: Might there be a safer, better place to live? But my worries are close to home: Luke is now taking the subway to art class one block from the White House. It recalls our terror at son Andy's being forced to huddle in his high school's basement for four hours with a thousand other Gonzaga students on 9/11, because the school is one block from the Capitol. It was with selfish relief that we learned the fourth hijacked plane — aimed at the Capitol dome and likely to descend right over Gonzaga's clock tower — was downed in Pennsylvania by the actions of some heroic passengers. Telephone lines out and huge traffic jams all over the city kept us from knowing Andy was all right for most of the day. D.C. is now ground zero for the next attack, as al-Qaeda tends to finish what it starts. Anthrax powder sent in letters to D.C. in 2002, one to a post office blocks from our house, had me opening mail with rubber gloves for weeks; it's been said the anthrax scare compelled President Bush over the edge into war with Iraq. The copycat sniper shooting of ten people all across Washington, one within a block of my work — the snipers rented their death vehicle purposely on the one-year anniversary of 9/11, September 11, 2002 — has me walking zig-zag to my car and the entire capital traumatized for a month. My Irish wife listens to my argument that coming to California may literally save the family's lives with fatalism beyond the so-called fatalistic Arabs.

Back in Los Angeles, under the reign of the savvy and ecumenical Schwarzenegger, who seems more like the president of the Country of California, there's precious little evidence of the terror threat or its flip-side, the quashing of civil liberties under the Paranoia, hmm, Patriot Act. Except when I visit the Muslims of Anaheim.

The public television station in Orange County wants to interview me about my new book on Arab Americans in the shopping district known as "Little Gaza," about a mile of Brookhurst Street between Ball Road and Lincoln. David Nazar, a sympathetic reporter with an Iranian Jewish background, sits me down on the sunny veranda of one of several Arab coffeehouses and we go at it. A few Arab men smoking and drinking *ahwey Turkiyeh* (Arabs still call their own coffee by the name of their former overmasters for five hundred years, the Turks) look over, listening. When Nazar wants to interview them, too, they balk. It's no surprise; since 2004, police have been jotting down license plate numbers throughout Little Gaza. "It has been a very uncomfortable situation for a very long time," says Syrian insurance company owner Belal Delati.

Nazar asks me to intercede, stepping back with his cameraman into the parking lot. I speak a little Arabic to the coffeehouse owner, telling him this is public television, they usually are more fair-minded than the networks or CNN. "Take this opportunity to speak as an American to Americans," I say. "Just being there on television shows you normal, eases the sense of threat. I mean, Christ, you're a small businessman. That's the mother lode of America!" I use my bona fides as the author of *The Arab Americans*, and give them a copy. The storeowner is grateful, puts his hand to his chest, bows his head, and says in Arabic, "Thank you. God praise you. Good. Let's do it."

"You know," I tell David Nazar later, "Some cops thought all these beauty salons and offices and restaurants and butcher shops were fronts for Hezbollah."

He laughs.

"But wait, here's the point. These people are almost all Sunni Muslims. Hezbollah is Shiite!" I sit for a while when the reporter leaves, drinking my Turkish coffee down to the grounds, flipping it to read the pattern. It's illegible. How much has changed! When I was young and bicycling these Anaheim streets, I was the only Arab boy around. Our living room was "Littlest Gaza." I was often taken for Italian or Mexican and that was fine with me. And now I was a go-between for this new community from Syria, Jordan, and Palestine, cowering in their new-found land, not safe in the old home and not safe in the new.

Maybe this is my home, a pontoon bridge over the treacherous waters moving fast from white to brown Los Angeles, indeed, a brown America. Anonymous or too known, perhaps an "outsider" minority is well positioned to stand on that bridge.

In Santa Monica one brisk winter night, Pat and I walk along the cliff. I remember being there in the daylight long ago with my new wife and two babies in tow. But I stifle the memory. We walk down the steep coiling steps of the palisades. Pat won't let go. And I remember something that has receded in my life — holding onto someone who holds onto you. We cross the Pacific Coast Highway in the wind and land, shoes doffed, sinking feet into the fine cold sand. In the darkness ahead, breakers sough and hiss.

Down shore turns the old Ferris wheel lit with many colors of the palette. It's Pacific Ocean Park, which caught fire and burnt to the ground when I was a boy, the old roller coaster charred, broken, hung over the sea like the road to nowhere. But now it is resurrected. The riders cry as they fly around a curve. Then silence.

We collapse in the sand as if we were sand, the colors from the Ferris wheel snapping on and off our bodies. Pat's blond puff of hair flares red, blue, green, then goes back to gold. The wind is up. The whitecap curls into the darkness.

It's August 2006. I'm in Washington, ready to concede defeat in the marriage, about to leave for Los Angeles for good, when the phone rings. I soon realize my wife's health is at stake. As if she has understood our ordeal, Aunt Jen pushes all her Madonnas toward me, and one night pulls the feeding tube out of her stomach. She points at me and smiles as if to say, "I know you." Within a week, she is dead of no food in this world.

On a long hike at ten-thousand-foot Mt. Baldy where the San Gabriels bend into the San Bernardinos, the freshets of an early spring thaw pour down the mountainside underneath a light snow pack. It's warm on our faces, but cold on our legs. My companion is generous: in body warmth, hand going to my forehead.

"You're going back," Pat turns on the trail suddenly to look at me. Her eyes are forlorn. They take in the sea. And then me again.

"Yes."

She turns to continue hiking and I follow her to the falling source of the stream, a waterfall small enough to show no whitecap splitting into two rivulets down the smooth rock-face before joining together and crashing at the bottom. I go to it, dip my head in. Pat stands back, looking down, looking out.

Two days later, Pat's boyfriend discovers it all for the first time and goes crazy. She is frightened and guilty and angry. She doesn't want to see me. She doesn't look me in the eye and her voice is raw: "I would think less of you if you didn't go back and give it one more try."

It's over. The fall bends wide on the rock.

You take who you are everywhere. For a time, I was unfaithful, then faithful. As St. Augustine knew, more than choosing in this life, we are chosen. Contract fulfilled, my job was completed. I was going home, I was leaving home. Home is where they love you in spite of what they know, where you sacrifice and are sacrificed, where you belong. I had to go to my wife; it was as certain, and perhaps more so, than my love of the West. The sun that exalted also exposed. I craved what changed as the earth changes in a moment, as it nudges one shoulder blade against another and shakes everything; and I hoped for what could last. I was an Angeleno. I lived with extremes, was happy with tides, welcoming of the peoples of the world standing on a fault. I had a shattered love, this Coast. I was going East to where the light begins, towards a sun now halted in the emergency, a frigging miracle, the love still retained. Would it rise? I didn't know. I would add my hand to the jet stream. I was an Angeleno.

Fante said of that moment at the Columbia Buffet as Arturo Bandini watched Camilla, "Everything here was holy." And it is. The tongue long, longing, the sand at the end, the spiders along the refrigerator waiting for crumbs, the crushed pomegranates of September, the split freshet, the wife coming out of the dark amazed at the sun, the son happy in the surf, Pat's grace, the paralyzed aunt drawing the Blessed Mother in a rest home with no rest, the blessed, the insane in Pershing Square and Fifth Street, my father turning over for a dream of this life in his tomb overlooking the sea, the sea I have joined with my saltwater blood, the sink of the mountains, a most azure love bringing the high low, as if the earth were a Muslim and the Pacific, God.

II

Arab America

Shall We Gather in the Mountains?

Not long ago, my family got lost in the mountains. Poet James Wright once bowed to the saving grace of suffering in *Shall We Gather at the River?* Plenty of my family gathered not at the river but in the mountains, and some fell off—or rather came close to falling off—a cliff, four exactly. And it struck me, as one family member after another was swallowed by the San Gabriels, lured to be a hero, that a short story was taking place before my very eyes. Or rather, by my flashlight.

Three flashlights, actually. My cousin had two and I one, though when I asked my cousin why he wasn't shining both of his on the treacherous path, he said, "I'm preserving the batteries."

There's a lot of preserving the batteries among Arab Americans. Couldn't we just blast out those flashlights full bore and to hell with the batteries? Once in a blue moon? That's what I want my writing to do: full bore, flashlights ablaze, flying deeper and deeper into the mountains.

So here I'm going to put the flashlights on and try and write this short story based on a March 2006 fiasco in the foothills behind Pasadena's Jet Propulsion Lab. And as I am writing it, I am going to lay bare how I write, how I take the real world and knead it and need it and bank on it and not bank on it because it doesn't make any money to need it and knead it, but love it, and show how, by loving it, we make a story. Frank Conroy, the memoirist and late director of the Iowa Writers Workshop, said that writing is an act of love of the world, of those out there from whom we are cut off. So in a way, when you are writing, you are in the dark mountains. And you may go deeper. Or you may flee down the slope and get killed.

At the same time, I may reveal here some themes I think are common to the literature of Arab Americans, but don't count on it. Don't count on me paying close attention to family, war, and love in this strange culture we find ourselves set down in, as I would if I were wearing a critic's hat, that stiff homburg. No, I am wearing no hat and going up into the mountains.

Let's get the facts right before we distort them to tell the truth. My cousin has a son adopted from the Lebanese Civil War named Christopher. Now twenty-two, Christopher was as an infant abandoned on the steps of a church in Beirut. This was before he became an American football player, wrestler, and apprentice fireman. Christopher was the last person you would think would get lost in the mountains. But he did. He and his buddy, who did fall off a cliff—which was either ten feet or a hundred feet down, give or take a zero—they started up the trail in the San Gabriels on bicycles at 3:30 in the afternoon. Not smart. They had no lights. Less smart. Their cell phones had only enough battery charge for one call. Least smart.

By ten o'clock at night, there was no word from Christopher and his friend. My cousin's wife was getting worried, and naturally she was getting angry at my cousin. Wasn't it his fault that Christopher was lost?

"My fault? What do you mean? I didn't tell him to go up there."

"But you should have stopped him."

"But he is twenty-two years old and bigger than me."

"It doesn't matter. What if he falls off a cliff?"

You can see where this is going. And I'm going to have a good time going there. But I may have to change something. My cousin's wife is part Mexican and part Greek. I like that about her, but it is distracting from what I see developing here. I'm going to make her Arab American. I think her insouciance is the important thing, and the crazy insularity and clinging to family I may want to emphasize, the pull to the fire of family as obliterating as a dark mountain. I realize I am losing something in making my cousin's wife of the tribe, so to speak. One could emphasize her sense of being outside of it all, and the anger that must whip up, or the incessant need to prove oneself worthy, or the sense of pride in being apart and able to survive in the outside world without reference to the West Bank and Gaza, or *kibbi nayyi*.

Anyway, that's my choice for now. I'm going to call her Fairuz. She sings a lot—at people. I'm going to make her more old world than the real wife of my cousin; the cousin character may just realize that getting the real thing from the old country isn't exactly a guarantee of wedded bliss on these shores. She's a loud one, this Fairuz. But we'll give her her due yet, up on that mountain.

A call comes in, the one call. Christopher says not to worry, they are miles into the mountain, halfway to Mount Wilson, really, and it's cold, they only have shorts on, and they have no lights, but they are going to ditch the bikes and walk out. Not to worry. They'll make it in two hours. They are on a fire trail.

This sounds promising. So we call off the rescue team, which sends the wife into a fit. But I think I'll take that fire trail whole into the fiction. Because the trail my cousin and I discover is anything but a fire trail. It is a narrow thing along a precipice. This is true. We decide to meet the descending boys with some light. (We do not say we are afraid they don't need us.) We take the wrong trail right from the start — the one marked with a sign "El Prieto Trail." We fail to take the other trail because it is unmarked, thinking: Wouldn't anyone rather take the marked trail? And right there, we have a failure of judgment. Twenty-two-year-old kids love an unmarked trail. It is we at fifty who need the markers, not the kids. The kids plunge into the mountains like an uphill cascade. They don't long; we long. They long not to long; we long to long. And two hours into our hike in the darkness uphill with hard shoes on, we are really longing. We are longing for our son, our nephew, our cousin, and especially, hiking boots. We have one bottle of water and it is going fast. Our backs are betraying us. The only thing we are thankful for is that my cousin's wife can't reach us to yell at us. Because our cell phone's batteries are dead.

You don't own anyone in this life. A critic of Eugene O'Neill's work said that. And that is hard for us, we of Arab stripe, to admit. I fought it for years. I laughed at Gibran's "Your children are not your children, but life's longing for itself." How ridiculous! He never had children, that's why he feels that way, I said. But the older I get, the more fallible I see people's love, the more I see that the American drive for identity and comfort can destroy that love, here where love is the first thing people spend for and the last thing they get, because it is not a getting thing, is it? It is a blessing and an act, an act of great courage, like going into the dark mountains not knowing where your loved ones exactly are. But wanting them, and wanting to matter, even if you don't own them, owning up to that, yes, that you need this holding and touch. Above money and position and the house and the mortgage and quasi-identity of a thousand sorts. You need this belonging, this touch. This real identity that you are finally able to give up to the other, and in the giving, gain it. How do you know who you are if you do not love?

I mention Eugene O'Neill because I saw this great documentary on his life lately, and that happens with fiction. Something untoward enters the story. I've been an O'Neill man for a long time. An Irish American playwright enters my story now. A great man of tragedy, who lost a brother to alcohol, a mother to morphine addiction, another brother to measles, and a father to Mammon. Who left a wife with two young children to plunge into the ravine of his past with a woman named Carlotta. This is not an Arab American proclivity, to abandon your children for the past. Or is it? What is the terrible pull of those mountains? And their darkness? And the hope of joining at the glistening peak, the source of all this longing and pain of family you don't own, touching in the darkness what God meant, perhaps, the unity of an early day in life when you looked at the sky where the sun touched the top of a mountain and said, "I want to be there. Maybe then I will know why I am here."

I confess that O'Neill appeals to me in another way. My own wife is Irish American, and there is poetry in that and beauty and longing and great luck. There's also stubbornness, Irish stubbornness, which may have its counterpart in Arab stubbornness. (I wonder sometimes, though, if flexibility, this drive to blend at all costs, may be the Arab Americans' particular cross.) In any case, Irish and Arab certainly both share a sense of being on the outskirts of empire wanting in, of longing for the core. And though there are not as many mountains in Ireland as there are in Lebanon or California, our lands share a love of the sea, green or blue. And that is a lot of longing. O'Neill loved the sea off Connecticut as a boy. And off Big Sur as a man.

So maybe we encounter an Irishman on our journey up the wrong trail of the mountain, and maybe he helps us, like a stranger really did. My cousin and I came upon a light in the woods, a tent lit from the inside. A voice spoke: "What are you doing here?"

In truth, the man never came out of the tent. We were scared by the stern tone of his voice. It was late — past midnight. Did he have a woman in there, a man, a dog? A gun? We had no weapons but flashlights. We spoke across the stream at this eerily lit tent in the darkness, like a huge firefly lit down on earth. We spoke of our mission. The man's voice said, "No one has been by here since 4:30 this afternoon and they were going the other way." I looked at my cousin. "We are on the wrong trail," I said, shining a light on my watch. It was two in the morning. We turned around and plunged into the darkness.

Why do I think now of Edward Said's memoir, *Out of Place?* As he says, "All families invent their parents and children, give each of them a story, character, fate, and even a language. There was always something wrong with how I was invented and meant to fit in the world of my parents and four sisters." Edward says it took him fifty years to feel "less uncomfortable" with his own name, "a fancy English name" as he calls it, hard to link with "its Arabic partner." Said goes on: "I would rush past and emphasize 'Said.' At other times, I would do the reverse, or connect these two to each other so quickly that neither would be clear." Why does that sense of disorientation occur to me now? After all, I am here. I made it down the mountain.

For that mountain moment I knew fear, but more: pure waste. The sense of being foolish, off-kilter. Maybe that's why I think now to bolster the story by adding the Irishman. However productive I am in the outside world, I feel something of wasted time when I'm apart from my wife and hope she feels the same. You build a life with shared memories, like the one my cousin and I now have getting lost in the mountains. Anyway, I'm creating a character out of love for my wife and the need to be near her — but I am going to make her into a man, this man in the tent who is going to help us. He will give himself away as Irish by his brogue. He is going to pour us coffee. There's going to be something wounded about him. He may have a dog named Joyce. He'll read us a line from "The Lake Isle of Innisfree" about a house of "clay and wattles made" where "peace comes dropping slow." And for just a bit, my cousin and I relax, forget about our search for the lost boy, even wonder if the man has two more sleeping bags.

But something in the solitary man's demeanor, something strange, snaps us out of it — maybe it's the way he scratches the scar on his forehead. We realize we are needed elsewhere, at least we hope so, and we go back down the night trail.

Come the hoot owls. The croaking frogs (frogs fiction, the owls fact). We scream into the darkness of the other ridge, knowing that's where the boys are. But there is no answer and our cell phone is deader than the Green Line of Beirut or the Great Wall of Israel. We shine our lights at the ridge. Nothing. No answer to our light or our voice. Now my story is beginning to sound like the American critical response to Arab American literature.

On the other ridge there's the shadow of a tall radio antenna. We shake our heads, because one of the last things Christopher said before the phone went dead is that he was near a tall antenna, and we thought the one on our ridge was it. We have been fooled twice. And now I think of the mistaken identities, sometimes lethal, in Arab American fiction. Like the character of Martin Habib in Vance Bourjaily's *Brill Among the Ruins*, who is murdered in a jealous rage walking out of a plumber's shop, mistaken for someone else. Of the many wrong paths heroine Mayan Atassi takes searching for her father in Mona Simpson's *The Lost Father*, hoping at one point that maybe he'll have the appeal of Yasir Arafat, standing for something, instead of being what she finds him as — a waiter in a restaurant in Stockton, California. Yet for all his flaws, he is hers. Would that people who walk deaf, dumb, and blind into the Middle East would have the moral courage to simply see Arabs as Mona Simpson finds Mayan Atassi's father: "He was only a man."

My cousin and I take several wrong turns going back, criss-crossing the stream, and we are getting lost. (This is not what happened — because I marked the trail, having lived two years in Alaska and being familiar with woods — our path back was near perfect. But I want these two to really get confused, afraid, maybe even terrified — or more accurately, they want me to be that way for the time of our story.) I love that title of Joseph Geha's short story, "Everything! Everything!" We have such a hunger for life, and this story is beginning to have a terrible drive in it, a complete swallowing of darkness. Something on the order of the chaos Hemingway's Nick Adams senses in the swamp at the end of "Big Two-Hearted River."

Lo and behold, a picnic table emerges in the dark! A real one! With real fictive opportunity. There the would-be rescuers rest, drink from a water bottle (I think I'll make them more intrepid and contingent — throw out the water bottle — and bow them low to drink from the polluted stream in all their confusion.) Getting their bearings, they open up to one another, two cousins who have lived many years and miles apart and don't really know each other as they once did, if they ever did.

Now part of this took place. My cousin and I did speak some important things to each other. But we didn't look up at the top of the mountain, think of Mt. Sannine in Lebanon, its snow-capped beauty and dread (poet Mikhail Naimy lived in Baskinta at the top in "The Valley of Skulls"), and I didn't ask the lost boy's father about how and why he was adopted during the Lebanese Civil War.

And soon they are speaking of that terrible fratricidal war and the current war on terror waged so blindly by our leaders. They might turn on Israel's second attack on Lebanon in the summer of 2006, or it is the third? The fourth? Israel's always had this "thing" for Lebanon, all the way back to the Song of Songs ("The fragrance of your garments is the fragrance of Lebanon"). You want the mistress to sit still and let you be, no matter what is left unsaid or undone that continues to kill in the night. Christopher's father — his character — might wax on being pulled out of line at the airport and fondled by a guard (is this that I just saw the movie *Crash?*). How he lost a contract after 9/11 for electrical parts. How Christopher says he wants to find his blood mother and father and can't stand America. This now is fiction. But this is the story I feel compelled to tell about the woods behind the Jet Propulsion Lab in Pasadena in the Year 2006.

I'm in a tradition. Gibran castigated the Lebanese over its factionalism in World War I, blasted the West and the Turks for the starvation of 1916, but people only remember him for his storybook of aphorisms, *The Prophet.* We still want the Arab to be wise and shut up. Wise, not a wiseacre. Samuel Hazo has his American couple kidnapped and a Socratic dialogue on terror takes place between a guerrilla leader and the couple in *The Very Fall of the Sun,* a prophetic, long out-of-print book published in 1978. The wreckage of war, physical and spiritual, riddles Naomi Nye's poetry and begs her to climb out. The first Iraq war haunts the lover in Diana Abu-Jaber's *Crescent.* As for the interior damage of war, Patricia Sarrafian Ward displays it with great sensitivity in her stunning novel, *The Bullet Collection.* There the Lebanese Civil War intersects with the personal agony of parent for damaged child: "My parents learned the truth first about Alaine; they locked cabinets and drawers; they slept on full alert, ready to spring up at the slightest provocation. The war outside was nothing; we slept through whole bombing raids, laughed at our own lassitude, but Alaine, the sound of her stirred even the deepest slumber."

So in the dark of the mountain, my cousin and I are going to talk the damage of war, the damage of inner war, that is, mental illness. We may talk about the suicide of my sister, and his worry for Christopher being lost down more than mountain trails. I'm going to change Christopher's name to — what? I don't know yet. But I want to protect the real Christopher, who is actually a balanced, sweet-hearted fellow who wants to be a fireman. I have no real idea of how his orphanhood from Lebanon may affect him inside, but my story can explore that.

You see how fiction grabs reality and wrings from it some inner obsessions, hidden truths hard to tell? They need out, because that is how we love, we writers, by shining the light in a dark mountain, a light that hurts the eyes and flares the heart into pumping.

We are pumping madly downhill and they're all there suddenly; we've found the way by sheer grace, including an uncle who walked blindly up another trail, cell phone a-blazing. Several aunts, uncles, cousins mill about, rubbing their heads, groggy, as it is halfway through the black morning. There are the glaring lights of the rescue SUVs, as well as Christopher's friend's mother, who put the final rescue call in. "Fayrouz" jabs her finger, wrist jewels tingling, at my cousin's chest. Maybe I'll have her file for divorce (as she really did). I don't want to distract with some predictable misery from the mystery of that collective dive into the mountain. It's quite a scene, enough to rouse the Jet Propulsion Lab security guards: police, ambulance, the friend leaned back on a cot with his broken ribs and gashed leg. And there the helicopter lifts away. In truth, the boys made it nearly all the way back before they were beamed. And actually, there was no need for our rescue, or the other rescue with its thousand-dollar price tag. It was all unnecessary.

Except for the need for my cousin and I to get lost. And talk. One by one, relatives went into the mountain wanting to help. It was all unnecessary. It was all a function of the hankering need to be a part of something greater, some dark mountain where we are as essential to each other as tree, rock, and brook. If I don't get into divorce court at the end, I could give Christopher's friend some permanent injury. There are mountain lions up there, you know! But that's too much. Life is relentlessly excessive; it is fiction that zeroes in, to the island in the rapids, to the mountain before dawn, the wonder before the explosion. Wonder may precede disaster, it may follow it. Either way, I want to be on the side of wonder.

In truth, people die of and kill with the best intentions, though, thank God, no one did that night in back of the place where America's spaceships are monitored long through the night so that even an astronaut is not alone. Not in this world, not with this family and its terribly beautiful love.

Baghdad with a Human Face

Before our bombers lock on to that vague splotch (Baghdad) lying below them along a serpentine green line (the Tigris River) in the desert, I would like to list a few targets I hope they will miss, most especially my artist cousin Wedad Orfali.

Wedad is proprietor of the only privately owned art gallery in Iraq. I first met her in 1986 during my only visit to Baghdad when I was a guest, with ten other American writers and poets, at an Iraqi-hosted literary festival.

Quite a character, a sort of Arab Gertrude Stein, Wedad Orfali had a home that was a salon for Iraqi artists, writers, musicians. Walls were covered, mosaic-like, with paintings, photographs, tapestries. At one point, Wedad pointed proudly to some Marc Chagall originals. "I adore him," she said.

An accomplished artist of magical cityscapes, she treated me to a virtuoso performance of "Strangers in the Night," first on a zither and then on a piano whose keys seemed to have buckled in a rainstorm.

"Stranzhers een the nyyyeta!" she intoned, calling over her shoulder playfully as her legs pumped the pedals and her hands pounded the warped keys. Her husband Abu Abbas, a taciturn ex-diplomat who had retired the very day Saddam Hussein invaded Iran in 1980, looked at me as if I were a hapless victim, a gleam in his eyes over the rim of his demitasse.

He was wrong. With Wedad, it was love at first *abrazo*, at first wrong chord.

I had never heard of her, nor do any of my relatives come from Iraq. But when Nasira al-Sadoun, an Iraqi novelist and bookstore owner, caught my last name at the al-Merbid festival, she insisted that we meet.

About sixty, short, but tall of voice and wide of smile, Wedad was convinced we were related. When I protested that my grandfather Orfalea

was born in Syria and was Christian, she grabbed my wrist, sat me
down in front of a dozen plates of *mezza* and told me she was studying
about Urfa.

Urfa is in Turkish Armenia, and Wedad had figured that we were all
Armenians at one point and that Urfa was the motherland. Our lives in
the Arab world were a wandering. "My dear, it's easy to figure," she
squawked. "The Christians of our family went to Syria and the Muslims
of our family went to Iraq." This was a most intriguing notion of family,
and I believed it on the spot.*

I also hope our bombers miss Nasira al-Sadoun, whose bookstore
features Melville and Hawthorne. Possessed (strangely, as was true of
many Iraqis we met) of a white blotch in inky hair — which bespoke of
agony within denial — Nasira's eyes were bituminous coal. Her novel *If
Shade Comes* is about a woman coming of age in a society of loosening
strictures and of war. She suggested that "shade" meant "peace."

Clearly, there was a propaganda purpose in gathering a thousand
writers from all over the world to Baghdad — the Iraqis at that time were
fairly desperate in the senseless battle with Iran. There were the expected
panegyrics against Khomeini and hymns to the greater honor and glory
of Saddam, whose visage on billboards was so ubiquitous, pictured in
garb so eclectic, as to be laughable.

Nevertheless, there also were moments of the real poetic thing. Ku-
waiti poet Suad al-Sabbagh lambasted the al-Merbid festival itself —
"Our seats are bored with us" — and called for a "homeland without
secrets, prisons, executions." She attacked "dinosaur" Arab regimes —
and, amazing as it seems in recollection, might have been including Iraq
itself; a police state gets no awards for freedom of speech, but Iraq did
alright that day.

Exiled Syrian poet Ahmed Suleiman Ahmed hushed a huge crowd
when he lamented, "We are a dead people, and there is no harm in
burying the dead twice."

Baghdad itself was personified in many a poem we heard, a city
standing endangered, tormented. And I think even now as we teeter on
the brink of attacking the very country we were supporting then, it
would be wrong to underestimate the pride that poets from all over the
Arab world evoked over the sacrifice Iraq made in shielding them from

---

*In addition to Armenian, over the years I have heard people insist that the Orfaleas of
Urfa are Kurds, Assyrians, or Jews. The origin of our name remains a mystery.

Khomeini. Wedad Orfali compared the ayatollah to Halagu, the Mongol invader who destroyed Baghdad in 1258.

Will we be seen any differently when we come bearing bombs?

Amid the almost feverish, yet genuine, hospitality of the Iraqi people, there were foreboding signs. An ancient sculpture at Babylon of a lion pouncing on a man was replicated in modern design at the airport. A palpable tension and paranoia in the streets, arising from Iranian missile attacks and the Iraqi secret police, were brought home to me when a woman grabbed my camera and tried to smash it as I photographed a fruit vendor and his pomegranates. The bird-blue camouflage uniforms of Iraqi Pioneers, or boy scouts, on close inspection revealed themselves patterned with maps of the Arab world. That blue cloak and their fervent chant, "We will die for you, Saddam," seemed sad, pathetic.

When I brought up the subject of chemical weapons used against Iran, one frank official said, "Look. If the United Stated were invaded by Mexico, you would use any weapon at your disposal." A year later, though, Saddam gassed the Kurds—his own people—morally indefensible on any grounds. I declined a re-invitation to the al-Merbid festival, citing the horrific event at Halabja.

At the end of my 1986 trip, we were taken to the war front near Khanaquin on the Iraq-Iran border. There, an Iraqi general touched his heart, indicating the solace the presence of Americans had for his troops, and stunned us more with his statement, "We are fighting your war." A leather-faced Army corporal stared at me intensely with hazel eyes. "My name is Abdulwahab," he said quietly. "I have been fighting for seven years along seven hundred miles. I am an English teacher."

I think I know what he was saying; it's a question troops massed throughout the Gulf are probably asking themselves, too, under all the rhetoric: *Why am I here?* I think it was the subtext of the impatient GI responses that Secretary of State James Baker received as he toured the dunes.

I do not mean to imply that war with Iraq should not be undertaken under any conditions, nor even that we should never countenance attacking first. I have neither the naiveté nor the radical, courageous solitude of the total pacifist. Torture of hostages, for example, may be enough of a reason to go to war.

What I am saying is this: Among rulers, the history of vengeance and temerity is a rather common and bloody one; the history of foresight and forbearance more rare and worthy. Both the tyrant Saddam Hussein and the righteous George Bush seem by turns perilously lacking in forbearance and suffused with temerity.

As we slide toward war, I find myself drawn not just to precious geography, ancient ruins, but people I met four years ago and to whom I am now linked, who walk and breathe in a looming killing field. Human beings, tens and perhaps hundreds of thousands, may suffer and die underneath bombardment, in a chemical mist or nuclear fire, or in the aftermath of ruin. They will be from many nations. Their lives and maiming will be linked to millions more — relatives, friends, anonymous avengers. Their dreams will be undreamed; their children-to-be unborn. Most of these will be Iraqis no fonder of Saddam Hussein than we are.

And so, calling up the faces of Wedad Orfali and Abdulwahab, the dutiful, haunted corporal, I would like to ask our president, burdened in this solemn hour more than anyone of us can realize: Have we yet done all we can to avert this horror? Is it clear that we will not destroy or unleash more than we will rescue? It isn't yet to me. And I don't think I'm alone.

Where Is the Outrage Over Iraq?

Did My Lai come to Iraq? The March 16–19, 1968, massacre of at least 347 civilians at My Lai (the monument says 504) contributed to the fall of the U.S. president and produced a quantum blow-up in Vietnam war resistance. Could such outrage finally get us out of the vortex of Iraq? Could we best remember our troops with the truth?

The answer to the last is yes; the former, doubtful.

On May 27, 2006, the first news reports surfaced of a November 19, 2005, massacre of twenty-four Iraqi civilians in cold blood at Haditha — six months after the killings. This tracks the My Lai scandal, though that bloodbath took twenty months to surface in the U.S. news media, a turgidity caused by deep embarrassment and a cover-up. A thirty-one-year-old major named Colin Powell, who arrived at My Lai just after the massacres, was put in charge of answering an early complaint letter by a soldier who asserted that the killing of Vietnamese civilians was becoming routine. Powell downplayed the problem, saying relations between GIs and the Vietnamese people were "excellent." This is the same General Powell who, as secretary of state, addressed the United Nations in 2003 with dramatic evidence of Iraqi malfeasance that helped launch the U.S. invasion of Iraq. The evidence was bogus.

After having been lied to repeatedly about a nonexistent Iraqi nuclear, chemical, and biological weapons capability, its supposed linkage to al-Qaeda exposed as fiction, one would have thought the troops, if not the president himself, would have been given the collar by now. War under false pretenses? Nixon and Clinton were impeached for far less (lying about a two-bit robbery at a hotel and a round of oral sex). No one died as a result of Nixon and Clinton's improprieties, but more than 4,000 American soldiers have in Iraq under the second George Bush, and at least 150,000 Iraqis, many civilians.

The enduring mystery of the Iraq war has been the passivity of the

American people during its execution. What does it take to wake us? There were half a million marchers in Los Angeles in 2006 over Mexican immigration. Nothing like those numbers have yet surfaced over the Iraq war. The Haditha massacre may have pricked the American conscience, though none are holding their breath for a generation raised with more community service consciousness than any other to flood into the streets in protest. There are jobs to be had, BlackBerrys to consult as if they were post-modern Ouji boards, and faces to search on Facebook. If you are saving anything, you are saving face. And, of course, there is no draft fanning consciences.

The media was late to question the myths on which the war in Iraq was based. But long after its skepticism should have been sharpened to a razor's edge, it was swallowing at face value Bush's claim that a 2007 "surge" of thirty thousand more U.S. troops had single-handedly reduced violence and put the war on a winning track. Few pointed out that cold cash (to the tribal leaders in the Sunni triangle) was as efficacious as extra khaki, and that political accord between Iraqi factions and sects was as distant as ever. In fact, Basra in the south, which had been a quiet front, suddenly exploded *after* the surge. Media schizophrenia on Iraq had no better demonstration than a November 28, 2007 *Washington Post* back-paged article headlined, "U.S. Troops Kill at Least 5 Iraqis at Checkpoint," including a child. What illustrated this all-too-gruesome story? Certainly not the murderers or the dead — rather two incredible photos, one of Washington Redskins cheerleaders mixing with the troops and another of Iraqi boys in a bicycle race in Fallujah! Message: Forget the story, the Surge is Working.

As for massacres of civilians or POWs in wartime, it must be admitted, they are less of an exception to the rule for any troops, ours included, than we care to acknowledge. About such unseemly events, especially in the so-called "good war" in Europe in the forties, our historians have been hesitant to probe. When I revealed in my 1997 book two instances of the shooting of POWs by my own father's decorated battalion in World War II, it was the first time names had been put to such murders in fifty-two years since the "good war."

My rule of thumb was one witness, no witness. There had to be at least two observers of each incident for me to report it. I'll never forget Jim Guerrant telling me about an incident at the Battle of the Bulge: "Private Harold Magnuson and Private Denny Downes took about six to eight German prisoners over the hill and executed them. We'd seen what they'd done to us at Malmedy, and these Germans were wearing U.S. tanker coats on the ridge. I guess everyone was pure outraged." Sergeant Thames Anderson corroborated it.

That same day — January 3, 1945 — Sergeant Duke Spletzer tommy-gunned twenty to thirty German prisoners. His commanding officer who witnessed the carnage, Lieutenant Phil Hand, didn't buy the excuse that they ran: "Hell, they didn't run. He just deliberately killed them." Spletzer's POW shooting was corroborated by PFC Forrest Reed.

Life, if not the courts, has a way of exacting retribution for such crimes — Magnuson and Downes were killed in a car crash spree in New York in June 1945, and Spletzer ended up as a prison guard, dying at fifty-eight.

Total war is total rage. In answer to the ferocity of Japanese armies in Manchuria and the genocide of the Nazis, hundreds of thousands of civilians died from our firebombings of Germany and Japan and the subsequent dropping of atomic bombs on Hiroshima and Nagasaki. Historians will forever debate these awful events and whether they kept the American death toll in World War II from climbing substantially higher than two hundred thousand. There is a decent argument that we gained nothing from the firebombing of the Axis cities, and it is a well-established fact that before we dropped the atomic bombs, the Japanese had signaled they were willing to surrender to us if they could keep their emperor.

We answered with the mass death-by-remote of bomber planes, which the poet (and former bomber pilot over Japan) James Dickey called "this detachment / The honored aesthetic evil / The greatest sense of power in one's life / That must be shed." But there is something about face-to-face executions that turns the stomach, and, let us hope, conscience, so directly that it cannot be shed or swathed as occurs in the suburban quotidian of Dickey's masterful poem, "The Firebombing."

As with the Bulge campaign and Vietnam, apologists for the rouge Marines at Haditha argued the lethality of civilians ("insurgent sympathizers") or some other loophole that "allows" such shooting of the unarmed (the Germans at the Bulge wearing GI "tanker coats" might make them executable as spies). In the spirit of Guerrant's suggestion that the Nazi SS massacre at Malmedy "explains" what Magnuson and Downes did, we were told that the blind anger of GIs at Haditha was mitigated by the car bombing of their fellows. But they're going to have a hard time explaining away the killing of the four Khafif girls ages fourteen, ten, five, three, and one, or the Ali children ages eight, five, four, and two months.

War debases. But it is not just our debasement that should be our concern with the Haditha killings. We are not just fighting for the hearts and minds of the Iraqi people, but twenty-two Arab countries, and, in fact, the entire Islamic world. At least that is the task the Bush administration set forth for us when everything else was proven false. Al-Qaeda sent copies of a journalist student's videotape of the Haditha massacres to mosques in Syria, Jordan, and Saudi Arabia. Laced across one of the Haditha houses was this angry graffiti: "Democracy assassinated the family that was here."

Whatever our good intentions, the face of our "democracy" campaign in Iraq has too often been ugly. Haditha, no doubt, stoked the recruitment campaign for Islamist terrorists and broke down distinctions between our civilization and the barbarism we decry.

We have not brought Iraq more clean water or rule of law or jobs, electricity, or more hope than Saddam Hussein, and, in fact, we have brought a good deal less of everything but fear. And then we were revealed not only as torturers as at Abu Graib, but as executors of the young and old.

One would have hoped the alleged killers would be swiftly tried and convicted. In December 2006, four men were indicted for unpremeditated murder and four for failure to report or investigate the deaths. One would have hoped the alleged killers would be swiftly tried and convicted. In December 2006, four men were indicted for unpremeditated murder and four for failure to report or investigate the deaths. For six of these eight men, charges were dropped. By December 2008, only two remained: Staff Sergeant Frank Wuterich, his charges reduced to voluntary manslaughter; and Lieutenant Colonel Jeffrey Chessani, for dereliction of duty. Lieutenant William Calley, who ordered the shootings at My Lai, was convicted of first-degree murder and sentenced to life imprisonment, though he ended up serving only 3.5 years under house arrest at Fort Benning. I doubt Wuterich and Chessani will get even that. We learn so little and excuse much in ourselves, though less in others. And the world continued to watch.

Bush and Company see no end in sight of this miserable endeavor; we must reverse it for them, let us hope, with the election of someone in 2008 who saw through the Iraq war from the start, such as Barack Obama, or at least someone who sees through it now. Certainly not

Senator McCain, who likes to repeat the old saw about the American people losing the war in Vietnam, not the military, as if the two had no relation to each other.

Elders Cheney, Rumsfeld, and Richard Perle learned nothing from Vietnam. It's time we took the country into our own hands and taught these insensate people a lesson. Haditha and Abu Graib do not constitute the America I respect and love and never will. But bad policy leads to atrocity, and atrocity, magnified a thousand times by the Internet, equals terror. It's as certain as Newton's Third Law of Reciprocal Actions.

The Arab in the Post–World War II Novel

About five months before the Israeli invasion of Lebanon in 1982, Lewis Lapham formulated in a syndicated column a composite of a "good old-fashioned reliable American villain" for Americans beset by economic recession, unemployment, nuclear confrontation, and attacks on their embassies. The closest comparison to any living man, Lapham opined, was Mu'ammar Qaddafi, though the villain would have to be of larger stature and broader education. Yasir Arafat, too, might lose out on the height requirement. But Hafiz al-Assad fit the bill well. Indeed, about a year later for the first time in history, the United States attacked the forces of an Arab country — Syria — with the resultant loss afterward of 241 servicemen by a horrific truck bomb in Beirut. By 1986, though the recession had receded, the great terrorist bogeyman had not, and U.S. aircraft actually bombed Qaddafi's residence. Enemies had almost been goaded into creation, and the results were tragically bloody.

Lapham's analysis appeared more ominously prescient when, after a decade of intermittent harassment, intimidation, and violence against Arab Americans, in 1985 an Arab American was killed in Los Angeles by a trip-wire explosive when he entered his office one morning. The leader of the Jewish Defense League, Irv Rubin, said he "shed no tears over the incident" and that Alex Odeh "got what he deserved." Such violence came to darker flower when, in the wake of the carnage of September 11, 2001, up to eleven Arab Americans and others were killed and seven hundred subjected to hate crimes as various as beatings and torchings of religious sites. None of these people or places had anything to do with Osama bin Laden. The backlash wasn't a national pogrom — there are three million Arab Americans — but its effect, injecting fear into the hearts of an entire ethnic group, was not too far from one.

In 2002, two members of the Bush-appointed U.S. Civil Rights Commission, during public testimony in Detroit, Michigan, stated for the record that should there be another terrorist attack on U.S. soil, Arab Americans would be rounded up in camps. Peter Kirsanow and Jennifer Braceras didn't say they were for such a thing. They intimated it was just common sense that it would happen.

Hurled from their homes, torn from their businesses and farms, humiliated in a hundred ways during World War II, Japanese Americans know well the costs of such "common sense." And Arab Americans aren't exactly reassured by that historic precedent.

Such startling pronouncements from the U.S. Civil Rights Commission do not emerge from a void. True, Lapham's Arafat is dead, as is Assad (though his son Bashar is already getting horns and tail in our press). Qaddafi is now our friend for renouncing nuclear ambitions (though hardly a friend to his people). But you don't bombard and invade a major Arab country without a long dehumanization campaign. Thus Saddam Hussein, certainly a murderous tyrant, was overblown into a Hitler by the Western press, and by implication, made a larger threat to the United States than the man who masterminded September 11. The country of Iraq—its plumbing, electricity, roads and bridges—all had to be destroyed, and the Baath Party members thrown out as Nazis. No surprise that when we turned to the Iraqis to provide security, there was hardly anyone left to provide it.

How did all this happen? The University of Chicago's John Mearsheimer and Harvard's Stephen Walt have made a riveting case that our going so far off target by swerving blindly toward Iraq after 9/11 is at least in part the result of years of lobbying by neoconservatives whose chief concern was not the United States, but Israel. Their 2007 book, *The Israel Lobby and U.S. Foreign Policy*, may be the most important work on international relations since George F. Kennan's writings on containment of the Soviet Union in the fifties.

My concern here, however, is with the devolution of the image of an entire people that allows a president to get away with such an invasion as that of Iraq and even to secure the approval of Congress. This devolution in popular culture and literature, and the fear it engendered, provided an atmosphere that encourages the president to go even further: publicly contemplating launching attacks on Syria and Iran with no countervailing force. The Democrats huff and puff, but blow no houses down.

Again, how does this happen? My focus is that of a writer and reader, and it is as such that one sifts a half-century of writings about the Arabs as if one were walking through sludge. Social and cultural biases have simmered in popular American journalism and literature, creating an atmosphere of distrust and even hatred that ultimately manifests itself in public policy. A casual sifting-through of political cartoons, product advertisements, television and movie scripts, gives plenty of evidence of American society's fixation on "the bad Arab." In 1980, the stereotype achieved governmental sanction when the FBI dressed up agents in *kufiyahs* and burnooses to catch unscrupulous congressmen in Operation ABSCAM. By 2005, the FBI had sought face-to-face interrogations with more than twenty-one thousand Arabs and Arab Americans in the wake of 9/11. What began as ABSCAM bloomed into the Patriot Act.

Edward Said traced the problem of the image of the Arab in particular, and "the Oriental" in general, in his classic work, *Orientalism*, back to the literature, history, and philosophy of nineteenth- and eighteenth-century Europeans, who were in the process of encountering, then conquering the Middle East. Analysis of American popular culture's stereotyping of the Arab has become something of a cottage industry; there is no lack of material on this subject. Jack Shaheen of Southern Illinois University has done exhaustive, groundbreaking work on the image of the Arab in film, *Reel Bad Arabs*, and in the summer of 2007, Shaheen unveiled his own film, a documentary on the same subject.

One aspect of the problem has been neglected, however, and that is the skewing of the image of the Arab in contemporary literature, specifically prose fiction. It is that corner of the problem, particularly the American novel over the past half-century, that I will take up here.

Since the founding of the state of Israel in 1948, the Middle East has been a growing favorite of fiction writers, and until very recently — the post 9/11 world, really — the Arab has been universally and emphatically *not* the hero.

I will discuss here four types of novels that have appeared in English since the end of the World War II in which Arab characters are found: spy thrillers; historical tours de force and adventure stories; novels of oil blackmail and international financial pressure; and finally, novels that have nothing to do with the Middle East. At the end of my piece, I will also take a look at new work by Arab American novelists (and a literary lion, John Updike in *Terrorist*), many of whom couldn't get published before 9/11, who are trying at a very late hour to right this stereotyping ship in favor of the real world and the blessed imagination.

The highest purpose of fiction, of course, is the evocation of the truth. Beauty, as Keats suggested, is critical, too, the beauty of language, and it is truth evoked in moving language that gives us readers a twinge inside, or the Houseman-like hair-raise on the back of the neck. We readers live for that effect. The best imaginative fiction cannot, by definition, utilize stereotype, which is the antithesis of imagination. Stereotype causes the hungry reader a wince, rather than a twinge. Stereotyping involves a breakdown in the perception of the plenitude of existence. Simple laws of perception admit reality's diversity. The keen eye, ear, and heart of a storyteller will not allow for the reduction of the individual to a mathematical equation or one characteristic (Italians are lovers or criminals, or criminal-lovers; Jews are stingy, Arabs are wily, Blacks are slow or fast, unfairly rich or fairly poor).

It's appropriate at the outset to mention two novels, one written just before and one just after World War II, in which the stereotyping of the Arab is not only avoided, it is not even considered. Again, this is the pre-Israel period.

In his 1940 autobiographical novel *My Name Is Aram*, about an Armenian boy coming of age in Fresno, California, William Saroyan devotes a chapter to "The Poor and Burning Arab." We know Khalil, the Arab, as an individual because his sadness is expressed "by brushing a speck of dust from his knee and never speaking." In one gesture Saroyan captured a man, where Leon Uris in *Exodus* and *The Haj* fashioned only tanned mannequins.

In *The Alexandria Quartet* (1957), Lawrence Durrell constructed one of the masterpieces of contemporary literature, its four books revolving around pre–World War II Alexandria, Egypt. In it is a dazzling array of émigrés, cabbalists, philosophers, diplomats, spies, decadents, Muslims, Copts, and closet Zionists. (The gorgeous Justine ultimately leaves a trail of lovers in Alexandria for a kibbutz in Palestine.) Durrell dispels stereotypes because his eye is keen, his ear tuned, and his nose inundated — not with the undifferentiated stink that Uris will identify with the Arabs of Palestine — but with real, specific odors of saffron, incense, tobacco, myrrh, as well as dung and sweat. Nothing is one in Durrell; all are many, and people are as labyrinthine as the four novels' interlapping affairs and intrigue. Here is Durrell's description of the summer home of Nessim, the Egyptian Copt and husband of Justine:

Here the Bedouin, overtaken by the involuntary hunger for greenness which lies at the heart of all desert-lovers, had planted a palm and a fig whose roots had taken a firm, subterranean grip upon the sandstone from which the pure water ran. Resting with the horses in the shade of these young trees, Nessim's eyes had dwelt with wonder upon the distant view of the old Arab fort and the long-drawn white scar of the empty beach where the waves pounded night and day.

This is sumptuous writing, blessed with the gift of telling metaphor (that beach is a "white scar"). Here the Bedouin is not a shiftless marauder but someone who actually plants. It had to help that Durrell lived in Egypt for a number of years, as a diplomat and teacher, and that he would come to know the dreams of bedouins.

The avoidance of stereotyping is not just a matter of grinding a single scene to imaginative powder. Durrell gives us street scenes in Alexandria in which the attitude toward existence is salubrious in itself. In one such scene in *Clea*, the last of the four novels, Durrell sees not only fruit, but the brilliant-colored papers underneath it. The skin of Ethiopians isn't "black," but "plum-blue." Chaos and terrorism are not in Lebanese eyes, but their skin is "pewter" in cast. Specificity — and a keen eye — combats the stereotype.

So much for verisimilitude and imagination in Saroyan and Durrell. Let us move on to *Exodus*.

Leon Uris' 599-page novel published first by Doubleday in 1958 and then by Bantam, *Exodus* is in its ninetieth printing. By the eve of the June War in 1967, it had sold twenty million copies worldwide. It has been translated into fifty languages and, along with *Gone With the Wind*, has been considered one of the most successful bestsellers of all time. No other book has so influenced Americans on an issue of foreign policy: with at least ten million copies sold in the United States alone, one American in thirty has read *Exodus*. It could be called foreign policy's *Uncle Tom's Cabin*, though the Arab character it presumes to describe is more debased then the docile Uncle Tom of the nineteenth-century abolitionist novel by Harriet Beecher Stowe.

Uris stereotypes in two directions: he elevates the Israeli to a Superman but portrays Arabs as filthy, cowardly, and cutthroat. Indeed, it would not be an exaggeration to say that *Exodus* set a pattern in the stereotyping of the Arab that became a blueprint from which fiction writers continued to draw.

Kitty Fremont is the central character of the novel, an American nurse who has lost her husband and child to war and disease and who is wounded internally, searching for a sense of belonging. It was ingenious of Uris to pick Kitty as the central character through which he provides "insights" and his own version of history. Sympathy is achieved not only through an Israeli, but an American WASP. Thus American goyim were drawn into the story.

Though at first skeptical of the fighting spirit of the Jewish irregulars in Palestine, Kitty falls in love with Ari Ben Canaan, a smuggler of refugees and the captain of the *Exodus*, a boat that successfully runs the British blockade of Palestine. In fact, at novel's end, Kitty has become so transformed that she refers to the indigenous population as "a quarter of a million kill-crazy Arabs at your throats." (The narrator himself uses virtually the same phrase at another time, stealing from his own character!)

The only developed Arab characters are Kammal and his son, Taha, of the fictitious village of Abu Yesha. Kammal is a nice guy who cooperates with the Jews before they become armed as the Haganah and Irgun. His son, a boyhood friend of Ari, becomes by the end a typical, lust-filled Arab whose apparent patriotism is undercut when he froths at the mouth for Jordana, a red-haired *sabra*, demanding she come to his bed or else Abu Yesha will resist the Jewish fighters. In short, there is not one Arab Palestinian (and the word "Palestinian" is used almost exclusively to refer to Jewish occupants) even remotely sympathetic.

Uris says in his dedication that "scenes are created around historical incidents" and, in his very imitable style, admits that figures like Churchill, Truman, and Pearson appear. However, Uris manipulates the line between fiction and fact for his own purposes. For instance, Arab historical figures earmarked as fanatics and bunglers—such as al-Hajj Amin al-Husayni or Fawzi Qawaqji—are referred to often, and hate-filled words are put into their mouths. Because they are historical figures, we are led to believe these phrases are "on the record." But which are and which are not? It is virtually impossible to tell, though it is hard to believe Qawaqji would have said, of a Jewish settlement: "You will lay open Gan Dafna. You will level it to the ground and you will wash your hands in their blood or I will set your carcass out for the vultures."

The rub is this. Historical figures on the Israeli side who would not have served Uris' purpose—such as Menahem Begin, who led the terrorist Irgun, or Yitzhak Rabin, whose memoirs document the forced eviction of tens of thousands of Arab residents of Lydda and Ramlah—are absent or heavily disguised and quickly dismissed with fictitious names.

The same dishonesty occurs with events. There are pages of exaggerated detail on the Arab-Jewish riots of 1921 and 1929. In the entire book, only one paragraph is devoted to Dayr Yasin, where 254 civilian Arabs were massacred by the Irgun. Uris does not even give Dayr Yasin its name. On page 523 of the novel, the massacre becomes Neve Sadij and it is dismissed as a "strange and inexplicable series of events." Begin himself was not so circumspect when he detailed the auspicious effects of the deed in his autobiography, *The Revolt*.

This twisting of fiction around fact and the de-emphasizing or elimi-nation of unsavory fact is mentioned here not to dispel the notion that compelling fiction can be written around historic events, such as E.L. Doctorow's *Ragtime*, but to suggest that with ongoing tragedies, such as the Middle East crisis, in which enormous stakes hang in the balance, the distortion of political fact in fiction is dangerous at best and at worst, a kind of literary crime. It is all right for Doctorow to play around with what F.D.R. might have said during the Depression. Such a crisis and its real actors are long gone into the realm of metaphor. But not so the Middle East crisis. Uris' distortions have the force, not of understanding or even of a glaring light, but of a novelistic incendiary bomb.

Early in the book, a British brigadier talks about "Arab sellouts" and Arab collusion with Germany during World War II. The connection between Arab and Nazi is made often by Uris. Later the narrator men-tions that "Farouk was thrown out of Egypt by a clique of militarists who spoke the pages of an Arab *Mein Kampf*. Intrigue and murder, the old Arab game, raged at full force." Gamal 'Abd al-Nasir, the champion of Arab nationalism, "inflamed the Arab world like a would-be Hitler."

The myth that might makes not only right, but Jewish identity, is exploited fully by Uris. An American Jew who is helping run refugees to Palestine says to Kitty, "Let me tell you, kid. Every time the Palmach blows up a British depot or knocks the hell out of some Arabs he's winning respect for us." American Jews such as Albert Einstein, Hannah Arendt, Nahum Goldmann — not to mention the eminent Israeli theolo-gian, Martin Buber — would not have agreed, but theirs was not a per-spective Uris sought.

Uris' disdain for the Arabs is demonstrated in his descriptions of their surroundings. Abu Yesha has a "road filled with camel and donkey excrement. A lazy dog lay motionless in the waters of the open sewer to sun himself . . . The air was foul with the mixed aromas of thick coffee, tobacco, hashish smoke and the vile odors of the rest of the village." For the Bedouin, Uris reserves the appellation, "the dregs of humanity." Ari Ben Canaan warns Kitty, who is visiting a bedouin encampment, about eating the food: "You can throw up later." He goes on, "Unwashed fruits were served, and the meal was ended with thick, sickeningly sweet coffee in cups so filthy they were crusted."

Other Arab stereotypes Uris uses include: the Arabs never ask a direct question; they steal; an Arab only understands the fist; he is a double-dealer by nature; and Bedouin are murderers. One extraordinary Urisism occurs after two pages of diatribe in which Arabs are seen as compassionless, cruel to one another, mistrustful of all outsiders, and stirred to religious hysteria by the least provocation. Jossi Rabinsky is then said to have become "fascinated with the many-sided Arab character." The many sides are curiously monolithic.

Part of a speech about refugees spoken by Barak Ben Canaan has appeared in propaganda of the Israeli lobby through the years:

> If the Arabs of Palestine loved their land, they could not have been forced from it—much less run from it without real cause. The Arabs had little to live for, much less to fight for. This is not the reaction of a man who loves his land . . . The Arabs tell the world that the State of Israel has expansionist ideas. Exactly how a nation of less than a million people can expand against fifty million is an interesting question . . . Israel today stands as the single instrument for bringing the Arab people out of the Dark Ages.

Bringing the Arabs out of the "Dark Ages" is certainly a loaded statement; as for the "question" of expansionism, the intervening years have answered it.

One would have hoped that twenty-six years would have sobered Uris. Unfortunately, *The Haj*, which in 1985 became a paperback bestseller, was more biased than *Exodus*. Told from the point of view of a Muslim Arab named Ishmael, it is not only arrogant; it is absurd. *Moby Dick*'s hero is called Ishmael, a Hebrew name. The Arabic equivalent is Isma'il. But for Uris, it is Ishmael, son of Hagar, whose father, Ibrahim, is stupid, murderous, and an adulterer. "I am Ishmael," the protagonist announces at the outset, a pretentious allusion to Melville's classic—and more subtle—opening line, "Call me Ishmael."

"I was born in Palestine during the riots of 1936," says Ishmael in *The Haj*. Uris dismisses as "riots" what for Palestinians was a serious three-year resistance movement (1936–39), which included a six-month nonviolent general strike. Ishmael croaks an explanation that is supposed to cover Uris' narrative liberties (and distortions of history):

"Other events happened here when I was not present. Aha! How could I know of these? Do not forget, my esteemed reader, that we Arabs are unusually gifted in matters of fantasy and magic. Did we not give the world *A Thousand and One Arabian Nights*?" In *Exodus*, Uris bewailed the Arab lack of imagination; in *The Haj*, Arabs are guilty of too much imagination. There is certainly little of the innocence and saving grace of Sheherazade here, though she was a Persian queen and the *1001 Nights* of Persian, not Arab, origin.

In *The Haj*, the women are scorned and the men hostile. In an extremely tasteless scene, Uris has Ishmael's mother fondling his genitals while she listens to her husband make love to another wife in the next room. Polygamy is harped on, and Arab men are portrayed as patently unaffectionate toward their children.

The novel ends with the 1967 June War; subsequent history, no doubt, would not have served the author's purpose, though it is not unlikely that Uris would have found a way to turn the occupation of the West Bank and Gaza, the annexation of the Golan Heights and East Jerusalem, and the invasion of Lebanon into rapturous events. In the finale, an Arab doctor, Mudhil, gives this assessment to Ishmael after his father, the hajj, has died:

> We do not have leave to love one another and we have long ago lost the ability. It was so written twelve hundred years earlier. Hate is our overpowering legacy and we have regenerated ourselves by hatred from decade to decade, generation to generation, century to century. The return of the Jews has unleashed that hatred, exploding wildly, aimlessly, into a massive force of self-destruction. In ten, twenty, thirty years the world of Islam will begin to consume itself in madness. We cannot live with ourselves . . . we never have. We are incapable of change.

It might be compelling — if darkly pessimistic — if the "we" here referred to "humanity." But it refers, of course, only to Arabs.

Interestingly, both *Exodus* and *The Haj* were panned as polemics in major reviews; but judging by sales, it may be that the distortion of the Arab in fiction is one case in which bad reviews do not matter. What Uris emblazoned in royalty gold from his two novels about the Middle East has become commonplace in American fiction: the Arab as villain, subhuman, incapable of change, and even bent on the destruction of the world. These themes may be found in dozens of spy thrillers that utilize "the Arab terrorist," in adventure stories and tours de force set in ancient times in the Holy Land, in tales of high finance and oil blackmail, and, finally, in novels that have little or nothing to do with the Middle East. Some of these books are contrived, some feasible, but all utilize the convenient "ugly Arab" as a representative of the forces of darkness.

Sometimes the subject matter is clear from the paperback covers. *Kamal* by D. W. Arathorn, for instance, sports a hairy arm holding a machine gun. *The Gaza Intercept*, subtitled, "A novel about the Arab plan to explode an atomic device above Tel Aviv," by E. Howard Hunt (of Watergate fame), shows a dagger stabbing a Star of David, with a falling drop of blood. Others are not so blatant. *Triple*, another runaway bestseller by Ken Follett, gives little away on its cover, though by page six we are already getting the Arab-Nazi connection: "The Arabs are murdering you people our there. Jeez, Nat, you only just escaped from the Germans!"

Kamal (1982), called by the *Kansas City Star* "a first-class novel," like *The Haj*, is told from the point of view of an Arab. (This became a new wave—letting the Arab himself do the stereotyping.) The book is about an Arab American named Kamal Jibral (read: Jibril, the surname of the leader of a radical, anti-Arafat splinter group). According to the jacket blurb, Kamal "is poisoned by his father's litany of hatred against those who took his homeland. Intoxicated with the violent romance of killing." He describes himself: "How does a Kamal Jibral with a scimitar nose like this one, and these lethal cheekbones which make the eyes seem like bats peering out of caves . . . how does he come to be carrying an American passport? Let me tell you." Arathorn does.

As for *The Gaza Intercept* (1981), the dialogue is filled with such jewels as this:

> "The Cairo nursery bombing."
> I felt my throat tighten. "Seventy-two kids."
> "*Ach du lieber, ja?*"
> "*Ja mit spades.* Al-Karmal. Aside from killing kids, do they have a program?"

The Nazi-Arab connection, reinforced by the accents, stands an historical atrocity on its head. Hunt's "they" refers to the PLO, but the only factual events that come close to this description are either the sabotage of British and American installations in Cairo in 1954 or the bombing of an Egyptian schoolhouse at Bahr al-Baqr in 1970 that killed forty-six children. Both were done by Israel.

The long-running bestseller *Shibumi* (1979), by Trevanian (who, if he is an Armenian, should really know better), contains one of the more unlikely stereotypes. The book is about a superhero survivor of Hiroshima and arch-secret agent pulled out of semi-retirement to track down the Palestinians who killed the Israeli Olympians in 1972 in Munich. During a meeting of secret agents at the CIA, an Arab is brought in "whose Western clothes were dark, expensive and ill-fitting. The shabby look was not his tailor's fault; the Arab's body was not designed for clothes requiring posture and discipline." The premise is that the Arab's body, by nature, is not like *our* bodies.

In one scene, the hero is told by a Basque raconteur: "One must confess that the British are bungling, the Italians incompetent, the Americans neurotic, the Germans romantically savage, the Arabs vicious, the Russians barbaric, and the Dutch make cheese." There is no mistaking that in Trevanian's Great Chain of Being, the Arabs and Russians are the lowest of the low.

In 1973, the year of the October War, the popular spy writer Eric Ambler, considered a cut above the norm in technique, wrote *The Levanter*. Its subtitle on the cover reads: "The explosive thriller about *the* Arab terrorist underground." In a discussion between two Americans concerning a Palestinian radical named Ghaled, one of them insists, "They're all far-out fanatics. By hatred out of illusion, the lot of them. They have to be. They couldn't survive otherwise." The other retorts, "No moderates at all? What about Yasir Arafat?" The response: "He isn't a guerrilla, he's a politician. He's against Palestinians killing Palestinians instead of Israelis. If he ever so much as hinted that a peaceful settlement with Israel might someday be possible, he'd have his throat cut within the hour." I can't resist the aside — thirty years later, after the real Arafat recognized Israel repeatedly, signed the Oslo peace accords, and shook hands with Rabin at the White House, it was Rabin who was assassinated by one of his own; Arafat died of natural causes in a hospital in Paris.

Many of these novels were and are made into blockbuster movies. Otto Preminger actually found *Exodus* so "anti-British and anti-Arab" that he failed to reproduce some of the novel's most offensive scenes, which made Uris disown the film. Another classic example is *Black Sunday* (1975) by Thomas Harris, in which an Arab terrorist gang hijacks the Goodyear blimp and fills it with explosives before trying to land it on the field of the Super Bowl. Football, nutty Arabs, Goodyear blimps: surely this is the stuff of which millions are made. In *Black Sunday*, a theme recurrent in recent spy novels appears: the Arabs will not compromise and are out for some kind of final Holocaust. Arabs thereby take the place of Nazis in Jewish nightmares. About the commander of Black September named Najeer, it is said: "The restoration of Palestine to the Arabs would not have elated him. He believed in Holocaust, the fire that purifies."

Probably only two spy novels since World War II show a glimmer of humaneness in their Arab characters, and they are both written by British authors: *Saladin!* (1976) by Anthony Osmond and *The Little Drummer Girl* (1983) by John le Carré. Le Carré was blasted in some circles as being sympathetic to the Palestinians, though most agree he is an excellent prose stylist and the premier spy writer of his time. What B'nai B'rith and others objected to, it must be suspected, was more what le Carré did than what he wrote. Just before the 1982 Israeli invasion of Lebanon, the author visited Beirut, met with Yasir Arafat, and toured the refugee camps. During the siege of Beirut that summer, le Carré wrote a stinging condemnation that reached American newspapers. He may also have committed the unpardonable sin of sympathetically portraying Palestinian life in the camps.

However, it would be going too far to claim that *The Little Drummer Girl* is biased toward the Arab side. The book's central character, a sexually loose, extremely gullible British actress named Charlie, is hardly as vivacious and strong as Kitty in *Exodus*. Charlie gets caught up in a schizophrenic jostle between the spy games of both Israeli and Palestinian agents. The only Arab character given real attention in the book (there are at least three thoroughly developed Israelis) is a shadowy terrorist named Khalid who apparently belongs to an Abu Nidal–type group that attacks both Jewish synagogues and Arab moderates. This is certainly a far cry from the mainstream Palestinian disposition, though after the betrayals of Oslo, the 2005 ascension to rule of the Palestinian Authority by Hamas, which condones suicide bombings against civilians, was extremely troubling. (Hamas was later unseated in the West Bank by the mainstream Fatah party, but remains in power in Gaza).

After spy thrillers, the second group of novels that stereotype the Arabs is comprised of the historical tours de force and adventure stories, a category Uris' books fit into. Examples of biblical forays include *The*

Tenth Measure (1980), subtitled "An Epic Novel of Love and Heroism in Ancient Judea," by Brenda Lesley Segal; *The Books of Rachel* (1979) by Joel Gross; and *The Source* (1967) by James Michener. Segal's novel deals with mass suicide of Jewish zealots at Masada. Gross' book traces Jewish history through the ages via a succession of Rachels. *The Source* is a massive explication of the same history by means of examining the findings from various eras through an archaeological dig.

Michener's immensely popular 1,088-page epic came out just before the June War, in which Israel invaded Egypt, Syria, and the West Bank. The book — which topped the bestseller charts for a year — gives expansive treatment to the historic Jewish presence in ancient and medieval Palestine, blurring whatever rights the last thousand years might have conferred on resident Palestinian Arabs.

A "decent" Arab or two pops up in Michener's thick tome. The Islamic era is afforded about fifty pages, in which two Arabs are presented: Abu Zeid, who whispers "like the utterances of a serpent," and Abd Umar, whose marked compassion for the Jews is rather offset by his summary decapitation of a pagan.

A pleasant "boy Friday" Arab, Jamail Tabari, appears occasionally in the book as an innocuous guide of the archeological dig. By the time he surfaces for a not unsympathetic tête-à-tête with Ila Eliav, the Israeli dig director, concerning the fate of Arab refugees, the reader has been bombarded for a thousand pages with a point of view so overwhelming in detail — and even reverence — there is no refuting it. Whatever misgivings Michener may have about the rigidity of Orthodox Judaism in contemporary society or the bad treatment of Arab refugees, they do not prevent him from twisting certain facts in a way reminiscent of Uris: "In 1948, against every plea of the Jews, some six hundred thousand Arabs evacuated this country. They did so at the urging of their political leaders."

The last page of *The Source* has Eliav squashing metaphysical troubles brought on by his debate with Tabari into an obliterating reverie that tells him "no religion defended so tenaciously the ordinary dignity of living" as did Judaism. As for Tabari, he will, in his own words, "always be an Arab," and the reader watches him turn away, abandon the dig, and presumably take up the life of Arabs, that is, rejection of compromise.

Refiner's Fire (1977) by Mark Helprin is an interesting example of an adventure and search-for-identity story that contains a few shadowy Arabs written by a highly praised present-day novelist. The story centers on a timeless American hero named Marshall Pearl, who is born and quickly orphaned on a refugee ship to Palestine. Pearl grows up in New York City, adventures in the Rockies and the Alps, and gives up skiing to seek "roots" by enlisting in the Israeli Defense Forces to fight Arabs in the 1973 War. The novel ends in an encounter with some anonymous Syrian soldiers on the Golan Heights.

Pearl ruminates at one point with the contradictory thinking typical of the Israeli Labor party: "Since the tenth of June, 1967, he had been firmly against the occupation of Gaza or the populated West Bank. He understood the hateful stares. But he felt the strong acid of his own imperative . . . 'To hell with them. To hell with them,' he muttered. 'Survival is moral. In itself alone it is right.'" Thus the heroic Marshall Pearl gains sympathy for an all-or-nothing, them-or-us attitude.

The third type of novel that engages in Arab stereotyping is that of international intrigue and finance, such as *On the Brink* (1977) by Benjamin and Herbert Stein. The plot of *On the Brink* deals with devious Arab and Iranian members of OPEC who seek revenge on the West by increasing petroleum prices. One exuberant OPEC member mouths these sentiments: "Does this mean that the Zionist racist swine are going to be thrown into the sea?"

As for the last collection of novels in which the malevolent Arab pops up — those which have nothing to do with the Middle East at all — the list is endless. Any randomly selected novel written since World War II — serious or not — may evidence the stereotype. Works by three authors — Herbert Green, Saul Bellow, and Joan Didion — widely divergent in theme, style, and quality will be examined here. The latter two, of course, are counted among the premier authors of prose fiction in America.

Karpov's Brain (1984) by Herbert Green deals with the KGB and Jewish dissidents in the Soviet Union. As early as page two, we find the first (and I believe last) cut at the Arabs in the thoughts of one character named Malik: "Why not let all kikes out? The whole stinking crowd. Open the gates, load them on trains and planes, let them crawl or swim to their Zionist desert. And let the Arabs finish them off."

On the other end of the quality spectrum is the Nobel Prize–winning author, Saul Bellow. A masterful stylist, Bellow was an important ruminator on and celebrator of our agonized, dizzy age. Yet on the Middle East, he revealed some biases. In his nonfiction work, *To Jerusalem and Back*, he notes, "Such injustices as have been committed against the

Arabs can be more readily justified by Judaism, by the whole of Jewish history, than by Zionism alone." He urges the Arabs to accommodate "the trifling occupancy" of Israel.

Bellow takes a veiled swipe at the Arabs in the book that won him the Nobel Prize, *Humboldt's Gift* (1975). The novel concerns a successful Jewish intellectual's debt to a poet friend, Von Humboldt Fleisher, whose life took a tailspin and ended in suicide. Despite the fact that the story has nothing to do with the Middle East or the Arabs, on page thirty-two Charlie Citrine, the narrator, jokes about a wandering university colleague with Humboldt: "Damascus! Among those Arabs he'll be the Sheik of Apathy." We are meant, of course, to see the professor, Sewell, as a lazy bum and the quip elicits a laugh. But the implication is that Sewell will thrive in his post in Damascus because there is favor among the Arabs for those who are apathetic.

Finally, there is Joan Didion's *A Book of Common Prayer* (1977). The novel deals with Central America and a woman caught between the opposing styles of a first and second husband. In one short exchange between Warren, the charming dissolute, and Leonard, the activist lawyer, Didion smartly puts the stereotype into stark relief: "How exactly did this creature come to your attention, Leonard? He rape an Arab? Or is that possible? Actually I believe that's a solecism. Raping an Arab." Leonard returns, "You've had that Arab in the wings, I can tell by your delivery."

Thank God for the intelligence of Joan Didion. One might ask at this point: are there *no* American novelists besides Didion since World War II who have avoided stereotyping by trying to evoke a broader, deeper view of the Middle East and the Arabs, writers who in a sense have heeded Didion's warning? Up until the nineties, and the groundbreaking work of Mona Simpson and Diana Abu-Jaber, this writer found only four authors and six books, none of which are in print. *The Heart of the Dog* (1972) by Thomas Roberts sympathetically portrays the case for Palestinian self-determination, but was limited to one hardcover printing by Random House. *Discovery!*, a short novel set in 1933 Saudi Arabia, by Wallace Stegner, was published by a press so obscure (Export Books) that the publishing date is not mentioned. One may ask why so esteemed an American novelist as Wallace Stegner had to resort to this publisher.

The other novelists who combated the stereotype in significant literary isolation were two lonely Arab American peace warriors, Vance

Bourjaily and Samuel Hazo. I have written extensively about both in an essay on the Arab American novel, and will treat each only briefly here.

Though he never enjoyed stunning commercial success, Vance Bourjaily was one of the heralded authors who came out of World War II. The acceptance of his first novel, *The End of My Life* (1947), was one of the last acts of the legendary Scribners editor of Hemingway and Fitzgerald, Maxwell Perkins. Jack Aldridge praised it in his own landmark book, *After the Lost Generation* (1951): "No book since *This Side of Paradise* has caught so well the flavor of youth in wartime, and no book since *A Farewell to Arms* has contained so complete a record of the loss of that youth in war."

The End of My Life is about an ambulance driver during World War II stationed in Beirut and later, Ba'labakk. The hero, Skinner Galt, is not of Arab descent, nor are any of his friends (though his best friend, Benny, is of Jewish descent). It is puzzling that Bourjaily would not feel compelled, as did other novelists coming of age at the time, such as Bellow, Malamud, Mailer, and Shaw, to write from his own ethnic vantage point, though he did once indicate that not having grown up in an Arab American colony precluded a deep interest. He did, however, include penetrating, non-patronizing, but humanized portraits of the Arabs in Beirut: "The Arabic-speaking people are warm people, with a long tradition of hospitality. They offer enmity where enmity is offered them; they respond to friendliness with friendliness; they are, except when angered, or when one tampers with their customs or ceremonies, humorous, humble and wise."

One of Skinner's fellow ambulance drivers, Rod, an itinerant jazz player in the United States, hears Arab fluting one night and succeeds, amid a crowd of Arabs in the street, in playing the flute himself:

"Salaam i-ehdik," said the old man.

And Rod, who couldn't have known what it meant but could sense that it was a high compliment, returned it to him: "Salaam i-ehdik." Later, they learned its meaning: Blessed be your hands.

Bourjaily does not romanticize. He calls the "tough part" of Beirut, its southern, mostly Muslim section, "Hell's Kitchen, the Lower East Side, the heart of the city," and admits rumors of gruesome muggings there. Although there is no single fully developed Arab character in the book, the milieu is faithfully described. Like Saroyan, Bourjaily has no ax to grind. *The End of My Life* is about the loss of innocence and the foreboding sense of a world gone mad.

Bourjaily did not return to writing about the Middle East until his fourth novel, *Confessions of a Spent Youth* (1960, rereleased in 1986). Here the hero, Quincy, is part Lebanese and visits his ancestral village of Kabb Elias in the mountains of Lebanon. The hero's grandmother, Nafi, is portrayed as a wonderful, earthy, and profound character. But Quincy is alienated—by America, his dual identity, and his sophisticated philosophic quandaries—from the homespun wisdom of Kabb Elias. It is, to the best of this writer's knowledge, the only American literary novel published since Amin Rihani's *The Book of Khalid* in 1911 with a non-stereotyped Arab American main character until Mona Simpson's *The Lost Father* and Diana Abu-Jaber's *Arabian Jazz*, both of which appeared in 1993—a thirty-three-year gap from Bourjaily and eighty-two years from Rihani.

It is not easy to classify poet Samuel Hazo's *The Very Fall of the Sun* (1978); because it is so drained of particulars, its relation to the Middle East is purely allegorical. Hazo's novel suggests the archetypal world of the guerrilla. In a kind of extended Socratic dialogue, it pits a vacationing American couple against a very intelligent and angry guerrilla-terrorist who has kidnapped them. The setting is not specified. It is tropical, southern, and could as easily be El Salvador as Lebanon. The nationality of Melchior, the guerrilla, is not specified. Melchior does allude to Tammuz (an ancient Babylonian mythical figure) and the American husband, Constantine, seems named to suggest penetration of the Arab world by the Christian West. But why all the subterfuge? Why not identify the place, the people? In an interview, Hazo said that he purposely removed particulars to effect a timeless debate between an American and a Third World revolutionary. Nevertheless, when Michener or Bellow wanted to evoke universal empathy for the struggles of the Jewish people, neither felt it necessary to avoid the "ethnic" specifics. And neither did Roth, Malamud, or Singer.

Published with a short life as a paperback by Popular Library, the film advertised as forthcoming on the cover never materialized. Perhaps *The Very Fall of the Sun*'s analogue to the plight of West Bank Palestinians was too close for Hollywood's comfort.

We come now to some final questions. How did a national literature participate—consciously or not—in the vilification of an entire people, a complete culture? And, most importantly, what can be done, in fact is beginning to be done, to address the situation?

First, the post–World War II novelists produced works that embodied a centuries-old Western attitude: that the Orient (and the Near East) is an alien, exotic realm inhabited by essentially subhuman figures who are to be analyzed, erotically enjoyed, then subjugated. Joseph Massad, in his recent virtuoso study, *Desiring Arabs*, elaborates on the sexual component. From the Near East, Western writers as various as Chateaubriand, Flaubert, and Paul Bowles sought not the just truth, but titillation. As Edward Said showed in *Orientalism*, the West has refused to see the East as it *is* and reduced it to a condition of subservience, pathos, and cultural backwater. It must be remembered that it was a novel — *Altneuland* by Theodor Hertel — that proposed to "redeem" Palestine through the utopian vision of Zionism. Authors from the powerful European states tended to ratify the conclusions reached by their government field offices that the Orient needed civilizing, Western discipline. George Orwell and Joseph Conrad were virtually alone in expressing reservations.

Second, America's insularity and isolationism increased the distortions wrought by orientalism. Though American Protestant missionaries proselytized in the Levant in the nineteenth century, the contact of American writers with the Middle East was about as limited as U.S. involvement was. Mark Twain's account of his tour of the Near East in 1869 that became *Innocents Aboard* was a somewhat humorous exception, though to Twain "Palestine sits in sackcloth and ashes . . . desolate and unlovely." What did Westerners seek in the Holy Land? Anything shy of milk, honey, and a golden-hued salvation seems to have thrust them in the other direction entirely. Certainly the simple beauty of olive groves and the Ramallah hills didn't do it for Twain. As the Palestinian diarist Raja Shehadeh notes in his exceptional *Palestinian Walks*: "It is as though once travelers took the arduous trip to Palestine and did not find what they were seeking, the land as it existed in their imagination, they took a strong aversion to what they found."

Prior to 1948, limited American contact came with the discovery of oil in the Gulf in the early 1930s and in the North African theater against Rommel. The first real "splash" of American foreign policy in the Middle East accompanied the creation of the state of Israel in 1948.

Third, American fiction has shown a predilection for the underdog, the outsider, the waif who seeks to transform himself and the world. The establishment of the state of Israel came on a wave of extraordinary American sympathy for the plight of Jewish refugees fleeing the atrocities of Nazi Germany. Many of the best post–World War II American novelists were Jewish — Bellow, Mailer, Shaw, Roth, Malamud, Singer. Though it would be wrong to conclude that these authors had identical views on Israel (Roth, for one, showed subtle, satiric doubt in *The Counterlife*), most were enthusiastically Zionist and wrote tortured, compelling fiction on the legacy of the Holocaust. A unique literary-political convergence occurred: criticism of the Nazis' heinous crimes came to mean unquestioned support for the new state of Israel. The spell was cast not only on Bellow et al., but on William Styron, Walker Percy, and many others who took the Jewish experience in the Diaspora as *the* metaphor for modern man's rootlessness and helplessness. That Palestinian disenfranchisement might be as valid a metaphor did not — and could not — occur to them.

Fourth, because Israel was assumed to be errorless and noble (and nothing U.S. policymakers did qualified this stance), the Arab world in which it was implanted came to be regarded as an enemy. The Arabs were painted as aggressors; the 1967 war was seen as an American victory (Ronald Reagan toasted it as governor in Sacramento at the time), and Arafat was viewed as an embodiment of evil. Unless an American author were to plant himself for an extended period of time in a Palestinian camp, an Arab capital, or an Arab American community, he would have no way of viewing events except through the prevailing American prism.

Fifth, stereotyping in fiction increased incrementally after the October War in 1973, largely due to the Arab oil boycott. It was bad enough that the Arabs would not lie down and accept Israel's fait accompli in Palestine. But that they finally chose to "sting" the West by withdrawing their oil was a final straw of sorts. America was wounded in its all-important gas tank, and whatever legitimate concerns the Arabs might have had were taken as inherently illegitimate. The isolated cases of Palestinian hijackings in the early 1970s and mid-1980s added a new plot to the old story of the bad Arab, and of course the onset of suicide bombing in the late 1990s and the 2000s only confirmed the stereotypers in their worst assumptions. Few took time to try to understand the anger and desperation that led some guerillas and family victims of Israeli terror to terrorism themselves. Novelists who want to sell — and few do not — could not help but read in this sequence of events that portrayals of Arabs as thugs and blackmailers sold far better than portrayals of the idealism, frustration, and struggles of the downtrodden and humiliated.

Finally, a natural pool of novelistic experience that could have helped correct the situation — namely, Arab American authors — has been, at least until very recently, too small and too easily dismissed by the publishing powers-that-be. Though their numbers are growing, few Arab Americans have pursued the literary arts, partly because of encouragement in other directions from entrepreneurial parents and partly because of the community-wide perception that there is no future — financial or otherwise — in the arts. On Arab American topics, there is some truth to this, given the repressive publishing climate. Though multiculturalism has been in vogue for a while — and we have seen everything from *Roots* to *The Joy Luck Club* — Arab American ethnicity has never been popular and has had to struggle to be included in the multicultural canon. It's instructive both of the abyss from which we came and the ongoing rough waters once we do land on a sandbar that after one of my poems appeared in the *Norton Introduction to Poetry* ("Arab and Jew in Alaska") in 1995 — a first, I believe, for the community in that estimable anthology — it was deleted in the next edition.

The one highly successful author of Arab descent, William Peter Blatty, has never had an Arab or Arab American protagonist in a novel. Though his multi-million dollar hit, *The Exorcist*, has an initial chapter set in Iraq, the book is about demonic possession. Blatty has written some funny, sentimental books of reminiscence about his Lebanese mother, but these are not fiction. In fact, in Blatty's one novel that does deal with the Middle East, *John Goldfarb, Please Come Home*, the protagonist is a Jewish pilot.

How, then, can the rampant stereotyping of the Arab in American fiction be averted?

First, American authors must begin to familiarize themselves with the Arab Middle East in a firsthand manner. It will not do to visit Tel Aviv for two weeks and then write a novel about Arab terrorism. Likewise, it will not do for a lecturer to land in Dhahran, Saudi Arabia, and then speed home thousands of dollars richer after glimpsing a superhighway in the desert from the American compound. We need authors with the lust for experience and hunger for humanity that compelled Lawrence Durrell to live some years in Alexandria; we need authors to live in Cairo, Nablus, and Damascus. (On this account our journalists may have a better start than our so-called serious novelists; witness the interesting novels by *Newsweek* Middle East Bureau chief Christopher Dickey and the *Washington Post's* David Ignatius.) Living in Israel — at least outside the grip of "official" sinecure or lobbyist trip — wouldn't hurt, either. It's a fact that far more trustworthy and deeply moving fiction is being written (and published) by Israelis about the Israel-Palestine tragedy (David Grossman, A.B. Yehoshua, for example) than by Americans.

Second, Arab American authors must become more confident and assertive of their point of view. At the same time, the Arab American community should encourage the study of literature and the arts — not a hopeful prospect in a culture turning away from literature and toward CDs and iPods.

There's preliminary indication, post–9/11, of some progress on both these fronts. On the latter issue, second- and third-generation Arab Americans, less inclined to the back-breaking factory, restaurant, or other small business worlds of their parents, have been freed by that parental labor to study the arts. They are easier in the society, too, and less anxious about being critical. Likewise, the children of highly educated recent immigrants, growing up in the age of the Internet, are more cosmopolitan and confidently verbal than earlier voices. This, too, bends them towards the arts. I might also add that a publishing renaissance in the community in the past decade has supported native writers like no time since Gibran's circle in the twenties. The Minnesota literary journal *Mizna* is a superlative example.

Who are the exciting new voices publishing first novels since September 11, 2001? Interestingly, most are women. They include Laila Lalami, a Moroccan American; Mohja Kahf, a Syrian American; Alicia Erian, a Lebanese American; Laila Halaby, a Palestinian American; and the 2007 winner of the first ever Arab American Book Award for the Novel, Libyan American Hisham Matar.

In her tightly written, insightful first novel, *Hope and Other Dangerous Pursuits* (2005), Lalami gives us an unusual perspective on immigrants fleeing across a border for a better life; in this case, it's not the Rio Grande, but the slit of the Mediterranean separating Morocco from Spain. They follow the path of the Moorish conquest in 711 by Tariq ibn Ziyad, but this time "instead of a fleet, here we are in an inflatable boat — not just Moors, but a motley mix of people from ex-colonies, without guns or armor, without a charismatic leader." Lalami delves into the complex motives of people who want to leave Morocco; in the case of the teenage Noura, the author debunks our expectations. The girl isn't fleeing for more freedom in the West, but less — in suburban Rabat, she's turned into a Muslim fundamentalist and aroused the wrath of her thoroughly secular Moroccan father, who muses on the eve of her flight, "Why did she have to turn to religion? Perhaps it was his absences from home, his fondness for the drink, or maybe it was all the bribes he took. It could be any of these things. He was at fault somehow. Or it could be none of these things at all. In the end it didn't matter, he had lost her again . . ."

Mohja Kahf's spirited *The Girl in the Tangerine Scarf* is one of the first in-depth studies in fiction of the coming-of-age of a young Muslim woman in America. This picaresque bildungsroman, though perhaps fighting one too many intellectual battles directly rather than trusting its story, is still full of life, Arabic poetry and song, vivid character portrayals, emotional and cultural clashes across generations, races, communities, families. It's irreverent; when Khadra has her first period, she's allowed to break her Ramadan fast: " 'Periods rock,' she mumbled with her mouth full." There are gradations of Muslim experience in the New World. Take the wayward Mishawaka Muslims: "They did shocking things in the mosque, like play volleyball with men and women together *in shorts.*" The admixture of Islam and Indiana is a treat in itself. When Khadra's family goes to pray behind the Kokomo Dairy Queen, her father gives her a Navajo blanket for a prayer rug, leaving himself with none:

> "What if the ground is impure?" Khadra said, remembering Islamic school lessons: purity of place required for *salah.*
>
> "The earth itself I consider pure, *binti*," he said. "All the world is a prayer mat." Even central Indiana Dairy Queen backlots were okay with God . . . Rising, her father brushed off bits of gravel that had embedded in his forehead.

Alicia Erian explores, with hypnotic, darker hand, the exposures of a woman coming of age, reared by a divorced Arab father in Texas. In *Towelhead* (2006), the confused girl is sexually abused by a neighbor — again, new territory for an Arab American author and difficult for any writer. Laila Halaby takes on an embattled marriage in Arizona of an Arab American couple in *Once in a Promised Land* (2007), coping with the small and not-so-small nightmares of the post–9/11 world. As for Hisham Matar, his brilliant evocation of the world of a boy slowly drawn into the horrors of the totalitarian regime in Libya, *In the Country of*

Men (2006), was shortlisted for the Booker Prize. The boy Suleiman is intelligent, but open, exposed, believing, terribly honest with himself and us readers, but lacking J.D. Salinger's anti-hero cynicism. Suleiman is not an anti-hero. He is a human being in the act of being deformed even as he is being formed. A little classic in its growing sense of dread — the climax is a neighbor's hanging on television — and the agonizing beauty of the Mediterranean seashore, Mattar's dark tale of a boy discovering evil deserves a place alongside *A Separate Peace* and *David Copperfield*. It's that good.

Clearly, the attacks of September 11 shook the nation and the intelligentsia, too. Some saw all their feverish fears confirmed and got us to attack Iraq, a complete fiasco and a stupidly destructive diversion from the difficult task at hand. What was that task? Not just the apprehension of bin Laden and his minions, but the need to address the injustices of fifty years of American policy off-kilter in the Middle East, which fueled al-Qaeda — most especially, the Palestine tragedy, but also our support for repressive Arab regimes in lieu of addressing Palestine. They are, after all, of a piece. We bought off Egypt in the Egypt-Israel Peace Treaty with billions of dollars in aid, but delivered nothing to it concerning freedom for the West Bank and Gaza. That got Sadat assassinated; one of the conspirators was Ayman Zawahiri, the number-two man in al-Qaeda, who was tortured in a Cairo prison, the place, says Lawrence Wright, that al-Qaeda was born. With no answer to his population for Israel's continued repression, Mubarak faced the increasingly radicalized Muslim Brotherhood with an increasing repression of his own. This self-destructive pattern has occurred throughout the Middle East. And our complicity in it is barely recognized.

Part of our intelligentsia finally began to speak about these painful realities, perhaps still not entirely the mainstream, but a growing opposition force that has fueled the anti-Iraq war movement. These thinkers have linked up with feminist forces most sensitive to being on the outside of things, to begin this new wave of Arab American fiction.

But there's a sobering note: with the exception of Alicia Erian, none of the new writers treated above have been published by a major New York house. And this brings me to my third and final point about what can be done to destroy stereotyping of the Arab in fiction. The mainstream New York publishing world must become sensitized to the pervasiveness of the Arab stereotype and the deleterious effect it has on the image of our country in the world. New York publishers must quit playing to the mob (or, indeed, creating it) and act responsibly. They must begin to allow novelists to treat the two-ton gorilla in the room (i.e., Palestine) with verisimilitude and empathy. It's extremely troubling, for example, that Diana Abu-Jaber, who has published two breakthrough novels with Arab American protagonists in the past decade, has repeatedly been rebuffed in trying to publish a fiction manuscript dealing with Palestine. Evidently, there are breakthroughs and then there are breakthroughs. In circumscribing such important subject matter and supporting stereotypes in fiction about the Arab world, publishers encourage hatred. It could be stated in more delicate terms, but that is the state to which the current situation has devolved.

The answer is not, of course, the production of counter-polemics—novels that skewer the Israeli as a devil-on-earth. This is no more acceptable than is the Arab-as-devil. Nor is uncritical support for Arabs the answer. That an Arab *can* be a terrorist or lazy or stupid is of course possible, just as an Israeli can be a terrorist or lazy or stupid. The point is that realistic characters presented in human settings will run the gamut of human possibilities. If the novel is to be the "great book of life" D. H. Lawrence called it, then one addressing America's blindnesses in the Middle East and their human toll has yet to be published by the major presses of this country.

A gritty recent exception, published in Ballantine paperback in 2007, may be John Updike's *Terrorist*. Updike isn't entirely slumming; he showed interest in the image of the Arab in literature as early as thirty years ago, at a landmark conference at Georgetown University at which Edward Said gave a paper from which *Orientalism* emerged. But from the very first sentence ("*Devils*, Ahmad thinks"), we are thrust into one-dimensional anger so unrelenting in its hatred of America and its mores that Updike's stinging critique of society is nearly burned away in it. As much as we resist—and I resisted to the point that I wanted to throw the book away at several points—we are sucked into Ahmad Ashmawy's decrepit northern New Jersey world, his relationship with a cynical mentor at the local mosque, distaste for his loose, ex-hippie mother, and inevitable seduction by terrorists. Of course, the Arab father is absent—a staple of current fiction treating Arab Americans that seems appropriated from African American—or plain old American—stereotypical life to portray alienation.

Because Updike is such a striking stylist—a master of setting and character—the book holds despite the monochromatic self-stereotyping of its anti-hero. For some reason, we accept Ahmad's Jeremiad, trusting, hoping that Updike's humanity will not desert us. It doesn't. Though I have my doubts about how abruptly the conversion takes place—and how late in the narrative—the reversal is stunning. On his way to the Holland Tunnel with a truck loaded with explosives, Ahmad is startled to find his high school counselor, a lapsed Jew named Levy, flying into the cab. An electrifying discussion takes place as they move toward annihilation. Ahmad quotes a merciless passage towards Jews from the Koran; Levy responds:

> Yeah, well, there's a lot of repulsive and ridiculous stuff in the Torah, too. Plagues, massacres, straight from Yahweh to you. Tribes that weren't lucky enough to be chosen—put them under the ban, show them no mercy. They hadn't quite worked out Hell yet, that came with the Christians. Wise up—the priests try to control people through fear. Conjure up Hell—the oldest scare tactic in the world. Next to torture. Hell is torture, basically. You really can buy into all this? God as supreme torturer? God as the King of Genocide?

Feverishly, Ahmad recalls in the same *sura* that praises the afterlife, praise to the Creator, and feels the shock of recognition. Life is what God wills. The explosion halts. And Levy lives to tell his student, "You're a victim, Ahmad—a fall guy . . . You're cool under pressure. You talk well. In the years to come, Arab Americans are going to need plenty of lawyers."

But Updike is an exception (and it is plain unsettling that he waits until the very end of the novel to unseat the stereotype). New York will occasionally indulge in publishing a political critique of Israel (such as Meirsheimer's and Walt's landmark book, passed off unfairly and inaccurately as anti-Semitic and used as counterpropaganda), but quality fiction—that by definition deals with reality empathetically and acknowledges its many facets—is too often held back when it treats Arabs or Arab Americans. When conditions are such that it is considered dangerous to evoke reality—indeed, when it is effectively taboo to do so—a nation's literature is not free and is to a certain extent a lie.

Great literature emerged from our nineteenth-century crucible, the American Civil War—Crane's *The Red Badge of Courage*, Bierce's "An Occurrence at Owl Creek Bridge," Whitman's *Drum Taps*, to name a few. A literature of depth and tragedy emerged from our nightmare in Vietnam. Why must our literary output on the Middle East be so shallow? It was hard enough to deny our deep involvement in the region after the gratuitous shelling by the U.S.S. *New Jersey* of Druze villages in the Lebanese mountains, the questionable attack on Libya, the absurd clandestine arms transfers to Iran tipping the balance against Arab Iraq in that pitiless war, the Pavlovian tolerance of the worst Israeli behavior. But it's impossible to do so now, with several hundred thousand American troops scouring Iraq and Afghanistan for the elusive Fountain of Terror. How long can our literature continue to pancake what is so unwieldy and sorrowful?

The answer may ultimately lie in the realm of the individual artist. As I have indicated, some are Arab American, some with long journalistic observation of the region, and some, like Updike, just sensitive to the nerve endings of our country and our country's victims since 9/11. These are true artists, gifted with extraordinary perception and apperception; Shelley called the artist "an unacknowledged legislator" — the conscience of the human race. It is to that lonely explorer of the mysterious depths of the human soul in all its joys, sorrows, hates, and loves that the problem falls. Vision, humanity, and an honest pen — along with courageous publishers — may yet go where politicians fear to tread.

To Hope

Hope, I am standing outside the green door of the Warner Theatre waiting to see your face after ten years. I do not know if you will remember me, or if, remembering, you'll march off down E Street by yourself. Surely you must be tired—this *Fiddler on the Roof* is good and robust—and you are a most beautiful Tzeitel. Until tonight I never thought I'd see this classic. Until two weeks ago you were a faded memory of a lively Jewish girl lodged back in the "college" section of the brain. I was called "The Arab."

I went to the Democratic National Convention in New York City to argue our side of the Middle East crisis with the Democrats, people of supposedly tender consciences. After day-in, day-out discussions with people who wondered what anyone of Arab heritage could possibly want of the Democrats, and weary from speaking of cluster bombs, settlements, and various Geneva conventions, I went out into the klieg-lit streets of Manhattan. It was lonely. Hundreds of gray sawhorses of the police blocked off Madison Square Garden. Putrid air came up hot from the subways. I angled back to the hotel room, discouraged, wondering if the Middle East would blow up no matter what candidate was elected. A word popped into my mind. Hope.

As if just a prelude, ten years shrank to a moment. I wondered: Was my cousin's friend, whom I would see on Thanksgivings in Brooklyn when I visited from college, still in New York? Indeed, was Hope still living at all? I looked into the phone book and sure enough, there you were. But when I called, a tape machine answered with your roommate's voice. I spoke into the tape machine three times that night, each time saying disregard the last.

When I finally got through, your roommate told me you were touring with *Fiddler* and would be in Washington soon. She seemed suspicious when I told her what I was doing in New York, and incredulous that I could be "pro-Palestinian." I tried to get off the phone quickly; I did not want anything to prejudice a reunion.

Tonight—opening night—I ambled up to the ticket window of the Warner Theatre in Washington, D.C. It's a warm evening. The sidewalks themselves could be rising like Arabic, like Jewish, bread. (Does Jewish bread rise? Maybe not. I am thinking of bagels, or matzo. They don't rise. So we will say tonight the sidewalk is Jewish bread that doesn't rise. And tomorrow it will be hot enough to take off like Arabic bread!)

I used to think matzo tasted like Holy Communion. This may seem to be a sacrilege to you; but I am thinking of things holy, and things holy for some should be respected. Sacredness is catchy. I met a man once who said he prayed to the pebble in his shoe. I said, why not take it out and then pray to it? He said, if I take it out, why pray to it? It's common after that. Hope, in ten years it is people like that who have remained with me.

There was a long line around the block for tickets; it looked like a sell-out. Would I not get in? Would I not get to know whom you were going to play, or if you would sing and dance, or if you still had a lovely figure, and braces? Had your cheerleading in high school paid off?! I asked the lady at the window if she had anything left. She raised her pointed finger. The last one, Hope. I bought the last ticket left on opening night. My head snuggled nicely against the ceiling of the theatre!

Before you emerge from this green door, I must contain the mounting emotion of watching this play with you in it. Many times I buried my face in my hands from a collision of joy and sorrow, while the fellow next to me remained impassive throughout the play. You may object to my even breathing the words. But *Fiddler on the Roof* could have been called *Oud on the Porch*. As I watched I felt I was watching my story, the story of my people who came to this country as a refuge from oppression. But Hope—my people and yours are at war.

It's no coincidence. The music in both our veins is Semitic. Your fiddle is our oud. The oud player strums his eggplant-shaped guitar and follows the dancer around, goading, enticing the dancer, even, as the fiddler does, in the midst of catastrophe. And Tevye—he's my grandfather! The one who came from farming land of almonds and lentils in Syria. "On the one hand, on the other hand"—his decisions in favor of the heart—that is my Grandfather Kamel, who is now dead. He came alive again in Tevye.

When the daughters came out, I strained, being so far back, to see which one was you. I remembered you as dark, dark skinned, with dark hair. A clear, heartfelt, independent voice rang out. Was this yours? I squinted. Like a night ten years ago in a smoky bar in Brooklyn. I was a sophomore in college; you were a freshman. We were to meet at the Gibbons, which later became the Studio. In the gloomy smoke of the bar I asked your friend, my cousin, "Where is Hope?" She shook her head. Suddenly you arrived in the hand of a tall blond fellow whom I knew to be your basketball-player boyfriend. I instantly turned toward the bar, and my own dark face. Thanksgiving was moody that year. I chided myself; after all, you had braces, didn't you?

Once I had identified you on stage, a pride welled up inside me. To think you had persevered and gone this far! Every time you had a line I mumbled: "That's it; tell 'em; that's good! That's superb!" The guy next to me moved.

I had to laugh when the matchmaker, Yenta, tells you of a bald man she's picked out for you, whom you reject. "If you want hair, get a monkey," cries Yenta. Hope, I used to be nicknamed "The Ape."

Tradition! How commanding is the music! How definite the pride! As your *hora* sways, so sways our *dabki*. As your bride and groom stand under the tent, ours turn in a circle with crowns. Your *yarmulke* jumps; our *kufiyah* flies! Your peddler of milk is our peddler of olive oil. Each is used for the healthy bodies of children.

Children, Hope. What will our love of tradition give to them?

I must admit I am ambivalent about this powerful "Tradition." There is something of the merciless in it, of the authoritarian. And when Tevye wrestles with himself over his youngest daughter's marriage to a Russian, he shouts, in a paroxysm of anguish: "There is no 'other hand'!" Tradition holds sway. He shuts out his last daughter. It is like Lear, abandoning Cordelia for not pronouncing her love in the way he feels befits him.

Hope, it is getting on toward midnight now, and most people have left the dark street as I stand here, waiting.

It has been ten years. Will we have to wait another ten, another fifty, to speak the truth? How many more will die while we stand on "tradition"?

The Arabs have a traditional dream of unity, and sometimes when it happened—such as with Syria and Libya—it looked like trouble. And Menachem Begin has *his* tradition—the dream of annexing Judea and Samaria—and that tradition is putting Palestinians through much horror. The playwright Jean Anouilh said in his play *Antigone*, "We are always free at someone else's expense." Must this be so? I think not. It cannot be so if our world is to remain — *our* world. But absolute freedom to enact all one's dreamy tradition is bringing your people, Hope, and my people, to the brink of an abyss.

At the end of *Fiddler on the Roof* the Jews are cast out of their Russian village, Anatevka, and made to wander. As they sway on the cold road — homeless, lost, wondering what they had done to deserve this — I thought of more than seven hundred thousand Palestinians cast out of their home in search of the same land your relatives hold dear. What did they do to deserve that?

The Russian soldier had promised Teyve he would protect the Jews of Anatevka. It reminded me of the many promises in the century given to the Palestinians that they, too, would have a state of their own.

Hope, the night air is getting cold and this street promises nothing but quiet for those who have been separated for so long. Maybe coming out of that door you will not want to hear these thoughts, but simply have a drink. You must be exhausted. Maybe you are not as robust as Tzeitel at all, like the old days when cheers would fly the tassels on your sneakers a foot off the ground. Maybe you have a date with the director, who will come out locking arms with you, and I will slink back into the night and walk down E Street until the White House and stare at the fountain through iron bars.

If you do exit here (is there another way out they haven't told me about — an underground tunnel?), yes we can talk of the Gibbons and our first bear-hug dances. We will wrangle over your Yankees and my Dodgers, and think with wonder of the green-lit spans of the Verrazano Bridge built in our green years, green as this door. And of course we will say to each other that we weren't born when the Nazis committed their heinous crimes, or when the Palestinians were shoved aside to make room for millions of suffering Jews. We ourselves did not have a part in the making of one of the most tragic ironies in history. We need not take up those items at all.

After ten years, dear Hope, we may have only an hour. Shall we not speak what is deepest inside us? Shall we not say that without compromise, the kind in which Tevye's love overcomes his salutes to "Tradition," we are all doomed?

A police car has just driven slowly past. Now its siren grinds to life and the flasher twists like a bloodshot eye.

I remember your eyes had a light that overcame the blood. Look with them, Hope! Our people are on center stage, and they may yet live side by side, in states of their own, when the tremendous and terrible pride of each may melt them together before it splits them completely apart. Otherwise, the stage will become quickly empty, the orchestra will play a dirge. No one will be left to toast "life," to say "l'chaim."

You are the last one to come out. And I am the last to leave.

Doomed by Our Blood to Care

Our youngest son is at the moment smiling with chicken pox. It is 3 p.m. and "heavy" (*lourde*, as the French say) after a summer storm. I've given myself the task of four paragraphs of this piece today, about the amount I figure I can get out before little Luke finds another wall socket (as he has just done, mid-sentence) or loses interest in the various toys and boxes I have sprawled over the floor to lure him. We'll dunk soon in a three-foot wide pool. I'm by myself this week with him — the rest of the family off on vacation.

The shrewd reader will find something Naomi Shihab Nye–ish about this beginning. I sometimes imagine her life-carvings going on in similar circumstances as she rears her own son, named after the framer of law (Madison) and not independence (Jefferson). Her work is faithful to the minute but essential tasks of our lives, the luminous in the ordinary. I won't claim luminosity, but this is a peculiar kind of aloneness the youngest boy and I have this week, which Nye raises up for examination in two of her most powerful poems. They enact in some ways a counterpoint to her overarching humanism, or communal warmth, drawing attention to a mysterious character. She affirms in these two poems the dignity of the separate, the role of the artist as connector of the disparate, discoverer of spiritual groundwater. She also, I believe, confronts in this anchorite's life a kind of tragedy of being.

I have been asked to reflect on the Arab and Palestinian sources in Nye's work. Inasmuch as she is the outstanding American poet of Palestinian origin, and one of the premier voices of her generation, this would seem appropriate. Nevertheless, of 155 poems in her first three published collections, only 14 had a recognizably Arab or Palestinian content — less than 9 percent. More deal with the Hispanic Southwest, where she lives, and Latin America, where she has traveled extensively, than the ancestral homeland of her father. Just as profitably one could delve into the extensive influence both the style and themes of William Stafford have had on her work—the plucky stoicism, the verbal magic. But, dutifully, I put my nose to the Arab grindstone, knowing her most lauded book is a culling of such poems (*19 Varieties of Gazelle: Poems of the Middle East*, a 2002 nominee for the National Book Award).

Little Luke has now found the nuts on my desk, the Central Filbert, as well as the typewriter, so seeing as I have met my goal of four paragraphs, and the heat and he are heavy, this, to be continued.

It's the next day. Luke takes a morning nap after a stroll during which he de-frocked a hydrangea in the alley (profligate of one-and-a-half years!), and I realize I could as fruitfully discuss Naomi Nye's fascination with her father in the lush, life-asserting "My Father and the Fig Tree" and his later, agonizing appearance in "Blood." However, I have decided to focus on another "double axle," two poems about her hermetic Uncle Mohammed. While riding this "two wheeler," I hope to veer in and out of some of the fourteen poems in her opus that deal with her heritage.

"For Mohammed on the Mountain" is the longest poem in Nye's first book, *Different Ways to Pray*. Its lines, too, are long. The voice in it is typical of much in that book—exhilarated, even girlish, stymied in this case by an uncle across the seas who has gone off to live a solitary life on a mountain. In her third collection, *Yellow Glove*, the lone figure returns in "My Uncle Mohammed at Mecca, 1981." Here the voice is older, grim, resigned in a way the uncle seems to have become resigned, but with a strange courage. The lines of this lyric are clipped, the questions whittled into something final. Yet the mystery, less scintillating than before, has deepened in the mature woman poet's mind. For Uncle Mohammed—as the Prophet himself—has literally disappeared. More on this later.

In the earlier poem, Uncle Mohammed is directly addressed in the first line: "you mystery, you distant faceless face." This non-traveler, incommunicado uncle nevertheless has hit the poet's antenna: "I think I know what you are talking about, / though we have never talked." She prefers her uncle, "in all your silence" to other distinctly American uncles who are pictured riding motorcycles, cooking steaks, or handing out goodies like "movie tickets."

Consciously or not, Nye is drawing on the life of Mohammed, the prophet, who concluded the Judeo-Christian tradition as, according to

Philip Hitti, "the greatest iconoclast . . . in history." But she is not about the task à la Salman Rushdie of debunking Islam and the myths surrounding its founder. This is not satire, but rather the story of a real uncle who happens to be called Mohammed whose twentieth-century life shares little with the twentieth century and much with that of a timeless quester.

Mohammed and Uncle Mohammed are drawn to mountains, "living close to the clouds," as Nye puts it. The prophet found his call as the messenger of God while sojourning in a cave on a hill outside Mecca, when a voice (later identified in the Koran as the Archangel Gabriel) exhorts, "Recite, in the name of the Lord, who created man from a clot of blood." This awakening is commemorated on the twenty-seventh day of the holy month of Ramadan.

Though Uncle Mohammed is not prophet or proselytizer, the poet wants to learn from him the secret of a secret life, that life we all harbor inside and about which we seem to know so little. She considers anger a source of his withdrawal, but discards it. Uncle Mohammed's own way of praying — and Nye's poems seem to be alternative prayers — is, to her, an example of simplicity and economy in living:

> This is what I am learning . . .
> It says, Teach me how little I need to live
> and I can't tell if it is me talking, or you,
> or the walls of the room. How little, how little, and the world jokes
> and says, how much.

Her uncle treasures life at its root — not its plenitude, but its being. From a mountaintop, all the suffering parts of the world-mosaic fit. Theirs is an abstemious celebration.

The vanity of human wishes she counterposes to her own withdrawal: "Money, events, ambition, plans, oh uncle / I have made myself a quiet place in the swirl."

Before our two older boys left for climes south with their mother, we spent two days rubbing peach pits on the sidewalk, showing them how to make a peach-pit ring, something I learned in childhood from my own uncles in California. A peach pit is hard; the task seems endless. Yet the hollow comes, enlarges, fits on a finger. Nye veers from contemplation of her uncle to thinking "how many shavings of wood the knife discards / to leave one smoothly whittled spoon." She follows "angles of light through the window" as an anchorite would, harvesting the simplest beauty. Being attentive to the day, Nye seems to imply, is the best work. Being attentive, too, to loss.

It is interesting that one of Nye's best "protest" poems concerning the arduous life of Palestinians under Israeli occupation is homage to a broom maker, a character similar to the mysterious Uncle Mohammed:

> It is a little song, this thumb over thumb,
> but sometimes when you wait years
> for the air to break open
> and sense to fall out,
> it may be the only one.
> —Naomi Shihab Nye, "The Man Who Makes Brooms"

It is not surprising, given the fifty-year nightmare Palestinians have lived—the tens of thousands of dead and imprisoned, homes bricked or cemented in collective punishment, water sucked from underneath by fanatics as wildly Western as nineteenth-century gunslingers—that some have taken to terrorism, more to poetry (and most to the roads). Smugly, America looks on like some high-tech Sphinx, refusing any culpability that "linkage" of its aid to Israel implies. Stifled for many years by the military authorities from any kind of meaningful political expression, outcry in verse is predictable; predictable, too, that, according to Palestinian writer and artist Kamal Boullata, much of it is bad. Poetry is, after all, an art and grace, not simply a function of necessity (though if necessity isn't in the spring, the river goes quickly slack).

A lesser poet than Naomi Shihab Nye might have succumbed to declamatory verse, trying to compensate for genealogical and geographic distance from the combat zone with righteousness. (The shrillest voices are usually on the periphery of horror. Those in the thick of it must invent: it is a matter of life and death.) As the American-born daughter of a Palestinian journalist from the West Bank city of Singil who was present at the Arab surrender to Moshe Dayan in 1948, Nye's slant is peculiar by nature: both close and distant. She has been asked and often asked herself: What is my responsibility in this tragedy as a writer with a gift? How is the gift deployed? One senses this is a burden she would not have chosen, as do our moth-poets flying into the fire of various conflagrations, the further away the better. As she ambiguously put it in an article in the *Houston Chronicle* (July 23, 1989), she feels "doomed by our blood to care."

Nye straddles the divide between the developing world and her native America, between community and self. On a trip for the USIA once, a Pakistani politician bewailed the lack of freedom of speech in his country and challenged her: "It is your duty to speak for us." But she ruminated, "Exactly how one speaks for another remained a concept less identifiable, since literature . . . must be more than preaching or sloganeering." (*Texas Journal*, Fall/Winter 1985).

Amid "voices chiding me to / 'speak for my people,'" Nye joins those marching "like guardians of memory / till we find the man on a short stool / who makes brooms." How easy it would be to shout down the settlements! Nye, to her credit, reveals her hesitance and patience. She does not want to commit an artistic version of political exploitation. She is not looking for a target, but rather revelation — the right cipher that will define resistance; it cannot come without love. And when she finds him he is a commoner, but resistant in his singularity like Uncle Mohammed: "I say he is like nobody, / the pink seam he weaves / is its own shrine."

In turning the volume down, she has turned the dignity up. In the midst of ongoing repression, she indicates the only sense left is a sense of continuity. If anything sweeps away the Israeli occupation, it may be something like that broom and its maker. The poem is a paean to human persistence, as masterful as anything written on either side of the Jordan, or the Mississippi.

There is then in Nye an emergent Palestinian consciousness: the art of staying put. (The title poem of *Yellow Glove* itself is a commemoration of losing something that, miraculously, returns — a yellow glove in the river.) Hers is not the grand elegiac sweep of Mahmud Darwish, nor the despair of Rashid Hussein. It has a strong element of American pragmatism, an ornery attachment to the land, a statement of love so unadorned and solid it is resistant to all that is not love.

The dedicatory aspect of her work has roots in the ancient pre-Islamic Bedouin poets' standard lament for an abandoned encampment. Nye declares in the opening poem of *Hugging the Jukebox*: "Facts interest me less than the trailing smoke of stories." A writer friend staring at a ceiling "before the dark came home to hold your hand," who "hiked railroad tracks dreaming of mirrors," stands in his room, "your black eyes birds barely landed, and learned the long river that was your voice" — another kindred soul, like the broom maker and Uncle Mohammed, fertile in solitude. "For Brothers Lost and Found" ends in exaltation:

For you, brothers.
For the blood rivers invisibly harbored.
. . . how strangely and suddenly, on the lonely porch,
in the sleepless mouth of the night,
the sadness drops away, we move forward,
confident we are born into a large family,
our brothers cover the earth.

It's now time to sum up, and to admit that six months have gone by since little Luke and I shared a delicious solitude. It is no longer summer; the year has turned and time has flown into snow.

Today Luke, now an ancient two, helped carry pieces of firewood his papa chopped from an old oak felled by a tornado. The air is chill. I marvel at this youngest one gripping wood with his little, determined hands, smiling as he plinks it on the pile, his breath going straight to heaven.

Mohammed went to heaven on a horse; Uncle Mohammed — possibly on the fender of a car.

There is much Arabic folklore and custom on which Nye draws that I have not indulged: her use of Joha, a kind of Arab "coyote" figure in stories; of the *zaar*, or town fool who may be "touched" but may also be inspired, such as Fouzi "famous for his laugh"; the omnipresent image of Arab food, fruits and vegetables (figs, peaches "marble-sized," the "purple shining globes" of eggplant, bitter coffee boiled to rise twice, served with a message of infinity itself — "There is this / and there is more." (That the Arabs read fortunes by the pattern of coffee grinds in an up-ended cup is seized by Nye.)

But it is the onion — an object of worship in Egypt before Europe discovered it — that will deliver me back to Uncle Mohammed, the broom maker, the solitudinous brother/writer, and my theme. For it is the onion, Nye says in "The Traveling Onion," that has "a traditional honorable career: / For the sake of others, disappear."

There is a selflessness and self-protection about this onion, and about Nye's notion of the role of the artist amid a chorus of suffering. Her stance is paradoxical: the fire of family and community requires that the artist withdraw *in order to fully commune*. This means neither cold detachment nor ephemeral intimacy. Nye's impetus is immediate: "Because my grandmother still lives high in the hills of her small Palestinian village, because my cousin's husband was recently rounded up in a large group arrested without charges by Israeli soldiers, and because I know what the stones smell like." ("We All Walk on Bones," *Houston Chronicle*, July 23, 1989).

She has been there, partly because it is unavoidable. And she has made the link of conscience with remarkable collection and aplomb. Take for instance her response to the Israeli border guard in "Olive Jar," who taunts her with questions — What kind of people do you wish to see? Arab people? Do you plan to speak with anyone? — "I wanted to say No, I have come all this way for a silent reunion." She doesn't take the racist bait but metaphorizes her "people" into "olive gatherers." In a short story "Local Hospitality," she fights the stereotypes subtly, humorously, as when word of homes for the aged in America are dismissed by an uncle as *haki fathi!* (empty talk). (How often during war with Iraq have we heard the pundits skewer "Arab exaggeration," the "Arab love of poetry," meaning ornate, and duplicitous, gibberish. As if none in America, our leaders especially, are guilty of empty talk!)

Yet there is some "doom" in caring so. Around empathy Nye finds a rind: "We develop by necessity a remarkable capacity to hear and think without feeling too much." There is as much regret as purpose here, a survivalism Eliot once called the capacity "to care and not to care." Witness gains by exposure, but can be lost in it, too. Witness requires at some point removal, perspective. Nye warns against those who "embrace only their issues . . . narrowing their ears." Because "Love means you breathe in two countries." At least.

Naomi Nye once wrote me, "Sometimes in moments of wistfulness about modern times and all that has been lost, I imagine porches to be the key to everything." It is an appropriate symbol for Nye's purpose — the porch. It is open to the world, but covered, raised above the street. It is both haven and thoroughfare, where one greets, shares, and where one perches alone.

In a recent Nye poem, one of her warmest, "How Palestinians Keep Warm," it is telling that she celebrates words (and states of mind) that are singular, removed: *alphard* ("solitary one"), *dirah* ("little house"), *mizar* ("veil"), and most importantly *adhafera* ("the one who holds out"). She announces a way out of deprivation: "When your shawl is as thin as mine is / you tell stories."

Or you are a story. One that begs to be told not by demand, but example — the broom maker, the writer in his solitudinous room, Abu Mahmoud and Aziz Shihab in their gardens, and Uncle Mohammed himself, who disappears on the only journey he has ever taken — to

Mecca. A man of singulars: one mountain, one journey, one gift (and off to pay homage to the great Oneness). His bizarre, rather mystical death is not one, though, but left for many to "complete":

> We search for the verb
> That keeps a man complete.
> To resign, to disappear, that's how
> I've explained you.
>
> Now I want to believe it was true.
> Because you lived apart
> we hold you up. Because no word connected us
> we complete your sentence.

Uncle Mohammed is many things: one who "holds out" by being himself (like the broom maker, shaping things in silence, in his case, olivewood birds). He is the vigilant one, who fights simply by staying put. But by cloistering himself in the mountain (did human woe do that?), he stands for pure Being, "The verb [intransitive?] that keeps a man complete."

The poet? She is fairly compelled by Mohammed's silence, his sad aloofness, to speak, to "complete" him. Thus Uncle Mohammed becomes both source and product of poetry: the individual.

There rests the human tragedy, as well. How did Uncle Mohammed die? Nye is mystified as much by what is known as what isn't. She told me in a letter that he left his bus to Mecca, went out on the road; his body ended up in a morgue in Jiddah, apparently hit by a car. Nye's exquisite elegy ends:

> Uncle of sadness, this is the last pretense;
> you understood the word was no pilgrim,
> and were brave and wise,
> and wanted to die.

There is great pathos here, and a skepticism that cuts — her whole inflation of him as saintly in his resignation could be "pretense."

But Uncle Mohammed's life is a command — to live with dignity, to die with it. Like the poet Randall Jarrell, as legend has it, tipping his hat, leaning into the taxi that killed him.

In her work, Naomi Nye has done something rare: spoken for a whole people's resistance to unrelenting loss, and her own day-by-day human persistence, as well. Luke is tugging at my pant leg. Ah, yes — doomed to care.

No. Not This.

No. Not this way. Not now. Not ever. In that way lies doom.

I do not know quite how to express my revulsion over the death and destruction wrought in Israel this December 2001, when two Palestinian suicide bombers in succession killed twenty-six people in Tel Aviv and Jerusalem.*

What insensibility, sheer lack of conscience and humanity, has brought this about? The dead were young people, children at the beginning of their lives, gathering on a weekend, letting go for a moment of the first grasps of terribly difficult things that adults must settle someday, pray God, so that they might just mix with each other, enjoy some music, breath a little, sigh a little, dream a little. Suddenly they are dismembered, headless, gone. On a bus or in a square, or having just walked the street together.

These were not just Jews or Armenians or Arabs. They are souls, people fashioned in the image of God, who must be hiding His face. What godforsaken image is in the visage of a lost boy or girl with explosives strapped to the waist? Let us not think for long that this is the Land of the Incarnation, where human beings barely breathe now — Israeli or Palestinian — without wondering if the next breath isn't the last.

How can people live like this for half a century?

I am going to resist discussing the Palestine-Israel crisis, the fact that though Ariel Sharon is a man with a bloody history, even a war criminal, he could move towards redemption, as Yitzhak Rabin was redeemed in the eyes of many Palestinians who suffered from his policies because he

---

*From 2000 to 2003, more than one hundred suicide bombings took place, most by followers of Hamas and Islamic Jihad, but some by the al-Aqsa Martyrs Brigade. During this period of the so-called Second Intifadah, 2,500 Palestinians and 700 Israelis were killed, most of them civilians.

admitted crimes of the past, saw no future in bloodshed or righteousness. Only in compassion, a reaching out, not back.

No, no, no. I do not want to talk about the insanity of declaring war on Arafat, leaving the leadership of the West Bank and Gaza to suicidal maniacs. Let us not dwell on the impossibility of rounding up Islamic Jihad and Hamas murderers if the Palestinian Authority's jails are blown up.

Let me just express, as an American, as someone whose grandparents came here from the Arab world a century ago, a deep sorrow and solidarity with the Israeli families and friends who have suffered such horrifying losses these past months. There is no excuse for such madness. We are all taught that two wrongs do not make a right. How many more innocent young people who don't know about the Balfour Declaration or the Oslo Agreement or Deir Yassin or Ma'alot, how many of them will have to surrender breath so that men of fear and hate can reign? Worse, how many young people who do know of these things, who are spoiled or twisted by wealth or poverty, by prejudice and half-truths or plain lies — how many of these will go down the road of the bomber Maher Hibashi or Yigal Amir, the murderer of Rabin, before this river of blood dries?

I can say the obvious if anyone is to get out alive from the place called the Holy Land. Hamas and Islamic Jihad must foreswear suicide bombing and terrorism or be opposed. Such people are living on a fantasy that Israel will be destroyed. Two wrongs don't make a right. You can't throw millions of people out of their homes, most of whom had nothing to do with your original disinheritance, any more than the American Indian can do that to the mass of Americans today. One genocide, or mass expulsion, does not justify another.

But don't expect Arafat or any one of his successors such as Mahmoud Abbas to crack down on extremists with hands and feet tied, their people bulldozed in their beds, or stopped every tenth foot for an ID check by Israeli soldiers. That is cynicism in the extreme.

As for Israel, it must get out of the West Bank and Gaza, plain and simple, and forget the cookie-cutter, humiliating approach to peace that kills the Palestinian middle. Military occupation is violence of every conceivable sort. Israel must not only stop the settlements, pure salt in the wound for forty years; they must dismantle most if not all of them. Israelis know better than I how corrosive these things are to their own national life.

Sharon wouldn't do any of this; I do not think he is a leader; I think he is an ideologue who wants the West Bank, if not Gaza — which is so poor no one wants it — and is only too happy to destroy the very jails Arafat would use to bottle up Hamas, because he wants Hamas for himself.

Enough of this. None of it will transpire. Arafat, who teetered on the tightrope between legitimate resistance and terrorism his whole life, will not outlaw Hamas or the Al-Aqsa Martyrs Brigade unless he has the boot off his neck and the political freedom to do so. Sharon will not outlaw the settlements because they embody a religious fundamentalist expansionist creed he has held to his whole life.

We are left begging for sanity from other people. Let us hope Mahmoud Abbas and the successor to Ehud Olmert are those people. We are left saying once again how horrible we feel, cheap as that emotion may be from so far away, for Israeli youth who died at the hands of empty, manipulated, desperate Palestinian youth. John Ruedy, my old mentor at Georgetown, has said of these suicide massacres they may more resemble student gun violence in Littleton, Colorado, than September 11.

As for the Palestinian kids gunned down and old men shot by Israeli soldiers and settlers (terrorists by another name) and the thousands made homeless by the crimes of extremists, I hesitate to say what those heinous acts remind me of. Collective punishment has become a way of life, a modus operandi of the Israeli occupation, and it echoes some of the crimes of Germany in the thirties and Bosnia in the nineties.

I pray the souls of good men and women come to the fore in Israel and Palestine, new leaders who may stay the hands of vengeance and truly go on a new path. Murderous anger is blindness. And complete numbness. Is there no one with a pair of eyes? Is there no one who can feel?

Snuffing the Fires of Radical Islam

Just as Saddam Hussein was a handy punching bag for U.S. fury over Osama bin Laden, Yasser Arafat had, long before his death, become a convenient scapegoat for failures in Western diplomacy over the fifty-year-old Palestinian tragedy. We just don't get it, and we'd better soon.

The relationship between the Palestinians and the rise of al-Qaeda, between Arafat and the rise of Israeli Prime Minister Ariel Sharon, needs to be deconstructed. Our whole "war on terror" (and of terror) will continue to be quixotic, if not self-destructive, if we don't take the opportunity of the Palestinian Authority president's death to set a new course, not based on a personality but on history and the needs of the region. At least a pinch of the salt of our own ideals in the soup of the Mideast wouldn't hurt either. And I don't mean force-fed "democracy."

I met Arafat in Beirut on the brink of the Israeli invasion of Lebanon in 1982, the event bin Laden referred to—with portent few caught—in his missive to the West just before the 2004 U.S. presidential election. I didn't know it at the time, but I was following in the footsteps of my father-in-law, Robert Rogers, who was the first major network reporter (NBC) to interview Arafat. He was also the first network documentary producer to openly criticize the Vietnam War ("It's a Mad, Mad War," 1964), showing courage we see too little of today over Iraq.

That afternoon in a crowded Beirut hovel, with U.S.–made Israeli warplanes overhead, Arafat seemed to offer hope for pluralistic coexistence when he reminded journalists of St. Peter's trip to Rome: "He did not capture Rome, but he captured the hearts of the people of Rome. This is the meaning of the *terra sancta*. This is the lesson of history. And one more time, sooner or later, we will give another lesson for the history."

I am not naive about Arafat. He was corrupt, and under his watch, if not his direction, extremists did horrid things. In this, he was little different from those leaders who sullied their records and their souls with the King David Hotel, My Lai, Irangate and Abu Ghraib, not to mention Sabra and Shatila. But what struck me that day in Beirut was Arafat's admission that the hot war on his doorstep was lost. That, to him, was a given and a smaller matter. His message was remarkably spiritual for a head of state, or state in waiting, and presumed the moral tradition of the Holy Land (terra sancta).

Far from being the unregenerate terrorist described by those who put Israel's interests above all others, Arafat never went back on his sixteen-year-old historic acceptance of Israel, nor his belief in peaceful coexistence with Israelis. The devil, of course, is in the details, and the settlement offered by Ehud Barak in 2000 — touted as the "deal of the century" — left the vast majority of Israeli settlements intact and cut the West Bank into a Swiss cheese of cantons with huge bypass highways to the settlements, patrolled by Israeli tanks. Even in the days of Jim Crow America, blacks could walk on the public roads. These roads in occupied Palestine are forbidden to Arabs, the vast majority of the people who live there. If this is freedom, one commentator noted, it is freedom unlike any freedom in the world.

Unnerving as he could be, Arafat was not the devil that Israel-firsters made him out to be, but probably the best Palestinian that Israel had going for it, certainly when compared with Hamas (or with the Saudi, bin Laden, a man Arafat chastised as cynically appropriating the Palestinian cause). Yitzhak Rabin understood this. One part of the Israeli soul knew this; otherwise Mossad would have done in Arafat years ago. The other part, however, the Likud part — unprepared to make minimum concessions to Palestinians, such as giving up the settlements and East Jerusalem and allowing some semblance of a right of return — had to make Arafat out to be the devil incarnate. As journalist I.F. Stone once said, "There is something in the Israeli soul that prefers the Arab extremist to the Arab moderate." You don't have to concede anything to extremists.

The key issue now for Israel is not how to force, or cajole, Palestinians into accepting the stale roses of an old "deal." The key for Israel is making the concessions necessary to new Palestinian leaders that will give them incentive to either crack down on Hamas and Islamic Jihad — to strengthen the middle — or to include them in a coalition government if they give up targeting civilians and accept a pre-1967 Israel. The key for the United States, which faces a far more dangerous force in bin Laden and his minions, is to finally grasp the centrality of the Palestinian cause to the phenomenon of bin Laden. The United States has to disengage itself in concrete ways from funding a messianic state in the Middle East, Greater Israel, whose current leaders believe they have a God-given right to land that was acquired by war. This state has made the very heart of the Arab world in Palestine suffer for half a century, on our dime.

There are those who say that President Bush saw the region primarily in religious terms, as ground zero for an imminent, God-ordained Rapture. If this continues, there is no reason left in American foreign policy. Let us hope for something better from our leaders than an apocalyptic fantasy that plays into bin Laden's hands—and that the country founded on the Enlightenment and separation of church and state prevails, not some kook West Bank settler or suicide bomber.

In October 2004, one of the 9/11 commissioners, John Lehman, spoke at Pitzer College at a conference on the subject of 9/11 and the writer's imagination and conscience. He acknowledged that evil would not disappear from the Earth if the Palestinian-Israeli conflict were settled. But, wouldn't a whole lot of the oxygen be drained from bin Laden's recruitment message if it were? Lehman agreed emphatically. Snuffing the "oxygen" of terror was the right metaphor, he said.

To President Obama: Save a lot of money and lives and sanity. You don't have to capture bin Laden. Just make him quaint.

Meditations on Lebanon, 2006

It is a painful thing, knowing that my Christian grandparents fled Lebanon and Syria seeking asylum and opportunity in the United States a century ago, to observe, with helpless anger and despair, yet another destruction of Lebanon with the aid of the country they put so much faith in. This irony touches the very marrow of the bones. As I watched Lebanon's third flattening in my time, two texts separated by almost ninety years began to fuse in my mind. The recent one, written by Richard Cohen on July 25, 2006, in the *Washington Post*, states: "Israel is, as I have often said, unfortunately located, gentrifying a pretty bad neighborhood."

One wonders how he forgot that Israel has treaties with the borderlands of Egypt and Jordan and has been offered one by Syria and every other Arab state, as recently as 2002. What would have been a better neighborhood? Uganda, as the early Zionists thought? Europe? Germany or Norway? An eminent Arab American academician at Princeton, Philip K. Hitti, testifying to Congress in 1944, suggested "the unoccupied plains of Arizona or Texas." But of course, that wouldn't have gone over too well with the tolerant people of Arizona or Texas. So why not a "pretty bad neighborhood" of Arabs?

Document two comes from 1917. That year the prime minister of Great Britain, Lord David Balfour, threw the great weight of the West behind the Zionist project to create a national home for the perennially persecuted Jewish people, "it being clearly understood," Balfour said, "that nothing shall be done which may prejudice the civil and religious rights of the existing non-Jewish population." That sounds reasonable. But listen to this (and you won't find it in an American textbook). David Balfour said in a secret memo to the British Cabinet later that year: "Zionism, be it right or wrong, good or bad, is rooted in age-long traditions, in present needs, in future hopes of far profounder import than the desires and prejudices of the seven hundred thousand Arabs who now inhabit that ancient land." FAR PROFOUNDER IMPORT.

The two statements of Balfour and Mr. Cohen are separated by almost a century — in which we have learned virtually nothing about the Middle East, especially the Arabs who live there. In that period, hundreds of thousands have been killed or wounded, millions made homeless, millions more brought up in fear and resentment. To what purpose? If I may conflate the two men — so that a nation of "FAR PROFOUNDER IMPORT" may live in "A PRETTY BAD NEIGHBORHOOD."

Where did this "far profounder import" come from? It came from the British Empire on which no sun set. That empire — once worldwide — is now reduced to specks of islands in the Caribbean, as well as the Falklands. Correct me if I am wrong, but the first to rebel against this extraordinary arrogance of culture and spirit was a far-off place near Boston that the British must have thought "a pretty bad neighborhood."

The third destruction of Lebanon in two-and-a-half decades by Israel with our American weapons is spurred by a racial and cultural arrogance that could be the latest signal of our careening empire's demise, unless we act with the highest principles of a land that finds no man, no religion, and no civilization "of far profounder import" simply by birth. If we exist anymore on that high hill of our Founders' inspired beliefs, in spite of President Bush II's woefully wrong-headed, delusional policies in the Middle East, we exist to do right for those ravaged by history, to wage war only as an absolutely last measure to defend ourselves or those who cannot defend themselves, and to use our immense power and wealth to create circumstances of understanding and dialogue between people at odds, especially at odds because of our own dereliction of duty and of principle.

One can't give the Lebanese a pass on their own sufferings, either. Ninety years ago from New York, Kahlil Gibran himself excoriated his fellow Lebanese for their vicious sectarianism and clannishness in his poem, "My Countrymen":

I have called you in the silence
Of the night to point out
The glory of the moon and the dignity
Of the stars, but you startled
From your slumber and clutched
Your swords in fear, crying,
"Where is the enemy?"

One shakes one's head in despair knowing that sixteen years of civil war (1975–1991) netted few fundamental changes in Lebanon after half a million dead and injured. The confessional system still apportions political leadership according to sect, instead of being based on the popular will of one man or woman, one vote. There has been no Lebanese "Truth Commission" bringing Lebanese involved in mass killings in the civil war and assassinations to justice. Not even Syria can be used as an excuse anymore for Lebanon's weak democracy as it pulled out in the "Cedar Revolution" of 2004. Hezbollah still operates its "state-within-a-state" in the South, lacking a settlement of the Palestine-Israel dispute.

Ultimately, however, the havoc and destruction in Lebanon is a tragic sideshow to the sixty-year infected wound in Palestine, where the Palestinians need desperately to be free in their own land. The routinization of Palestinian suffering has to be resisted, rather than spread. As Mahmoud Darweesh, the great Palestinian poet, once noted, the killing of Palestinians was so regular throughout the last half of the twentieth century it was almost "seasonal," a kind of Israeli burn-off of forests and undergrowth too thick for comfort. A controlled fire, if you will, deemed necessary to prevent an even greater fire.

The events of August 2006 in Lebanon have made me wonder if Lebanon and the Lebanese, too, are part of the same seasonal killing, which Israel exhorts the West to simply put up with as a lamentable but necessary burning of the underbrush.

The underbrush this time is Hezbollah, at other times the Palestinian terrorists; then there are simply generic terrorists, and even, on occasion, Americans such as that upstart Rachel Corrie, who in 2003 had the temerity to stand up to a bulldozer in the West Bank about to crush an Arab home and paid for it with her life. Or the thirty-four sailors on the USS Liberty who were burned or shot to death by Israeli fighter planes who didn't want them snooping around the Mediterranean, an Israeli lake, apparently, during the June 1967 war. Or perhaps my father-in-law's best friend and boss, Ted Yates, who got it right in the forehead from an Israeli sniper while Yates was setting up his cameras for NBC in Jerusalem at the start of that same war. All these were more or less excused by Israel as "unfortunate incidents," cases of mistaken identity. You couldn't see that huge American flag on the Liberty ship, even if you passed over, as the Israeli fighters did, several times. Who knew Rachel Corrie was an American? Anyway, we warned her to get out of the way. And those cameras Ted Yates was setting up looked like machine guns, right?

That we have allowed ourselves and our core principles as a nation to be so abused, not to mention our own citizens and soldiers killed in cold blood by a country we have given so much to since the days when the United States more than any nation helped birth it, is one of the great mysteries of relations between states in history. Why should it be any surprise that Israel now flays Lebanon with impunity? You have to grant Israel its shadows, it seems. I sometimes wonder if there is more operating here than the standard explanations.

It is not the Israel Lobby, per se, or Western guilt over the Holocaust, or geopolitical positioning for oil, or a racist fear of Arabs, or even absurd evangelical millenarianism. Any or all of these may be involved in the extraordinary permissiveness we show towards Israeli actions inimical to U.S. interests and laws, Israel's own survival, and world peace itself. But even in concert, this litany doesn't quite cover a foreign policy skewed of all sense now for over half a century. Unless you subscribe to the theory that Israel is the spearhead of American imperialism in the region, naked and unapologetic. Maybe it is the last drop of optimism I carry in my heart from my immigrant ancestors, but I simply can't admit that. At least not yet.

Could it rather be nuclear blackmail? You'll put up with a lot of insult, not to mention bloodshed, at the prospect of nuclear war. We know the Jewish state has about two hundred nuclear bombs. What has prevented Israel from conveying to us, either directly or indirectly, "You take issue with our actions in any substantive way, and we will feel free to destroy any one of or all the Arab capitals in a matter of minutes"? We know Israel readied its nuclear arsenal in fear of the Soviets arming Syria with nukes during the 1973 war. What prevents it from feeling similarly exposed and confrontational if we cut off aid, for example, over settlements?

The United States, of course, helped create this leviathan. President Johnson looked the other way when fissionable material stolen from a Pennsylvania plant in the sixties and diverted from South Africa ended up in Israel. But we will ultimately have to take this problem on if, in the words of Israeli Knesset member Uri Avneri, we are to "save Israel in spite of itself," not to mention ourselves. Otherwise our righteous anger over nuclear proliferation in Pakistan and possible proliferation in Iran will continue to ring hollow. There is no Muslim who doesn't understand this essential hypocrisy.

About a thousand Lebanese, mostly civilians, and about a hundred Israelis, mostly soldiers, died in Lebanon in two weeks in 2006. For what? To what end? For a phantasm of pure safety? For the Evangelical Right's dream of the Rapture? Gaza laid waste over one snatched soldier? Lebanon destroyed for the third time in a quarter-century over two snatched soldiers? This isn't just a question of proportionality. It is a question of sanity.

Hezbollah basically shot rockets off in solidarity with the Gazans, bearing yet another Israeli full-scale military assault. How long does Israel seem to think it can get away with bullying its neighbors into submission without paying some sort of price? Does it think the Arabs will stand themselves to be defenseless forever? That they will never act effectively in concert? In some ways in 2006, Israel took the bait from Hezbollah, ready with its tunnels, a countryside of supportive Lebanese (and not just Shiites), and ten thousand rockets. But Israel cannot abuse its neighbors any longer without cost—to us as well as them. Our cities are no longer safe from attack. We are implicated, too, in this ultra-nationalism, and that, too, is terribly logical.

One wonders after all these years of conflict: Does Israel want the cost, need it? Does it need to be at odds with those who surround it? Has it known war so long (and cited it so much in its Biblical readings) that oppression from without is central to its identity? Does it gain its singularity because it is set upon? That certainly seems to be tele-evangelist and founder of Christians United for Israel John Hagee's interpretation of things. If this is true, is peace not only too expensive, but too dangerous, that is, too porous for a society that does not want integration with its neighbors in any real way? Is there any doubt that if there is ever real peace, Jew and Arab will become literally more intimate?

More worrisome, has this "wall" mentality catalyzed its mirror image in Arab society, the radical Muslim fundamentalist who gains identity in the fire of battle? To complete the triangle of righteousness, John Hagee and Company's Christian evangelicals want the battle of nations to commence, and goad Israel on to it. This triad of religious extremism intensifies at a ground zero that grows more nuclear every year. It matters less who started this absolutely insane round—Israel, bin Laden, or bin Hagee—than who will begin to throw cold water on it. We haven't.

What is needed to avoid a complete explosion of the region and several of our own cities? I believe five fundamental questions need to be raised. They need to be addressed with common sense, wisdom, and a sense of urgency by the next American president.

1. Isn't it worth our best minds to be sent to the Middle East at the beginning of a new term to secure a final peace agreement, rather than a half-hearted effort, doomed to failure, at term's end? Former President Jimmy Carter and former Secretary of State James Baker would make a formidable team, speaking to all sides with understanding and firmness, not insufferable arrogance. The Pope's presence, too, might underscore the importance to world peace. Groundbreaking, important initial sessions should be held with the Syrians and Iranians — diplomatic recognition offered for a reining-in of Hamas and Hezbollah — before intense sessions begin with Israelis and Palestinians. Gaining provisional Syrian and Iranian recognition of Israel contingent on significant concessions to Palestinians could be deeply motivating for all. The "lock 'em in a room till they come out with peace" approach of President Carter at Camp David may be preferable to Condoleezza Rice's one-day farce in Annapolis in November 2007. If it takes a year, so be it. No return to the States until peace is secured.

2. Does it truly help guarantee Israel's survival to keep sending $3 billion in aid each year while the settlements on the West Bank grow? How do you make peace while paying for more gas to be poured on the fire? In short, how do you make someone do what you want if you pay them not to? It will make a great deal of sense to suspend all aid to the three main parties to this conflict — Israel, Palestine, and Lebanon — until they do what they should do to come to a peace agreement, that is, until the Israelis dismantle the vast majority of their settlements and withdraw from the West Bank; the Lebanese disarm Hezbollah; and the Palestinians get Hamas to forswear suicide bombing, accept a pre-1967 border Israel, and thereby join a coalition government. Using the aid leverage is not only practical; it shows the world we are willing to stand on our principles and put distance between ourselves and both Israel and Palestine until both parties do the right thing. There is no better antidote to bin Laden.

3. If we understand that our aid is leverage, and that the world sees it at least now as destructive indulgence, why not add a carrot to the stick? In tandem with an announcement of an aid cut prior to peace, could we not promise, if a peace agreement is entered, a tripling of aid to Israel ($3 billion to $10 billion), and the same amount ($10 billion) to rebuild the devastated economy and society of Palestinians? Could there not be a similar package to Lebanon, so

hopelessly caught in the middle for so long? Why not enact significant financial incentives to peace? We spend fifty times more than this in Iraq for far less security.

4. Why does the United States keep promulgating a fiction, and a policy based on that fiction, that Israel does not have nuclear weapons? Isn't it long past time that we revealed exactly what we know — that Israel has around two hundred nuclear bombs — and with that finally out in the open, enter into immediate negotiations for a Middle East and Indian subcontinent nuclear-free zone? The concurrent dismantling of Israeli, Pakistani, and Indian nuclear weapons should be encouraged by a further deep reduction, if not elimination, of our own. You can't expect nonproliferation by others if you are sitting on the biggest pile of bombs yourself. We might also suggest that Israeli prisoner-of-conscience Mordechai Vanunu be released from house arrest and afforded a hero's welcome, if not the Nobel Peace Prize, for his uncovering of Israel's nuclear capacity, which cost him many years in an Israeli jail.

5. Why are we delaying a single moment more to get out of Iraq and concentrate on the real problem: Israel-Palestine? Our troops should be substantially out by the end of the new president's first year in 2009, and we should put in place a generous fiscal pipeline to rebuild Iraq's critical infrastructure needs for water, sewage disposal, roads and bridges, medical facilities, and the electrical grid. Iraqi and other Arab companies should be the beneficiaries, not Americans. Six years of no real political accord should have demonstrated by now that our military, even in its best moments, cannot solve Iraq's sectarian antipathies. Only Iraqis can do that. My guess is if we get out of the way, we give them a better chance to do just that.

What the Bush administration and Congress allowed to happen in Lebanon over the summer of 2006, and, in fact, their predecessors' lack of courageous action for half a century in the Middle East, is unconscionable, un-American, and self-destructive. It is long past time that over matters in the Middle East — not to mention the environment, health care, and gun control — the citizens of this country took back their nation. Hopefully, we can do it peacefully through our institutions and with the gutsy leadership of a new president; if not, we have the example of our own forefathers.

Facing the Wall

Arab Americans and Publishing

The important thing to say before any discussion of discrimination in the publishing, marketing, and review of books is how the odds are stacked against you before questions of race or religion are even addressed. That is, it is just plain difficult to publish a good book in this country no matter what your background is. This is a literate society with universal education and there is just a great deal of competition for the few spots available, at least those that are available after the obvious bestsellers are swooped up. When I was young, there were about seven Master in Fine Arts (MFA) in Creative Writing programs in the country; today there are at least one hundred, and most churn out capable and occasionally inspired writers. I remember one of my fellows from Georgetown quitting poetry after she faced seventy-five poets vying for a professor's golden touch at the Iowa Writers Workshop. Seventy-five poets! Could that be better than seventy-five lashes at the pillory? So the competition is brutal and has caused more than one writer to break pencils entirely or, as my writer friend, write in blissful anonymity.

Secondly, there is a shrinking market for books, especially literary ones — barring the mantle of Oprah, of course. The culture has gone visual with a vengeance. In Los Angeles, the pot of gold at the end of the rainbow is not a book that made you sweat blood, it is a screenplay, with its ubiquitous two-page "treatment" sent forward like a pick-ax in the Klondike. Can anyone doubt that it is probably easier to market a video-game than a retranslated *Anna Karenina* in this culture? (The exception that proves the rule is the newly translated *War and Peace*, which hit number-one in fiction at Politics and Prose bookstore in D.C. for a week or two.)

Thirdly, we are undergoing vast changes in the tastes of American readers that are difficult to anticipate or even understand. For example, a well-known agent told me in 2006 that one of the hardest book manuscripts to take around New York these days is the coming-of-age novel of a young man, whereas the coming-of-age novel of a young woman is still hot property. Is this a kind of reverse gender discrimination? Radical feminists, no doubt, would write this off as "a taste of their own medicine" after longstanding domination of literary circles by male authors. Still, how do half the authors in the United States — many of whom had nothing to do with such historical inequities — deal with such a thing? Change their protagonists' gender? Cross-dress?

Lastly, I should say that perhaps the hardest barrier to entry is yourself. Writing a good book is an ordeal. It's a little unsettling to hear someone who discovers that I am a writer say, "Oh, I have a book in me. I've been wanting to write it forever. What a life!" I don't go up to a heart surgeon and say, "I've got a good operation in me. I just wish I had the gloves!" I don't go up to a pianist and say, "You know, I play 'Chopsticks.' I've been playing it all my life. I know I have a symphony in me. If I only had the time!" If an interesting life were the only qualification for a writer and such stories put immediately to print, I have no doubt the country would be flooded with 250 million new memoirs.

Unfortunately, there is the matter of writing these books. And the time, concentration, love for and facility with the language, and above all, discipline, are things that even dedicated and gifted writers grapple with every day, not to mention the extraordinary tolerance of rejection someone must have in this calling.

Now, on to discrimination.

Of the four examples presented here, I do not know if my Arab American identity so much as my political activism on Middle East issues such as Palestine was the salient factor in rejections, but I do know that discrimination was partly an issue and that it is a mark of the difficulty in speaking about these things that I do so for the first time here. The first article I ever published on "Arab American issues" was an innocent piece called "Mideast Crisis: Clash of Two Nations." It was completely unoriginal. It relied heavily on George Antonius' *The Arab Awakening* and notes from Dr. John Ruedy's Islamic Civilization class. Published in Georgetown University's *Voice* student newspaper when I was a sophomore, the article elicited two scathing letters to the editor, one by a graduate student named Raphael Perl — a cousin of Richard? — who considered my piece "hate propaganda," the other from a professor of pathology. Both letters relied heavily on the myth that the Palestinians walked out of Palestine, as the pathologist put it "voluntarily," or as Perl shrugged, "Every war reaps its inevitable crop [of] refugees," metaphorically converting the ethnic cleansing of seven hundred thousand people into some sort of agricultural project. In subsequent years, several Israeli historians, notably Benny Morris and even one of the key perpetrators (Yitzak Rabin), refuted this central myth, though when I was an undergraduate the sources on the *al-Nahkba* were mostly British and Arab. Most unfortunate was a bizarre illustration of my article with two photos of the hanging of Iraqi Jews, a graphic I certainly would not have approved. These photos had virtually nothing to do with my minor piece on Palestinian rights. The bombastic attacks on it didn't get me thrown out of school, but they shook me up enough that I didn't take up the subject again for some time. (A codicil to this story: a student editor of *Voice*, Marty Yant, later went on to a distinguished career as an editor and syndicated columnist with the Columbus (Ohio) *Post-Dispatch*. After favorably reviewing my first book on Arab Americans, *Before the Flames*, Yant's column was summarily cancelled by his anchor paper.)

A second, more serious incident, at least as far as a professional writing career is concerned, occurred in the mid-eighties when Simon and Schuster considered my first book manuscript, the one that turned into *Before the Flames*. I was told there were seven members of the Simon and Schuster board that made final decisions on book acquisitions. Junior and senior editors would put forth their favorites to the board each year. In short, if you had gotten that far, you had gotten very far indeed. I had gotten that far with my first book. A young star editor at the time, Robert Asahina, who later became a Simon and Schuster vice president, presented that book on the history of Arab Americans to the seven-person board. He told me later his prior record was a perfect seven-for-seven books presented, books accepted by the board, and that this one was the best book of his yet. Well, *Before the Flames* was Asahina's first loss with his own company.

How did this happen? I only heard the story through my agents (one of whom went on to be a columnist for *Time*, Margaret Carlson) and Asahina himself. But I was told that several distinguished members of the board, including its chair Alice Mayhew and an editor named Fred Hill, were in favor of signing me up as a first-book author with Simon and Schuster. It seemed, in fact, that a majority of the board wanted it. But one man named Herman Golub did not want it, spoke passionately against it, and it was rejected. Asahina was almost as dumbstruck as me. I don't know who Herman Golub is; it was said that he had had a far-stretching conversion to the faith of his fathers. For whatever it is worth, Alice Mayhew outlasted him on the board.

The book ultimately was published by the University of Texas Press and didn't do too badly for a university press book. It was reviewed, for example, in the *New York Times Book Review*. Ten years later, in 1997, I finally published a book in New York, with The Free Press at Simon and Schuster, *Messengers of the Lost Battalion*. It was about World War II. I like to think Alice Mayhew smiled.

My third story is not about a publishing company, but Santa Barbara City College. I include it here because acceptance in academia has a direct impact on publishing, and vice versa. The two worlds for a literary writer are inextricably bound. Having taught with success at SBCC for two years of a full load at slave wages, I had applied for a tenure-track position. My best friend on the faculty, a tenured prof, was on the hiring committee. One day the committee was going over applications and my friend pulled out my application and said, "Greg Orfalea was quite popular here a few years back and he's published more than anyone else in the pile." Elaine Cohen, who was chairing the committee, grabbed the application and said, "No, no. He's anti-Israel and anti-Semitic." And into the wastebasket she tossed it. My friend was astonished. It was the source of embarrassment for us both for some years that he didn't put up a fight or protest, but it is exemplary of the chilling atmosphere over such matters that he sensed such a protest would get us nowhere. Twenty years later, we have the example of Joseph Massad at Columbia University, who hangs on by the skin of his teeth in a battle for tenure, under similar attacks.

My last example is perhaps the most disturbing. My second novel, *Mirage*, was set in 1936 Palestine and featured a marriage between an Arab and Jew in old Haifa. It was being taken around New York by a fine agent named Elaine Markson. So taken was she with the manuscript she told me, "This is not only going to be a great book. This is going to be an event." I told her, "Elaine, forget the event. Just get it published." Well, one day I received a phone call from Little, Brown's Frederica Friedman, a legendary editor who had done the bestselling historical novel on Japan, *Shogun*. She said to me, "Mr. Orfalea, you write very well. You are on an intriguing mission." I said "Ma'am, I'm not on a mission. I just follow my instincts and obsessions." She said, "I want you to know I like your book very much, but I am not going to publish it." "Why?" I asked. "Because of who you are," she said. For a second I wanted to ask her,

"Who am I?" But I just sat on the phone, speechless, until she filled the silence. "Greg," she said, "If you were Jewish, this wouldn't be a problem. People would believe the book. But because you are who you are, nobody will believe it."

I have thought about this portentous conversation for a long time. Intermarriages in old Palestine between Jews and Arabs were not common, but they did happen, as they do occasionally today in Israel. I've met several people who were products of such marriages and interviewed a daughter of one extensively. Naturally, their views on the Palestine-Israel conflict are complicated and I think fascinating. Freddy Friedman was basically saying she agreed with my presentation of this complex reality and attitude, but because I was of Arab background, I couldn't get it right. I was, by dint of who I was, perceived as unable to be fair. I was, de facto, an unreliable narrator.

And that was that. *Mirage* was never published. Elaine Markson was so discouraged she said I should find a new agent (I did; as with the valiant Ms. Carlson, he landed nothing). In fact, I have never had any of my four novels published, and though I have something of a reputation as a writer of creative nonfiction, and teach it, I chew sometimes on the thought that some of my best work is in the fiction. But who knows? Maybe plain old author's delusion.

I want to underscore something in conclusion. None of this singles out Jews in publishing as a nemesis of my work; quite the contrary. The most encouraging and helpful people in the publishing world for me have been almost to a person Jewish Americans, such as Elaine Markson. My editor at The Free Press, Adam Bellow, the son of Saul Bellow, is an exceptional editor and person. He was a great believer in my book on World War II and has engaged me ever since at other publishing houses where he has hung his hat, though he does no fiction. Some of my most supportive friends, such as Tobias Wolff, are accomplished Jewish American writers and academicians who vigorously support independence for Palestine and are deeply opposed to the Iraq war.

But there have been individuals who for either zealous political reasons of their own or unsparing assessment of the marketplace or simple prejudice probably stalled my literary and academic careers a sum of years. That they didn't kill them is as much a tribute to my Jewish friends as it is to my almost mindless tenacity.

How does all this stack up for other Arab American writers? It's not easy to say. On the panel that was the basis for this piece, I don't recall the other Arab American authors giving a specific example of a press or editor or institution as having refused their work due to their ethnicity or political stances. All, to be sure, felt anti-Arab prejudice in publishing and in general indicated suffering from it, but they may have feared blackballing. I don't judge them; I understand them too well, having been there; most are at the tender outset of their careers.

In an interview for my first history book, poet and novelist Samuel Hazo — in semi-retirement by then — indicated that the critics Helen Vendler and Harold Bloom entered into a meeting to choose the 1973 National Book Award (NBA) winner in poetry, for which Hazo had been nominated, and announced they were going to vote for A.R. Ammons, essentially foreclosing debate. (There has never been an individual Arab American winner of a major American literary prize such as the Pulitzer, NBA, or National Book Critics Circle Award — Edward Said never won one; Naomi Shihab Nye, whose work was pulled off the shelves by a Virginia public school after 9/11, has been the only other Arab American nominee for the NBA, in children's literature, a highly odd categorization, since the book was adult poetry.)

The critic Stephen Salaita has said, "Zionists, both liberal and right wing, stonewall in various ways Arab expression in the United States." Though this may literally be true, I don't think it is a conspiracy. I do think it is irrefutable that there are powerful people in powerful places — some Zionist, some not — who have almost reflexively erected barriers to our community's advance in the arts and media — the "expressive" professions. You add to this the aforementioned natural barriers to achievement in writing beyond ethnicity, and it is not hard to see Arab American authors working decades in the dark under very difficult circumstances to bring their art to light. Perhaps it has burnished our work, put it through more than the normal fire, and that may be to the good of the work itself, if the writer manages to hold onto his sanity.

As for the marketing and reviewing of Arab American books and the audience for them, I have contradictory responses. On the one hand, I recall with fondness the American Arab Anti-Discrimination Committee (ADC) getting vigorously behind my first book, *Before the Flames*, and sending me out around the country where I lectured to about a dozen chapters. The book was widely reviewed and ADC's support helped create that interest. On the other hand, eighteen years later a better and more valuable book on the subject — *The Arab Americans: A History* — hit a critical wall of silence. Though it has sold well, though it's in its second or third printing, and though it received the first starred review in *Publishers Weekly* that Interlink Press had achieved to that date (written I discovered later by a remarkable Israeli), there have been zero reviews in major newspapers or journals. Being published by an Arab American small press did not help it, perhaps, though I was honored by Michel Moushabek's great devotion to it and happy to encourage my own community's native publishing efforts, as had the esteemed African American poet Gwendolyn Brooks with her later work. I do know the silence was not from want of trying by Interlink.

To this end, I have a few suggestions for the Arab American community itself in taking ahold of this problem of discrimination. I would like to see young native Arab American critics emerge, such as Lisa Suhair Majaj and Nouri Gana; for too long, Evelyn Shakir and Eugene Paul Nasser labored virtually alone. We also need more readers in our community, more active solicitation of and organization for Arab American authors for lectures, workshops, and other presentations, not just in political organizations, such as the ADC, but in religious institutions such as churches and mosques. I'll bet more Arab American authors are invited to temples than mosques. It would be great to encourage our authors to do things that are not strictly Arab American. For example, Patricia Serrafian Ward is writing a fantasy novel a la *The Hobbit*. I happen to think Diana Abu-Jaber's striking, magnetic psychological crime novel, *Origin*, which has virtually no Middle Eastern content, is her best novel to date. You know you have a literary culture when the community supports you in work that has nothing directly to do with the community. We don't do that. We need to encourage the arts with our children, as a profession, but also as a joy in itself. I don't underestimate the difficulty of doing this in a culture intent on destroying the inner ear, not to mention the brain. Finally, I think it would be important for our writers to band together and pass resolutions against censorship and suppression in the Arab world, as well as America. RAWI (the Radius of Arab American Writers) might be perfect for this purpose.

I am sure there are those who would say the situation I describe is one that was obtained "in the old days," that is, pre–September 11, 2001, the day on which America discovered the Arab world. That was, needless to say, one reprehensible, terrifying way to get noticed, one any one of us writers would gladly exchange for a ton of published books. Rather than say a cultural wall has collapsed along with those sad towers, it seems to me a wall has definitely been cracked. Naomi Shihab

Nye reports getting more invitations to speak than ever after 9/11. New writers are indeed getting published, though most are with smaller presses; Arab American literature and history courses are at long last beginning to be taught (I taught the first one at Georgetown in spring 2007); the study of the Arabic language is in flower; and more of us are getting positions in academia in literature, the arts and media.

To return to my initial premise, this writing life is no easy row to hoe. If television doesn't get you, cell phones will. If a critical silence doesn't do you in, you get it from your own. You've spent years on a manuscript with nothing assured, then someone knocks you out of the queue with a book he wrote in a month with an advance, a ghost, and a morning cocktail. Your husband loves you but doesn't understand, your kids support you but don't read your books, your best friend points out a typo.

Take heart. Robert Frost didn't publish till his forties and was an English American. Mark Twain didn't write *Huckleberry Finn* until his fifties and was written off as a humorist. Herman Melville was considered an adventure writer whose *Moby Dick* had to wait fifty years after his death to even begin to be understood.

You take up this life of words following the tortuous path to the truth, and there are walls and walls. Sometimes the words themselves puncture a good hole.

Why Write?

My subject is both simple and impossible: Why write? I seem to be facing the void of late. This has been one of those times in a writer's life that questions the most fundamental assumptions about life and oneself in particular, and it seems unavoidable that if this self-sweeping is going on, then one can't help but consider the possibility that writing is useless. It won't help you eat, certainly, and it won't help you breathe, and it certainly won't stop the war in Iraq. Or Palestine. Or Canoga Park in Los Angeles, where the rate of gang violence went up in 2006 — and this in a vast middle-class suburb of the San Fernando Valley — while it has gone down everywhere else, including South Central L.A. My mother lives two miles from Canoga Park.

Why write?

The spondee makes you skip a breath. One way to address this age-old problem (surely it must have occurred to the carvers of sandstone at Joshua Tree, the first letter writers at Sumer, and the authors of the laws of Hammurabi) is to peel off, one by one, the standard answers and to inspect them for viability in today's writing world, a world in which the electronic image is God, the spoken word is contorted to hate and called poetry, and the written word seems at best waste, if not filler between the images on Myspace. The styrofoamization of the language surrounds us all.

First of all, some definition of terms. When I ask, "Why write?" I am not talking about the occasional act of writing, or writing a letter versus phoning someone, however much I am in favor of the letter, one of the great lost genres. I am not talking about making lists, or emails, or even a speech, per se. I address here why someone should take up the life of writing at all; I am considering the habit of writing, the habit of words, the practice of putting ideas and feelings to paper or screen on a more or less regular basis. Why do that? It's not natural. It certainly is not something espoused as a line of work in this or any society, outside that of Dark Age monks. It has been, certainly in these pragmatic States, a peripheral kind of calling, one that, spotted in high school or earlier, is whispered about by teachers and students alike as, at best, a blessed plague, something one is branded with, like the disability of echolalia. "Oh, he's the writer in our class." Is that ever said with the same relief and expectancy as "He's going to be a lawyer" or "She's good with numbers"?

Let's start with an obvious motive in a capitalist society. Anything that takes as much time as writing a book better pay off, and the way it should pay off in this land is with tender — not tenderness, tender. (Is English with its homonyms inherently oxymoronic — tenderness, tender? It seems like a thing can't be stated without containing its opposite. Perhaps all language is like this, all life. And we can't pretend to know life at its core without acknowledging, accepting, even welcoming its doubleness.)

Back to money. It may seem laughable, but there are ways to make money writing. A good lawyer today, a convincing one, had better be a good writer, or at the very least, a good logician. We've all known the English majors who end up as lawyers. These are the practical sorts who know they have a facility, even a blessing, with words but also have the humility and perhaps perspicacity to divine that that blessing is in fact a curse, guarantees years of drafty pockets — therefore little social standing and flighty girlfriends or boyfriends. In short, the English major turned lawyer has had a glimpse of forever and found it definitely wanting.

You can also make money shilling for others. I did it for the better part of twenty years. Words like popcorn. Public affairs, brochures, annual reports, advertising, ghost-written speeches, even, as I once did, cue cards in Hollywood. (Actually, that was not writing, that was printing.) I don't wish to be too cynical. Surveys show that 80 percent of all MFA and other creative writing grads will take up some form of public relations for a job, as opposed to teaching or rapping. There can be creativity in that line of work. The poet James Dickey invented jingles working for Coca-Cola. ("A Sign of Good Taste"?) The poet Dana Gioia worked for a long time for General Foods as head of its PR. Poet Joseph Awad directed PR for Reynolds Aluminum for many years. The novelist James Gould Cozzens, who won the Pulitzer Prize, worked in World War II as an Army public affairs officer. Whitman himself for a time wrote memos for the Bureau of Indian Affairs. We all have our favorite stories of writers who spilled their blood in the gutter as ghosts. Yes, it can raise children. It can bring home the bacon.

But is money the reason to write after you've come home exhausted, wrestled the children — or lover — to bed, and faced the blank page? Is this motive enough to wrestle your own demons? Doubtful.

The current money craze for writers — the equivalent in language of the 1848 gold rush — is the screenplay. There's a screenwriter on every block in Los Angeles. It seems there are more screenwriters waiting tables than actresses and actors. In fact, the actresses and actors are all writing screenplays, too. The bus drivers are writing screenplays, the accountants, the flippers of hot dogs and various buns. There's a screen-play, or potential one, in every pot, or pot belly. And why is this? Because dollar for dollar, it's short. Far shorter than a book, and potentially far more lucrative. A screenplay is about a hundred manuscript pages, two-thirds of which are blank. You only have to write talk to write a screen-play, but if you hit it, you'll never stop talking, at least to your agent, about that real drill bit for a gusher, the two-page "concept."

I don't wish to throw cold water on screenwriting. I am sure it has paid for many a backyard pool and front yard tuition. But it is essentially writing by committee — your words are pulled apart not just by an edi-tor, but a director, a producer, a star or two, and even the publicist. Have you noticed as you bear the Academy Awards yet another year, another year of absurd tears and bathetic thank-yous, that the co-authorship of screenplays is growing, causing a proliferation of Oscar statuettes to the point where the thank-yous get longer, the orchestra prompts for release from this torture more frequent? Am I the only person that seems to catch Stephen Spielberg now as a co-author of his films' screenplays? And what qualifies as a co-author? Two lines of dialogue? An extra camera direction? Or just the purse strings?

There can be genius in a screenplay — 12 Angry Men is my favorite, with On the Waterfront a close second. Of recent note, Michael Clayton was well done. But Hollywood nearly destroyed Scott Fitzgerald and Faulkner, both of whom were lured by its promise of easy money. It also redirected if not swallowed the talents of one of the finest American novelists of the twentieth century, John Fante. Consider this from Fante's masterpiece, his second novel, Ask the Dust, written just before Holly-wood manacled him and lead him away: "I went up to my room, up the dusty stairs of Bunker Hill, past the soot-covered frame buildings along that dark street, sand and oil and grease choking the futile palm trees standing like dying prisoners, chained to a little plot of ground with black pavement hiding their feet." The camera can pan that scene, but can it duplicate the rhythms, the pathos, the lived-in life, like the language itself?

So money might not just do it. But what about sex? Some have said that poetry is an aphrodisiac, that writing is sexy, that it might gain one favor in the mating game of ages. Andrew Marvell hoped so. That nerd with a pen in sophomore English, that four-eyed monster? He's sexy. That girl in black, with tattoos on every square inch of her body, with blue hair and rings in her eyelids and a notebook stapled to her forearm, she's sexy.

I'm not going to spend too much time with this. Let me just point out that Ernest Hemingway had four wives and loved the first one the most; that for every paramour brought to bed by a lyric, two have been repelled; and that Byron himself, with his club foot and Don Juan loves a-plenty, ended up throwing his life away on the battlefield in Greece, far from any bed.

So forget money and sex. Let's go up the ladder of Maslowvian fulfillment. Let's try a teaching position, respect. And definitely in that order — teaching position first, respect later, often much later, often never. But who needs respect if you've got tenure? The benefits seem obvious — five months off a year to write, for one. A captive audience every day for another. And even job security, something of a Golden Fleece for our itinerant Writer. There may even be among writers a certain kinship with the young, pulled as we are by the past, ever fixated on trying to find meaning, something most adults give up on with their first filing of a health insurance claim.

I'm stuck on teaching and learning and so would ordinarily support this motive for the writer. But careful. The competition is fierce; more than one hundred MFA programs churn out creative writers each year. Every job in writing at the college level receives between one hundred and three hundred applications. Dipping your résumé in purple dye won't help. You must have published at least a book or two for most positions — I was taught poetry and taught it well by a poet at Georgetown who did not publish his first collection for thirty years. That simply cannot happen today. On the other hand, if you've published several books, that may work against you. The "green-eyed monster" factor is a strong one at universities. For every productive colleague who is your comrade in arms, there will be two unproductive ones who will shoot arrows at your heels.

And then there is the time-honored conflict between the "writers and the scholars," that is, the English Department and the Writing Department, if they are so distinguished, or between creative writers and scholars in the Literature Department itself. This absurd divide persists, I am sorry to say, when we all know there is a great deal of creativity in the best scholars (Edward Said is an obvious example) and scholarship and research in the best of creative writers — take a look at the source notes in *Cold Mountain* by Charles Frazier or Eliot's notes to *The Waste Land*, or any volume of creative nonfiction by Joan Didion, most recently her *The Year of Magical Thinking*. But it persists — and this friction between scholars and so-called creative writers is a vicious one and has broken the heart of more than one writer (I am thinking of the rough going-over poet Kenneth Rexroth got at the University of California at Santa Barbara, or Nicolai Gogol, who practically invented the realist short story, reduced to muttering at the University of St. Petersburg in nineteenth-century Russia.)

Because most American literary authors end up in the Academy, the rhythms of the academic year affect the output and, I think, the quality, of the work. The so-called "summer novel" is real. If one takes teaching seriously, it is a labor-intensive job, and that leaves for a cramped pocket of time to put out a book. This may make for dutiful, competent, and compact writing, but is it fired in the hearth of human frailty and need? Does it come pouring out of a soul's struggles with death and life, which have no seasonal time frame? Which tend to grab one at the least expected moments and stun one onto the page or, as the case may be, silence? To be silent for the summer is a risky business for a tenure-seeking writer. But silence may be as important to a writer as speech. And the passion of inner battle is as important to the shape of a paragraph, a stanza, as the time limits of summer vacation. One has to surrender to one's inner demons and angels as a writer. That doesn't often square with the timelines of Academia.

So we have hacked off the vines of money, sex, and position. What is left? Well, of course, the loftier reasons we are always given to write: psychological health, social justice, and of course that great five-letter word, Truth.

Let's take each quickly — and why not, as any of them are not often got in a lifetime.

First, a healthy psyche. There are tomes and tomes about this, self-help books up the ying yang that espouse the healthy aspects of writing. One of my classmates at Georgetown, who later married and divorced Martin Scorsese, Julia Cameron, wrote a slew of books on finding your "inner self" and the power of creativity, advising all manner of journaling and self-plunging to massage the wounds of the inner soul. Her books became bestsellers, though evidently they did not massage the inner soul of Martin Scorsese who puts out, gallon for gallon, more blood in his movies than any filmmaker in history. In fact, violence becomes almost laughable in *The Departed*, and to some extent in my old classmate's work, so does creativity. Writing becomes a sort of purging mechanism, not unlike verbal bulimia, that clears the bowels and scours the esophagus. It also apparently lines pockets, though not the pockets of the readers.

There are serious authors who made careers about this cleansing aspect of writing. The poet William Stafford toured the country espousing something he called "Writing the Australian Crawl." I happen to enjoy Stafford's poetry, though I do not think it is, at core, very reassuring about human nature or the writing process. Stafford, and to some extent, Robert Frost, were selling snake oil, and no surprise that both poets are far darker than their good grey poet public images would lead us to believe.

The fact of the matter is that writing, serious writing, is isolating. It is also, if electric and beautiful, skating along the thin ice between sanity and insanity. Shakespeare understood this, as did Herman Hesse, not to mention Flannery O'Conner, or anyone who has ever spent eight hours staring at a wall. I am not saying that there may be something exhilarating, endorphin-raising if you will, in a well-formed sentence or page. Nor am I so cynical as to say that writing cannot help discover parts of human nature previously ignored, parts of your own self kept in shadow, or a spiritual connective with mankind. What I am saying is that these discoveries can be as psychologically shaking as they can be healing. That the one happens before the other is even possible is not reassuring. You must crack yourself open in this writing life, and you don't eviscerate a psyche without damaging it, or at least putting it through great strain. It is no surprise that Eugene O'Neill left his two most important and devastating plays — *Long Day's Journey Into Night* and *The Iceman Cometh* — until the very end of a prolific career. He wrote such plays that can take your breath away and drench you in sweat far out in the country in Big Sur near Monterey, living with his last wife, Carlotta, with no one but the moon to consult if she were worn out, as she must have been, for all her devotion to the greatest dramatist of the twentieth century. These two plays probably cost O'Neill his life. He never recovered from them. He hardly wrote again, coughed out *Moon for the Misbegotten* and lived for only a few years after his ink ran dry.

So much for psychic health.

Now on to social justice. Improvement of the species! How many times I have uttered this clarion myself! If we begin to write for a girl-friend, boyfriend, husband or wife, when that fails, bring on the masses! Storm the barricades!

The instinct to write, to express, to overcome the inchoate, to rescue things and feelings from oblivion, is related to outrage. There's no question about that. We pen pushers do not much cotton to hypocrisy and the suppression of what is evident and obvious, especially in the service of power. But recall: Plato felt poets were a danger to civil order, and not only because they were volatile emotionally, but because they "maim the thoughts of those who hear them." They pulled the chords of the heart only to arouse, not clarify. No ruler, certainly no ruler in ancient times, could stomach this independent force. So poets in Plato's Republic were marginalized, if not banished, and as Plato wrote all too compellingly, Socrates was put to death.

There is also something else serving this instinct to take on injustice. The more you write about human nature, the more you take pity on it. The more you take pity on it, the less you want to judge it. Political power is based on judgment and favor. It does not usually care about human suffering, as there is always a greater good to sacrifice lives for, including the greater good of one's own continued power. That is why in spring 2007, George Bush could with a straight face ask Senator Jim Webb of Virginia about his son serving in Iraq.

"I think we ought to get out of Iraq as soon as possible," said Webb.

"You didn't answer my question," said Bush. "How's your son?"

"That's between my son and me," answered Webb shrewdly and caustically.

It's no surprise Webb is a novelist. It would be an absolute miracle if he were to last more than one term.

There are all kinds of activists in writing, or writers in politics. The tradition is an honored one, from Thomas Paine to Walt Whitman, from Clifford Odets to Norman Mailer, Allen Ginsberg, Grace Paley, and Barbara Kingsolver. I wouldn't say it is the main strain of American literature, but it is a significant secondary strain. (What really worries me is that in the name of political righteousness, or correctness, non-mainstream activist writers, suddenly finding themselves tenured at universities and formulating a kind of mini-mainstream, exercise an alternative tyranny, but that is another topic, which might be called "A Good Reason Not to Write.")

It is not enough for many of us writers to reflect the world, to celebrate or damn it — we want to change it. It's a very natural outgrowth of our love of language, to make language serve the right and the just, to help not just our résumé or the bookshelf, but a human life. Some great writing has been put in the service of saving lives, or at least alerting us to lives that needed improving if not saving, such as James Agee (poor sharecroppers), Frederick Douglass (black slaves), Betty Friedan (suppressed women), the poet Ernesto Cardenal (slaughtered Nicaraguans), the poet Frederico García Lorca (butchered Spanish communists). Some, such as García Lorca, lost their lives in the process. Novelists have famously illuminated human suffering in the meat-packing industry (Upton Sinclair's *The Jungle*), the agony of Vietnam (Tim O'Brien's *The Things They Carried*), the destruction of Napoleon (Tolstoy's *War and Peace*). Social justice figures in some of the greatest works of literature. But beware even here at the threshold where the writer tackles matters of body and soul. There are two pitfalls. One, what if a novelist gets the social issue wrong? Consider for example a little-known German novel published in 1897 whose author was an obscure journalist named Theodore Hertzl. The book was called *Altneuland*, or "Old-New Land." It launched, in its fictive longing for a home for persecuted Jews, the whole movement of Zionism. For many Jews, especially those victimized by pogroms in Russia, Hertzl's vision contained not only justice, but salvation. For some, such as Hannah Arendt and Sara Roy of Harvard, what the novel posited was fraught with danger and delusion. And for Palestinians, *Altneuland*, which relegated the locals to little more than snake charmers, was nothing short of a nightmare.

Thankfully, we have a counterstrain in literature that questions utopic visions like Hertzl's, such as Thomas More's *Utopia*, Hawthorne's *A Blithedale Romance*, and George Orwell's extremely dark *1984*. More than one Israeli novelist has shown that my literary justice may well be your misery; I'm thinking of the superb work of A.B. Yehoshua and David Grossman. In short, the social justice spur to write needs watching. Think of Ezra Pound's *Pisan Cantos*, virulently anti-Semitic but barely hidden inside a rant for economic justice. I need allude to only one more poet, a Chinese one, and I don't mean Lao-Tzu, but Mao Tse Tung. I believe history shows us that poets and other failed artists (Hitler was a watercolorist) with social engineering visions are dangerous men and their metaphors murderous.

The second problem with the impulse to justice literature—one I have lived with most of my writing life—is that social and political problems you tackle often have no apparent end. This can lead not only to bitterness, but wooden if not shrill writing. Conversely, some of the best protest literature has been written after a historic debacle has passed. Take for example the aforementioned *The Things They Carried*, surely the best novel about Vietnam, written long after Tim O'Brien was out of the Army and fifteen years after we pulled out of Vietnam altogether. One of my favorite novels of World War I was penned eighty years later—in the 1990s, *A Very Long Engagement* by Frenchman Sebastian Japriscot. About the psychic damage of war—and the power of love—it is utterly transcendent.

I am not saying give up on writing poetry that matters. Not at all. Simply that in writing about injustices, tyranny, racism, sexism, social sadism, you must proceed with both courage and caution. You do not want to be hoisted on your own petard, for one, and you need constantly to keep in mind that literature ultimately lives or dies on the beauty and originality of its language, the grip of its story, and the richness and depth of its characters. Theme is important. But without humanity, feeling, human complexity, it is, at best, cant, and at worst—well, a fringe on atrocity.

As for the Truth.

I confess. I seek it. I'm drawn to writers who seek it. There is no writer worth his or her salt who doesn't yearn for it, pray for it, let blood and position for it, hunt it, dice it, and serve it raw to readers. But lest I strain the reader's patience more than I already have with this little diatribe, suffice it to say that more writers have died short of the truth than there are grains of sand in the Sahara. And sadder—almost as many have died because they have uttered a most disturbing grain of truth to a society otherwise blind, deaf, and dumb to it.

So, why write? Not for money, sex, or status. What left's if not for psychic health, social justice, or the truth itself? Why don't we all just give up the ghost before it breaks our hearts, our relationships, not to mention our wallet? (As they say on TV with no little menace, "What's in *your* wallet?")

Well, in my dilapidated wallet is a reason to write which keeps me going when all else fails: I love it! I love it because short of lovemaking itself, writing is one of the few human activities that can add more life to this sorry life that we have. As Anthony Hecht wrote, echoing Goethe on his deathbed and thinking of a Polish guard who gave his life for the Jews, "More light! More light!" Well, the writer who does it right can say, "More life! More life!" When you write, you are preserving like a flesh-and-blood museum facets of human desire and struggle and joy and pain as they were caught in the magma, as they were lived, breathed. And if you do this catching, this cooling of the ultra-hot, if you do it well, you preserve it past your own breathing.

Consider: There is no human instrument, not the fastest laptop — not even a legion of cameras — that can record life as it happens. Life itself is a tragedy because in its very enactment it is dying; each second dies to give life to the next. Even the most attentive person will not replicate or recall life's most portentous and fullest moments. But art — and literature especially — has the ability to distill, to choose if you will, the representative moments, distancing, combining, bending the real to a greater capital-R Real which transcends time.

To put it more simply, when you are depressed, when the Palestine conflict goes on and on, when the gun never ceases its passage from Dallas to Columbine to Virginia Tech — and the Iraq war goes on and on and on, beyond, it seems, any good pen's hope or effort, when your child is sick beyond the grip of words, when the editors nod and the agents flee — take heart. You are creating new life. You are giving life itself — and not the least, your life — a second chance.

Acknowledgments

The author gives grateful acknowledgment to the following publications and presses that first published these essays and memoirs in somewhat different form:

Los Angeles Times Magazine: "Kingdom of Rags," "The Barber of Tarzana," "The Teacher's Prayer" (formerly "That's My Soul. Why Don't You Draw Yours?"), and "An Act of Forgiveness"

Los Angeles Times: "Snuffing the Fire of Radical Islam"

Michigan Quarterly Review: "Valley Boys"

Washington Post: "Straight Shooters" and "Baghdad with a Human Face"

Smithsonian Institution Press: "Nazera" (formerly "There's a Wire Brush at my Bones") in *Crossing the Waters: Arabic-Speaking Immigrants to the United States before 1940*, edited by Eric Hooglund, 1987

Mizna: "We Were the People"

Cleveland Plain Dealer Sunday Magazine: "Contact: The War, Sandlot Football, and My Father," © 1996 the *Plain Dealer*. All rights reserved. Used with permission of the *Plain Dealer*.

Persea Books: "The Messenger of the Lost Battalion" in *Visions of America: Personal Narratives of the Promised Land*, edited by Wesley Brown and Amy Ling, 1993. Another version of the essay appeared as the introduction to *Messengers of the Lost Battalion: The Heroic 551ˢᵗ and the Turning of the Tide at the Battle of the Bulge*, by Gregory Orfalea, the Free Press/Simon and Schuster, 1997.

Arab Star: "No. Not This."

Jewish Currents: "To Hope"

Cambridge Scholars Publishing: "Shall We Gather in the Mountains?" in *Etching Our Own Image: Voices from Within the Arab American Art Movement*, edited by Anan Ameri and Holly Arida, 2007.

Journal of Palestine Studies: "The Arab in the Post–World War II

Novel" (formerly "Literary Devolution: The Image of the Arab in the Post–World War II Novel in English")

Paintbrush: "Doomed by Our Blood to Care" (formerly "Doomed by Our Blood to Care: The Poetry of Naomi Shihab Nye")

The author would also like to thank the Arab American National Museum, where two of these pieces were first presented as lectures ("Shall We Gather in the Mountains?" and "Why Write?"); the American-Arab Anti-Discrimination Committee, where "Facing the Wall: Arab Americans and Publishing" was presented; and Politics and Prose Bookstore in Washington, D.C., where "Meditations on Lebanon, 2006" (formerly "Some Thoughts on the Late Crisis") was delivered as a talk recorded by C-SPAN before a book signing. All of the pieces were originally somewhat different.